PENSION POLICY AND SMALL EMPLOYERS:
At What Price Coverage?

AN EBRI-ERF POLICY STUDY

By Emily S. Andrews

EMPLOYEE BENEFIT RESEARCH INSTITUTE

©1989 Employee Benefit Research Institute
Education and Research Fund
2121 K Street, NW, Suite 600
Washington, DC 20037-2121
(202) 659-0670

Library of Congress Cataloging-in-Publication Data

Andrews, Emily S.
  Pension policy and small employers: at what price coverage?
  (An EBRI-ERF policy study)
  Bibliography: p.
  Includes index.
  1. Pension trusts—United States. 2. Retirement income—United States. 3. Compensation management—United States. 4. Small business—United States—Personnel management. I. Title. II. Series.
HD 7105.45.U6A535   1989   658.3'253   89-12015
ISBN 0-86643-050-4

Printed in the United States of America

Table of Contents

List of Tables

List of Charts

Executive Summary

The U.S. retirement income system is facing a number of challenges today as a result of the economic uncertainties confronting the nation.

Evolving and maturing over the last 50 years, the retirement income system consists of a combination of Social Security, employer-sponsored pensions, and personal savings. Today, earnings of "retired" workers and in-kind benefits such as federal and employer-sponsored health insurance have become important supplements to retirement income.

Millions of Americans receive income in retirement from these sources. Many analysts predict that even more workers will benefit in the future as a result of changes in the work force and modifications in pension plan provisions. Despite this optimistic outlook for the future, however, some policymakers are concerned about economic trends that could have a negative impact on pension plan provision, such as sluggish growth in productivity, family income, and earnings.

These trends emerged just as the pension plan participation rate began to level off. With many millions of workers without pensions, policymakers are looking for ways to increase pension coverage. Some lawmakers believe the answer lies in encouraging or requiring more small businesses to establish pension plans, since studies show that the small-business sector accounts for the majority of workers without pensions. In 1985, more than 90 percent of full-time employees in medium-sized and large companies participated in retirement plans. The participation rate for full-time employees in small firms was 43 percent that year.

To judge whether recent proposals to increase small-business pension coverage through changes in public policy would be effective or even desirable, *Pension Policy and Small Employers: At What Price Coverage?* reviews the U.S. retirement income system, analyzes the effect of economic decisions on pension plan formation, and assesses the importance of factors that influence small businesses when they consider whether or not to establish pension plans. The study also evaluates the efficacy of past legislative efforts to expand the voluntary pension system.

The Future of the Retirement Income System

Social Security and employer-sponsored pension plans have developed over 50 years and are still expanding. In 1941, only 20 percent of those eligible for Social Security were receiving benefits, but by 1986, that percentage had risen to 93 percent.

The participation rate of wage and salary workers in private-sector employer-sponsored pension plans has also grown—from 23 percent in 1950 to over 45 percent today. And even though participation rates appear to have stabilized in recent years, the number of workers receiving benefits will continue to climb because of a time lag between plan formation and the retirement of workers. Since the employer-sponsored pension system is still relatively young, many workers covered by employer-sponsored plans are just beginning to reach retirement age and to start drawing pension benefits.

Over 70 percent of workers born during the early years of the baby boom can expect to receive pension income from employer-sponsored plans by the time they reach age 67. Recent changes in pension law are expected to increase the number of workers receiving benefits, particularly the provision in the Tax Reform Act of 1986 that requires many pension plans to reduce the maximum number of years of participation for vesting from 10 to 5 years (or 7 years, if graded). The effects of this change will be most pronounced for younger workers and for those yet to enter the labor force.

Despite this optimistic picture of retirement income system growth, fears about the stability of the system have also been increasing. These worries stem, in part, from economic uncertainties: the oil shocks of the 1970s, shakiness in financial markets, and sluggish growth in productivity. Questions also have arisen in the public mind about whether the Social Security system is still strong, despite a 1983 legislative "rescue" of the Social Security trust fund that ensured it would be in actuarial balance for many years.

In this environment, some younger workers no longer believe that the retirement income system will be able to provide them benefits comparable to those received by their parents and grandparents.

Faced with these uncertainties, some policymakers and politicians believe the foundations of the retirement income system need to be buttressed. One way to accomplish this goal, some say, is by increasing pension coverage in small businesses since these firms employ the most workers without coverage.

Studies show that pension coverage tends to be associated with workers who have a long-term commitment to the labor force. A sizable minority (46 percent) of uncovered workers either work limited hours, are relatively young (under age 25), or have reached retirement age. However, 68 percent of uncovered workers who were in the prime age group (from ages 25 through 64) and worked more than 1,000 hours were employed by small businesses.

But public policy proposals to expand small-business pension coverage have not been subjected to empirical analysis to determine their efficacy.

Whether these proposals will work depends on the economics of pension plan provision.

Small Employers and the Economy

Small businesses employ a substantial proportion of America's workers. In 1983, 45.5 percent of all private-sector civilian nonfarm employees worked for small companies and 41 percent worked for large employers. The rest worked for medium-sized firms.

Some observers have suggested that the small-business share of employment has been increasing. Such a shift would have a significant impact on pension coverage since small businesses are less likely than large businesses to sponsor pension plans.

But data show that the small-firm share of employment has not expanded. Nearly 46 percent of all civilian nonfarm employees in the private sector worked for small companies in both 1979 and 1983. The distribution of employment has shifted, however, toward smaller establishments or work-site locations.

Job creation data suggest a strong cyclical component to employment growth. When large companies reduce their work forces during economic downturns, small firms are allocated a larger share of total employment. Cyclical movements may help explain why small firms are less likely to take on the long-term commitment associated with plan sponsorship.

Other economic factors related to pension coverage include unionization, self-employment, and productivity. While pension coverage is higher among union members, a significant decline in unionization has taken place. Conversely, pension coverage is much lower among the self-employed, whose ranks are steadily increasing. Pension coverage also could be adversely affected by the slowdown in U.S. productivity and by the expansion of service-sector employment.

Examining the differences between small and large employers helps explain the conditions that favor pension coverage. Small businesses are not simply smaller versions of larger companies. They are less highly capitalized, less likely to be corporate entities, and more likely to be concentrated in service-related industries. Very small firms are more management intensive than others.

The work forces of small firms include more teen-agers, retirees, and part-timers. Employees tend to stay on the job a shorter period of time and are less likely to be unionized. There are fewer employees in professional or technical occupations. These are all factors that could influence pension coverage.

Small Employers and Pensions

The compensation packages provided by employers consist of both wages and benefits. Although the work forces of large and small companies are different, that alone does not account for the fact that large companies provide better benefits and pay higher wages than small companies. Several researchers have concluded that large employers are less able to monitor the performance of their workers and so must provide higher wages to motivate employees to perform well on the job.

A similar explanation may account for the greater prevalence of benefits in large companies. Employers might provide pensions to encourage superior job performance. Under this theory, a worker who is not vested would be less likely to risk job termination for poor performance because that could result in a substantial loss of pension benefits. And a worker who is vested in a final-pay defined benefit plan would be less disposed to change jobs because that would mean sacrificing the higher benefit accruals that come with long tenure.

Thus, it may be that not only large employers but also small businesses operate on the premise that continued employment leads to improved worker productivity. Consequently, they would hire workers for the long term and encourage long tenure with the firm through the provision of pensions. Under this scenario, the decision to establish a pension plan would depend on the management needs of the small-business employer.

Another useful step in considering the relationship between economic factors and pension plan formation is to look at businesses with pension plans and those without plans to ascertain whether the different characteristics of large and small companies play a part in the decision to provide pensions. Just as small businesses differ from large companies, pension plan providers differ from nonproviders in terms of production requirements, types of workers, industrial patterns, capital and management requirements, and the extent of unionization.

Covered workers are more likely to be in manufacturing than in services, but differences in coverage rates by firm size are as great as the disparity between firms of the same size that are in different industries. Workers in very large firms in all industries are more likely to be covered by a pension plan than workers in small businesses.

Firms with pension plans are more capital intensive, hire more higher-paid workers, and employ more managers. Workers with pension coverage tend to be prime-age and full-time workers who spend more years on the job than those without a pension. These facts seem to corroborate the argument that firms of all sizes offer pensions primarily for business reasons.

Five separate studies directly asked small-business owners why they decided to establish pension plans. Two studies were done for the U.S. Small Business Administration, by James Bell and Associates, Inc., in 1984 and by Justin Research Associates in 1985. Others were conducted by the National Rural Electric Cooperative Association (Korczyk, 1988) and the National Federation of Independent Business (Dennis, 1985); and a study was commissioned by the Employee Benefit Research Institute and the American Association of Retired Persons that built on the responses of small employers in focus groups.

Many employers listed the well-being of their workers, their own retirement needs, and tax advantages as reasons for having plans. Pension plans also offered a way, some employers said, to compete for and keep valued workers.

Many of the employers cited financial concerns as a major reason for not providing pensions: their firms were not profitable enough to justify the costs. A number of the employers also believed their workers preferred direct compensation to pensions.

Many small employers indicated that the decision to provide a pension plan depended on whether it was cost effective to do so. Pension plans are more expensive for these employers because their administrative costs are higher on a per participant basis than those of larger companies. And small firms must also consider the financial condition of their firm and the impact of the plan on profits and productivity.

If the benefits of sponsoring a pension plan lie chiefly in the plan's potential for increasing worker productivity, then small employers must balance that consideration against the costs of providing a plan for workers whose job performance will not improve. The decision to establish a plan also depends on the nature of the business. Small firms that are less highly capitalized and employ fewer skilled workers have less incentive to provide a pension plan to improve worker productivity and establish a long-term employment relationship.

Economic Influences on Pension Coverage

Even after taking into account differences in the work place such as industry and earnings, workers in large companies are more likely to be covered by a pension plan than workers in small firms. Longer tenure on the job and higher earnings are consistently related to higher pension coverage.

Since small employers face higher per capita administrative costs for operating a pension plan, even those firms that are in good financial shape need greater incentives for starting a plan than large employers. The likelihood of a small firm sponsoring a pension plan is projected to increase by 1.3 percentage points if administrative costs decrease by $10 per worker.

Gains in employment, job tenure, or average payroll all increase pension coverage rates, but increases have to be relatively substantial in percentage terms to make much of a difference. Firms with higher profit rates that are more highly capitalized are more likely to sponsor pension plans.

Unionization also affects pension coverage, as union workers are more likely to have pension coverage than nonunion workers. But increased unionization of employees of small firms is unlikely because of the difficulties of organizing the typically unskilled, decentralized work force of many small businesses.

The kind of information and advice that small businesses receive in regard to pensions also appears to be a factor in whether or not they establish a pension plan. Small firms that received pension information from accountants and insurance agents were less likely to offer a plan than firms whose primary sources of information were from financial planners, investment advisory firms, business consultants, lawyers, and bankers.

Small-business owners may also have their own personal financial reasons for providing pensions; business owners find tax deferral as attractive as the rank-and-file worker does. Whether small employers provide benefits primarily for themselves at the expense of their workers, however, needs to be assessed.

Through the Tax Equity and Fiscal Responsibility Act of 1982, Congress sought to ensure that owners and managers did not establish pension plans largely for their own benefit without a fair share for their workers. Even before this legislation was enacted, however, most small employers sponsoring plans did not exclude their employees from benefits. There is no evidence that most small plans are established solely to satisfy the personal financial considerations of owners and managers.

The picture is somewhat less clear, however, for employees of professional firms. Coverage among professional-services employees is higher than average, but participation is lower.

Policies to Encourage Pension Coverage Growth

For over 50 years, the federal government has sought to encourage the establishment of pension plans through tax incentives. At the same time, public policy has been directed toward ensuring that plans are financially sound and equitable. Some observers have questioned whether these changes are having the opposite effect and are impeding pension growth.

Early legislation such as the Revenue Act of 1921 and the Revenue Act of 1926 first provided tax-deferred status to pensions. In particular, profit sharing plans gave small employers the flexibility to forgo contributions in those years in which profits were low. The Self-Employed Individuals Tax Retirement Act of 1962 allowed small unincorporated business owners to start a pension plan for themselves and their employees for the first time through Keogh plans.

The most important landmark in pension legislation, however, came with the enactment of the Employee Retirement Income Security Act of 1974 (ERISA). Included in this law were participation and vesting standards, fiduciary and funding requirements, and strengthened reporting and disclosure rules. In general, ERISA focused on safeguards for pension plan participants.

Since ERISA, a steady stream of legislation changed the types of pensions that small businesses were allowed to sponsor. In particular, the Revenue Act of 1978 created simplified employee pensions (SEPs) as a low-cost way for small employers to start a pension plan. SEPs are personal accounts similar to individual retirement accounts (IRAs) that allow employers to make contributions on behalf of their employees.

The Economic Recovery Tax Act of 1981 (ERTA) raised Keogh plan contribution and benefit limits and the dollar limit on SEP contributions. These changes were intended to encourage small businesses to establish pension plans. The Tax Equity and Fiscal Responsibility Act of 1982 (TEFRA) placed self-employed businesses on an equal footing with corporations by making contribution and benefit limits the same for all pension plans.

Perhaps the most significant provision in TEFRA for small businesses, however, had to do with plans in which more than 60 percent of benefits were going to key employees—so-called "top-heavy" plans. Small-employer plans are more likely to be top heavy, because the ratio of shareholders to employees in the plan is likely to be higher, and because more employees have shorter tenure and lower average wages than in large companies. TEFRA required top-heavy plans to provide minimum benefits or contributions to rank-and-file workers, provided for faster vesting standards, and placed stricter limits on allowable benefits for key employees.

The pace of legislative change continued with the Deficit Reduction Act of 1984 (further reducing the limits on maximum plan contributions and benefits), the Retirement Equity Act of 1984 (reducing the minimum age of plan participation from 25 to 21), and the Single-Employer Pension Plan Amendments Act of 1986 (restricting the terms under which pension plans can terminate and increasing the termination insurance premiums that single-employer plans must pay).

The next major piece of legislation that affected small businesses was the Tax Reform Act of 1986 (TRA). Although this law includes numerous employee benefit changes for employers in general, several provisions have a greater impact on small employers. For instance, tax reform changed the way in which employers can integrate their pensions with Social Security. Very small plans are more likely than larger plans to have integrated benefits.

Pension changes were also included in budget bills in 1986 and 1987. In 1986, plans were required to continue benefit contributions or accruals regardless of age for workers participating in defined contribution or defined benefit plans. In 1987, the single-employer termination insurance premium was raised and funding rules were changed substantially.

Surveys of small employers reported mixed findings about the effect of government regulation on small-business pension plans. Some small employers indicated that constantly changing laws and regulations were a significant deterrent to setting up a plan or administering one already established. Others did not agree. Thus, the direct responses of small-business owners provide only partial information about the economic effects of government regulation.

Since employers must balance the costs of setting up a plan against the benefits, whether government regulations increase or decrease costs affects the decision to set up a plan. On the one hand, favorable tax treatment for pension plans reduces the cost of plan sponsorship, and employees regard pensions favorably because they can defer individual income taxes on pension contributions until retirement. On the other hand, other government rules increase costs through funding, fiduciary, and reporting and disclosure requirements. Other provisions such as the top-heavy rules impose additional costs on small employers, whose per participant administrative costs are already higher than those of larger firms.

Statistical analysis shows that coverage rates in 1983 were lower than in 1979, suggesting that pension legislation may have constrained pension plan growth in recent years. Other research suggests that recent legislation may have changed the types of plans provided. When federal regulations increase the cost of defined benefit plans, some employers will shift to defined contribution plans. Nonetheless, other factors such as profitability and the ratio of capital to labor may have had as strong an impact on plan provision as the changes in pension legislation.

Recent legislation intended to encourage pension provision in small businesses does not appear to have been particularly successful in achieving these goals. Only 5 percent of the self-employed have set up Keogh plans; only 12 percent of employees without pension plans contributed to an IRA in 1982, and only 6 percent of small employers sponsored SEPs in 1985.

As a result, many lawmakers still seek to increase coverage among small employers—even though some observers, including many small businesses, are wary of further changes that could threaten the stability of the system. Proposals for change that are intended to encourage pension coverage among small employers fall into four categories: (1) simplifying the plans available to small employers, (2) improving the regulatory environment, (3) reducing costs, and (4) preserving benefits for retirement.

Although SEPs were introduced as a low-cost plan for small employers, few have taken advantage of them. Some observers believe that many small employers have never heard of SEPs. Nonetheless, the idea of a simplified plan for small businesses continues to be attractive to some lawmakers.

Some provisions of pension law ease regulatory requirements for small businesses, including those that allow firms with fewer than 100 participants to file financial reports every three years instead of annually. But small employers are burdened with stricter regulations than large firms through the top-heavy rules. The top-heavy rules may prevent owners of small businesses from accruing pension benefits as generous as those of the top management of large corporations who earn the same salaries. Small employers must also pay substantial charges to the government to start up, amend, or terminate their plans.

Lawmakers have also been concerned about pension preservation to ensure that pension benefits are used to provide income in retirement instead of being cashed out and spent when employees change jobs. Cashouts are most prevalent under defined contribution plans that distribute vested benefits directly to the participant upon job change.

Legislative proposals in 1987, 1988, and 1989 that address these issues include the Pension Portability Act, the Portable Pension Plan Act, the Pension Portability Improvement Act, the Retiree Health Benefits and Pension Preservation Act, and the Small Business Retirement and Benefit Extension Act (SBRBEA). All three portability bills have provisions to facilitate SEPs, such as reducing reporting and disclosure requirements, and seek to maintain preretirement distributions in a retirement income plan. The Portable Pension Plan Act also requires Department of Labor outreach to small employers so that they may be better informed about their plan options.

SBRBEA would phase out the top-heavy rules on the grounds that they are costly and unnecessary as a result of tax reform. Also, this bill would directly reduce the pension costs of small employers by providing a tax credit equal to 14 percent of employer contributions for rank-and-file workers.

Judged from the economic perspective of small employers, most of these proposals would not have much influence on pension plan formation. Lower administrative costs for SEPs or eased regulatory requirements may not be enough to convince small employers that plan sponsorship would be an advantageous business decision. However, simulations indicate that a 14 percent tax credit would lead to a substantial increase in the percentage of small employers providing pension plans.

Had the tax credit been in place in 1987, projections indicate that 3.9 million more workers would have been covered by a pension plan, raising the pension coverage rate among private-sector workers in small firms from an estimated 22 percent to 34 percent of all employees. Since not all workers in a company with a pension plan become plan participants, a 14 percent tax credit in 1987 would have added fewer plan participants. The simulations indicate that 2.9 million more workers would have become plan participants, raising the small-firm participation rate from an estimated 17 percent to 26 percent.

A broader-based proposal for a "negative income tax" for all small employers whether or not they have taxable income leads to an even larger simulated increase in the percentage of small-firm workers covered by a pension plan. An estimated 5.8 million additional workers would have had pension coverage in 1987, leading to a 40 percent coverage rate, compared to the 34 percent coverage rate under the pure tax credit. The participation rate among those working for small employers was projected to be 28 percent.

Based on 1987 projections, the estimated annual cost to the government of a 14 percent tax credit would be $1.1 billion, and the cost of a 14 percent "negative income tax," $1.7 billion. The public policy issue is whether these costs are worth the increase in coverage. The tax credit might be politically more attractive if it were coupled with preservation provisions that would mean pension distributions were used solely for retirement income.

Real wage growth of 0.9 percent a year could increase the pension coverage rate for small-firm employees from 22 percent to 27 percent. But the prognosis for economic growth is uncertain. Even in an expanding economy, some small employers may not find setting up a pension plan to be a good business decision.

At What Price Coverage?

Businesses, workers, and the federal government are all concerned with pension policy. Employers provide pensions for business reasons—to foster continued employment among workers who are valuable to the firm and to regulate the labor force by easing workers out of their jobs at retirement age. For the worker, employer-sponsored pensions provide tax-deferred retirement income and pension benefits that are cheaper than individual savings at a given level of retirement income. The federal government encourages employer-sponsored pensions to promote retirement income security and adequacy.

Over the years, proposals have been made to mandate employer-sponsored pensions to supplement Social Security. Most recently, President Carter's 1981 Commission on Pension Policy supported a "minimum universal pension system" (MUPS) to be established for all employees over age 25 with one year of service and 1,000 hours of employment with their employer. The minimum contribution would have been 3 percent of payroll and vesting would have been immediate.

In the years after MUPS was proposed, the minimum plan-participation age was reduced to 21 by the Retirement Equity Act of 1984. Based on that age, the mandatory recommendation would have raised pension participation rates for very small employers from 12 percent to 54 percent in 1987. The cost to the federal government, however, would have been $12.7 billion in 1987—more than 10 times the direct cost of a 14 percent tax credit for small employers.

The long-run costs of a MUPS pension contribution, according to analysis by the commission, would be passed on to workers in the form of lower wages. Some workers would be forced to accept pension coverage rather than higher wages. But in such a mandatory system, all workers included in the legislation would become plan participants immediately.

Both mandated and voluntary pensions have their strengths and weaknesses. Under a voluntary system, similar workers do not always have similar coverage. But under a mandatory system, the costs of providing for retirement income would fall primarily on small businesses, their workers, and the consumers who buy goods and services from these firms.

Employment-related retirement benefits may be increased through a continuum of policies. Choices range from expanded Social Security to a mandatory employer-provided pension system and from additional tax incentives to regulatory relief. The question ultimately is: at what price coverage?

Foreword

When the issue of small-firm pension coverage is raised, the initial reaction of many listeners is to presume that the topic is of limited interest because it focuses on a relatively specialized segment of the economy. After thoughtful appraisal, however, most listeners soon realize that the issue of pension coverage within the small-firm setting is at the heart of much of the discussion about retirement policy. Although nearly one-half of the work force is employed by small companies, most small firms do not provide pension coverage for their employees.

Representatives of business, government, and labor are concerned that our nation lacks a coordinated retirement policy. Policy interest is focused on the mix of benefits that will be provided in the future and on federal incentives for their provision. In particular, the future of employer-sponsored pensions is in question. Some fear that recent legislation has eroded employers' incentives to provide pension plans. Others suggest that since plan provision is so limited in small businesses, additional incentives are needed to bolster pension coverage in the future.

The Employee Benefit Research Institute (EBRI) has long been committed to the accurate statistical analysis of public policy benefits issues. *Pension Policy and Small Employers: At What Price Coverage?* continues a long-standing EBRI tradition. The work draws upon four data bases to analyze the economics of small-employer pension plans. Based on this analysis, author Emily S. Andrews finds that small businesses sponsor pension plans for essentially the same reasons as larger businesses. Pension plans are shown to foster long-term relationships with those employees who will become more valuable to the firm after more years on the job. Pensions are also an important component of personnel policy, enabling employers to structure their work force through retirement. And wage deferral through a pension plan provides employees of large and small firms the opportunity to save for retirement on a tax-deferred basis. The statistical findings reported in this volume are in keeping with reported attitudes of employers toward plan sponsorship.

Although the incentives for plan provision are similar in firms of all sizes, even after taking into account differences in the work place, workers in large companies are more likely than those in small companies to be covered by a pension plan. Part of this difference rests with the greater per-capita administrative costs that small employers must pay. By contrast, EBRI research does not find that most small plans are established solely to satisfy the personal financial considerations of owners or managers.

Based on economic findings, Andrews provides estimates of the number of employees who would become plan participants if legislation were enacted to permit small businesses to credit up to 14 percent of their pension plan contribution against their income tax liability. The likely effects of other policy proposals to increase coverage among small employers are discussed as well. These include proposals to encourage the development of simplified employee pensions and to ease regulatory requirements for small plans. Andrews also studies the chances for coverage gains without legislative change. The impact of economic growth on pension coverage is evaluated. The potential for targeted marketing strategies is considered as well.

Pension Policy and Small Employers: At What Price Coverage? is a valuable resource for those interested in proposing a consistent retirement policy for the nation. The focus of the study is the small-employer sector—without the expansion of small employer plans, pension coverage will not grow. The background for the study is the entire retirement income system. The volume describes the current system and its uncertainties and evaluates the need for greater pension coverage in the future. The aim of the analysis is to provide information to help us reply to the question: at what price coverage?

The book could not have been written without the assistance of Jennifer Davis, who tracked down other studies, checked on the accuracy of the findings, and provided valuable insights into the volume's logic and readability. The research was also supported by the programming assistance of Jeannette Lee, Kevin Ward, and W. Hardee Mahoney. Mary Catherine Calvert produced several drafts of the study during its development. The study would not have been possible without the donation of the National Federation of Independent Business' December 1985 survey of benefits through the auspices of William J. Dennis, Jr. The final volume was edited by Barbara Coleman, with the assistance of Shannon Braymen and Deborah Holmes.

Finally, the thoughtful and thorough review of earlier drafts provided by EBRI sponsors and outside reviewers made this book possible. Special thanks go to John Cooper, Neil Donovan, H. Gray Hutchison, Paul Jackson, Francis P. King, Donald Segal, Herbert L. Spira, and Paul Zwilling. Additional thanks go to Catherine Armington, Jules H. Lichtenstein, Frank S. Swain, and Hazel Witte on behalf of the Small Business Administration. In addition, the reviews of Robert L. Clark, Olivia S. Mitchell, Gregory W. Welch, and Stephen W. Welch were most appreciated.

Thanks notwithstanding, the views expressed in this book are solely those of the author. They should not be attributed to the officers, trustees, members, associates, contributors, or subscribers of the Employee Benefit Research Institute, its staff, or its Education and Research Fund.

DALLAS L. SALISBURY
President
Employee Benefit Research Institute
June 1989

About the Author

EMILY S. ANDREWS, Ph.D., is director of research at the Employee Benefit Research Institute (EBRI). She is a specialist on the role of employer pensions and Social Security in retirement, and author of *The Changing Profile of Pensions in America*, published by EBRI's Education and Research Fund in 1985. Her most recent research has been on pension provision among small employers. Before coming to EBRI, Dr. Andrews held policy research positions with the Social Security Administration and the U.S. Department of Labor. She also served on the staff of the President's Commission on Pension Policy. Dr. Andrews received her Ph.D. in economics from the University of Pennsylvania.

Introduction

The U.S. retirement income system has matured over the last 50 years, leading to increasing numbers of retirees who are receiving pension benefits. But the pension coverage rate has leveled off since the late 1970s. Coverage declined from 56 percent of all civilian workers in May 1979 to 52 percent in May 1983, and is believed to have leveled off since then.

The gap in private-sector pension coverage for workers appears to be largely among small employers. The latest data indicate that more than 90 percent of full-time employees in medium-sized and large firms participate in retirement plans, while, by contrast, only 43 percent of full-time employees of small firms do so.

Some members of Congress and other policymakers have indicated concern about potential costs to society and to future retirees themselves if employer-sponsored pension coverage fails to continue the expansion of the past 15 years, supplementing Social Security and private savings.

To meet the challenge of providing additional coverage, a number of legislative proposals specifically aimed at small employers have been introduced in Congress in recent years. This study provides economic data on small employers as background for evaluating the possible effects of these proposals on pension policy. The study used four data bases to provide a fuller picture of the costs and benefits of plan sponsorship for large and small firms. These include: the Small Business Administration/Internal Revenue Service match of corporate tax returns with employment data for 1979; the May 1979 and May 1983 Current Population Survey pension supplements; the National Federation of Independent Business mail survey of its membership; and the 1984 Survey of Income and Program Participation conducted by the Census Bureau.

Chapter I provides an overview of the U.S. retirement income system, with a description of the role played by government and employers, the development of the system, and pension policy concerns for the future.

Chapter II examines the role of small business in tomorrow's economy to help forecast future pension coverage. Economic changes that may affect pension coverage are reviewed, such as trends in unionization, self-employment, industrial composition of the economy, and labor productivity. The chapter also compares a number of characteristics of large and small businesses such as organizational and labor force factors.

Chapters III and IV develop an economic theory of pension provision. Chapter III investigates the connection between wage and benefit payments, and reviews research findings on why small employers pay lower wages on average and provide fewer benefits than large corporations. Chapter IV examines the connection between higher wages and pension coverage, as well as other characteristics of the work place and the work force that are related to pension coverage. Also reviewed are the reasons small employers themselves give for sponsoring a pension plan.

Chapter V presents economic findings that assess the extent to which business considerations, worker demand, and pension plan costs influence the decisions of large and small employers about establishing plans. Two other questions are explored: Does the source of information about pensions affect a small employer's decision to set up a plan, and do small firms establish plans primarily for their own tax-planning purposes?

Chapters VI and VII look at the federal pension policy that has been developed through legislative enactments since the 1920s and the policies that are currently being proposed. Beginning with the Revenue Act of 1921, chapter VI traces the evolution of pension legislation as Congress has sought to ensure that preferential tax treatment for pensions has been accompanied by fair and equitable treatment of lower-paid employees. Chapter VI looks in particular at these nondiscriminatory provisions as they have been aimed at and have affected small businesses. Also reviewed are legislative provisions aimed at encouraging small businesses to set up plans. Chapter VII outlines recent congressional proposals and examines the potential impact of this legislation on plan growth.

Chapter VIII compares the strengths and weaknesses of proposals to improve the voluntary pension system with broader-based alternatives such as mandating employer-sponsored pensions or expanding social insurance.

I. The Retirement Income System and Small Employers

Introduction

Are small businesses the coddled children of an otherwise competitive economy or pioneers on the frontiers of economic growth? These kinds of starkly contrasting terms are often used to describe the importance of small business in the U.S. economy. Sharply contrasting views are also expressed about the nature of employee benefits offered by small employers. Do small employers shirk their social responsibilities and thus transfer that responsibility to others, or do they provide their workers the benefits they deserve? These questions are relevant to a debate over the role public policy should play in encouraging pension coverage.

Concern for the economic well-being of the elderly leads some observers to question whether small employers accept sufficient responsibility for their employees or whether those workers in retirement will become a burden to society. Several lawmakers have proposed legislation to encourage or mandate greater pension coverage by small businesses to address this concern. Yet it is not at all clear that such legislation would be effective or even desirable.

The benefits that small employers provide must be viewed within the context of the nation's retirement income system and the economy as a whole if we are to judge whether national needs are being met. Only within that context can we assess the necessity for proposed legislation. Chapter I provides an overview of the retirement income system as background for an evaluation, in public policy terms, of the benefits offered by small employers.

The Retirement Income System

The U.S. retirement income system is complex, and is traditionally viewed as consisting of a mix of government benefits, employer-sponsored pensions, and individual savings (table I.1). Government programs include employment-based Social Security benefits and welfare-based payments from the Supplemental Security Income (SSI) program. Voluntary employer-sponsored pensions are provided by many public- and private-sector employers and are regulated by the federal government through the tax code and the Employee Retirement Income Security Act of 1974 (ERISA) and its amendments.

1

TABLE I.1
Percentage of Older Family Groups[a] Aged 65 or Older with Money Income from Specified Sources, 1986[b]

Source of Income	Total	Under $5,000	$5,000–$9,999	$10,000–$19,999	$20,000 or More
Number of Older Family Groups[a] (in thousands)	21,583	3,724	6,237	6,186	5,436
Percentage with					
Earnings	20%	4%	9%	22%	43%
Retirement benefits	94	82	97	98	94
Social Security[c]	91	80	95	95	90
benefits other than Social Security	40	6	23	56	63
other public pensions	15	2	9	19	28
railroad retirement	2	1	2	3	2
government employee pensions	14	2	7	16	27
private pensions or annuities	27	3	15	39	41
Income from assets	67	26	54	81	94
Veterans' benefits	5	4	5	4	5
Public assistance	7	25	8	1	0

Source: Susan Grad, *Income of the Population 55 or Older, 1986*, U.S. Department of Health and Human Services, Social Security Administration, pub. no. 13-11871 (Washington, DC: U.S. Government Printing Office, 1988), table 8, p. 16.
[a]Older family groups consist of married couples living together—at least one of whom is aged 65 or older—and nonmarried persons aged 65 or older. Persons who are married but not living with their spouse are included in the nonmarried persons category.
[b]Components may not add to totals due to rounding.
[c]Social Security beneficiaries may be receiving retired workers' benefits, dependents' or survivors' benefits, and other special types of benefits.
Note: Numbers may not add to totals, as a person can receive income from more than one source.

In recent years, supplements to this retirement income package have grown in importance. These supplements include current earnings of "retired" workers and in-kind benefits. The latter include health insurance benefits that are provided through the federal Medicare and Medicaid programs or through employer-sponsored retiree health care plans.

The U.S. retirement income system is characterized by diversity and by a decentralization of public pension policy.[1] Many policymakers conclude that a clearly defined retirement income policy is needed to specify what the balance of income sources in retirement should be. One way to define this goal is to ensure that workers maintain their current living standards throughout retirement. Within that context, policymakers have voiced concern that small employers do not take enough responsibility for their retirees' pension and health care needs. To evaluate those concerns, we need to understand how the mix of retirement benefits and entitlements provides income in retirement.

The Government's Role—Two of the most widely recognized government benefits are employment-based Social Security (Old-Age and Survivor's Insurance) and welfare-based SSI. The Social Security Act of 1935 established pension benefits for retired workers related to earnings and years of covered employment. The original act was extended and supplemented over the years and now covers the vast majority of American workers. The system redistributes income—lower-wage beneficiaries receive higher benefits in proportion to their lifetime earnings than beneficiaries with higher incomes.

Through the SSI program, welfare payments are provided to elderly persons whose lifetime earnings did not entitle them to minimum Social Security protection and whose income and assets fall below set amounts. In general, workers with lower incomes will depend more heavily on the government for support in retirement.

The federal government also helps retirees aged 65 and over by paying for a substantial proportion of their medical care through the Medicare program. Enacted in 1965, Medicare provides hospital and medical coverage to persons entitled to monthly benefits under Social Security. Legislation enacted in 1988 also provides catastrophic health coverage for Medicare beneficiaries financed through a schedule of fees paid by the beneficiaries themselves.

Low-income elderly receive means-tested benefits through Medicaid. That program also finances costly nursing home care for retirees if they have exhausted their own assets paying for these expenditures. While this

---

[1]Several committees in the U.S. Congress have primary responsibilities in the retirement income policy area, and several different federal agencies administer the laws.

study does not address noncash medical benefits in depth, these in-kind benefits provide an important income increment for older Americans. Without these benefits, retirees would face higher out-of-pocket costs or be denied access to care.

The Role of the Employer—Many public and private employers voluntarily provide pensions for their employees. Private-sector employer-sponsored pension plans became widespread after World War II as a supplement to Social Security. Some public-sector employer-sponsored pensions, such as the federal Civil Service Retirement System, were intended to be the sole source of retirement income for workers not covered by the Social Security system. All new federal employees now contribute to Social Security and are also covered by a retirement system that includes a pension plan and a retirement savings plan. Some pension plans for state and local government employees are expected to provide full benefits at retirement while others provide benefits to supplement Social Security.

There are two basic types of pension plans—defined benefit plans and defined contribution plans. Defined benefit plans provide employees a specified pension (benefit) at retirement that generally is based on a fixed percentage of salary per year of plan participation. By contrast, defined contribution plans do not guarantee a specific pension at retirement. Instead, such plans ensure that contributions are made according to specific rules—those contributions define the plan. New hybrid plans are starting to emerge as well that define the rate of return provided by the plan. These plans are characterized as defined benefit plans.

Workers may have only one primary plan or they may have both primary and secondary plan coverage. In general, employer-sponsored pensions in combination with Social Security are intended to give full-career workers a certain target percentage of their preretirement earnings. Some employers also provide their retirees health insurance in addition to pension payments.

The Role of Savings—Retirement savings were expected to grow after the Great Depression of the 1930s as more families began to have the financial resources to save. Savings did grow, and many retirees now supplement their pensions with income from assets. Pension assets have also added to private savings for workers who saved the pension distributions they received when they changed jobs or retired. The most important asset for most Americans, however, is their investment in their home. Home ownership reduces the expenses of many older Americans who do not pay rent and are no longer burdened by a mortgage.

The Role of Earnings—The concept of retirement has changed significantly in recent years. Although many more Americans are retiring before age 65, many also embark on part-time work after retirement. Postretirement

4

employment provides earnings that supplement other sources of income to varying degrees. This new source of retirement income may reflect a movement away from the traditional concept of retirement, suggesting a growing diversity among older Americans that mirrors the greater diversity in the population as a whole.

How the System Works—The four components of the retirement income system serve different needs and, accordingly, retirees receive different combinations of benefits. Well-targeted public policy must take into account the sources of support received by different groups at retirement. Not surprisingly, those with lower retirement income depend more heavily on government support, while those with higher retirement income rely more heavily on their own resources.

The poverty rate among the aged is lower than that of the rest of the population, in part because some elderly who would be poor based on their own resources live with other family members. Nonetheless, pockets of poverty remain. Older women are more likely to live at poverty or near-poverty levels (125 percent of the poverty line) than men because of their limited labor force participation and lower earnings during their working years.

Older family groups (aged 65 and older)[2] at the lowest end of the income scale (17 percent of all older families), with income of less than $5,000 a year, are less likely to receive Social Security than those in higher income groups (table I.1). In general, low-income elderly are more likely to receive direct public assistance from SSI and less likely to have income in the form of earnings.

Most older family groups with income between $5,000 and $10,000 a year (29 percent of all older families) receive Social Security benefits. For the vast majority of these beneficiaries, Social Security payments amount to more than 60 percent of income.[3] Twenty-three percent of these elderly families also receive an employer-sponsored pension.[4] For one-third of the pension recipients, the pension benefit amounts to over 20 percent

---

[2]Older family groups consist of single individuals and couples aged 65 and older whether or not they live with younger family members who may officially be designated head of household.

[3]Figures on the importance of income sources to different income groups are based on tables in Grad, 1988.

[4]These figures distort the role of pensions within different income groups insofar as the receipt of the benefit automatically raises the income of the retiree. Unfortunately, no data have been available to compare retirement income with preretirement earnings. The only study was that by Fox, 1982, based on the Retirement History Survey (last taken in 1979), the only data base providing all the necessary information for that type of an evaluation. He found that the importance of pension income was greater for workers with higher preretirement earnings.

of income. Over one-half of the retirees in this income bracket receive income from assets, while fewer than 10 percent have income from earnings.

As retirement income increases, pension benefits, asset income, and earnings become more important. Fifty-six percent of older family groups with income between $10,000 and $20,000 a year (another 29 percent of the older family population) receive benefits from an employer-sponsored program. For the 51 percent of those receiving pensions in this income bracket, the pension provided over 20 percent of income. Eighty-one percent in this income bracket have income from assets, and 22 percent have income from work.

We do not know into which income categories former employees of small businesses fall. Do retirees of small companies rely on government support? Would legislation encouraging greater pension coverage mean that fewer retirees would face a declining standard of living after retirement? While these questions are difficult to address directly, they depend on the way in which small business pension plans are formed and the impact public policy has on plan formation—issues that will be studied in depth in later chapters.

The Development of the System

Regardless of its efficacy, retirement income policy is rooted in the experience of the past and in the promise of the future. By its very nature, retirement income policy is a long-term commitment. Even the Social Security system has only recently reached maturity, some 50-plus years after its birth. Similarly, recent changes in employer-sponsored pensions will only come to fruition 25 years or more in the future. One way to think about the future is to examine the results of the past.

History—Social Security and employer-sponsored pensions have developed over a half-century and are still expanding. The growth and gradual maturation of Social Security is well documented.

Although the Social Security Act was passed in 1935, benefits were not paid until 1940. Farm workers, the self-employed, public employees, and employees in the nonprofit sector initially were not included in the system. In fact, in 1939, only 55 percent of paid workers were covered. This percentage rose to 61 percent in 1949 and 86 percent in 1960. Today, 93 percent of all workers pay Social Security taxes. In other words, even this nationwide pension program has taken 50 years to provide complete career coverage to virtually all workers.

In the beginning, few older workers were eligible for Social Security benefits and even fewer received them. Eligible workers may have been poorly informed about their benefits or may not have been able to afford to retire on the benefits provided.

In 1941, only 20 percent of those eligible for Social Security were receiving benefits (Social Security Administration, 1988). This percentage rose to 59 percent in 1950 and 85 percent in 1960. By 1986, 93 percent of all eligible older workers were receiving benefits. While most retired workers now receive Social Security, in the early 1960s only 69 percent of all older family groups reported getting a Social Security check (Grad, 1977). In other words, the system has taken many years to mature.

The employer-sponsored pension system is still maturing. Since pensions are voluntary, the gradual adoption of plans by employers has been an important component of system growth and future pension recipiency. Participation in private-sector employer-sponsored pension plans grew from 23 percent of wage and salary workers in 1950 to 37 percent in 1960 and 44 percent in 1974 (Skolnick, 1976). While consistent figures are not available for subsequent years, the rule of thumb generally used is that the participation rate has leveled off at around 50 percent.

As participants have started to retire, the receipt of employer-sponsored pensions has also increased. Recipiency will continue to increase even though pension plan participation rates have stabilized. This is due to the inherent time lag between the formation of plans and pension recipiency.

After an employer starts a plan, most plan participants will work many years before they are ready for retirement. Consequently, in 1962, only 9 percent of family groups aged 65 and older received benefits from a private employer-sponsored pension plan or private annuity although coverage was already much higher. By 1971, recipiency rose to 17 percent. Recipiency growth continued, so that by 1980, 23 percent of family groups aged 65 and over received private employer-sponsored pension benefits and by 1986, that rate had risen to 27 percent. Including pensions sponsored by both public and private employers, 40 percent of family groups aged 65 and over received pension benefits in 1986, compared to only 35 percent in 1980 (Grad, various years). Employer-sponsored pensions are expected to continue to grow in importance as a component of retirement income, which will change the benefit structure for future retirees.

Future Implications—Growth in pension benefit recipiency reflects increases in plan participation and changes in pension law. Because the pension promise is tied to an individual's entire work life, the future impact of current policy must be examined to understand how many years may be needed to accomplish current retirement income policy goals. Although more retirees are receiving pension benefits than ever before, the number will continue to grow because of past increases in pension plan participation and changes in plan provisions.

Fully 71 percent of all future retirees born during the early years of the baby boom are expected to receive pension income from employer-sponsored plans by the time they reach age 67 (Andrews and Chollet, 1988).[5] This represents a substantial increase from a 48 percent pension recipiency rate estimated for workers who are age 67 and recently retired. In addition, income from pension plans is expected to increase to 38 percent of total retirement income (excluding income from assets) for those born during the early years of the baby boom, compared to 23 percent of income for those who recently turned age 67.

These increases in recipiency reflect, in part, changes made under the Tax Reform Act of 1986 (TRA) that require employers who sponsor pension plans to guarantee benefits to workers under the plan after only five years of participation (or seven years if benefit entitlement is phased in over that period). Under ERISA, most plans adopted 10-year cliff vesting—that is, benefits granted to employees only after 10 years of service under the plan. The more rapid vesting schedules became effective with plan years beginning in 1989. As a consequence, the impact of TRA will be most pronounced for younger workers and for those yet to enter the labor force. The more years an individual works under the new law, the greater the benefits of shorter vesting will be. Those who start working in 1989 will have the opportunity to accumulate benefits from each job in which they qualify for five-year vesting.

While projections have not been made for workers not yet in the labor force, the effect of five-year vesting on pension recipiency for women born during the early part of the baby boom will be striking. The projected pension recipiency rate for married baby boom women at age 67 is 56 percent under five-year vesting. Before tax reform, only 43 percent of these women would have received an employer-sponsored pension at retirement (Andrews, 1987).[6]

---

[5]These forecasts come from the Pension and Retirement Income Simulation Model (PRISM) developed by ICF Incorporated under EBRI specifications. The model takes particular age cohorts (in 10-year age ranges) and simulates their career paths based on probability matrices until age 67. At each job change, workers are assigned an appropriate pension plan (also determined according to a probability matrix), and the benefits accruing from each plan are calculated at retirement. For a fuller description see Kennell and Shiels, 1986.

[6]Five-year vesting is projected to have a much smaller impact on older women since it affects only their current job and any future jobs they may hold. Before tax reform, 27 percent of married women who were in their fifties in 1985 were projected to receive pensions at age 67. After tax reform, the pension recipiency rate is expected to reach only 29 percent. The pension recipiency rate for women in their fifties at retirement is lower than that of baby boom women retirees because older women tend to have had fewer years in the labor force. Increasing labor force participation rates have lengthened the careers of women in each successive generation.

If current policies are maintained with no further legislative changes, the pension system will continue to grow and provide better retirement income to more American workers. But many wonder what the future will bring if the economy stagnates and the budget deficit continues. Uncertainty about the future of the economy has raised concerns about the future of retirement.

Pension Policy and Concern for the Future

The stability of the retirement income system for employees working in both large and small businesses depends on a combination of factors that are not all directly related to retirement income policy. Although most realistic forecasts of the retirement income system are optimistic, public concern about the future has grown. Some fear instability in financial markets. Others worry that sluggish growth in productivity, family income, and earnings may undermine the retirement income system. After decades of strong economic growth, for example, the oil shocks of the early 1970s led to an era in which gains in family income were limited at best (chart I.1). Analysts with a pessimistic view of the future are more likely to advocate policy adjustments to accommodate these circumstances.

Other economic uncertainties have fueled fears about the retirement income system. Unfriendly corporate takeovers have been accompanied by raids on overfunded pension plans, which brings into question the ongoing nature of the pension promise. Similarly, plant closings and plan terminations have raised fears among workers despite the benefit guarantees under the federal Pension Benefit Guaranty Corporation (PBGC). Although these incidents affect relatively few plan participants, in a world of greater economic uncertainty they amplify concerns about the stability of the U.S. pension system.

Income Inequality—While a sharp downturn in family income has not taken place, greater fluctuations have been apparent in recent years. Many young people who can foresee only limited economic gains for themselves wonder whether they can expect economic security in retirement. Recent studies have shown that, except for the aged, family income may have become less equal. For instance, Radner (1987) found that income has become somewhat less equal among younger families and more equal among older families. He found relative declines for most younger age groups. The Congressional Budget Office also reported a less equal distribution of after-tax income between 1977 and 1984 (U.S. Congress, 1987).

Analysts disagree about the interpretation and importance of these findings, however. Some warn about a trend toward greater income inequality, while others note that the shifts in income distribution are relatively small.

9

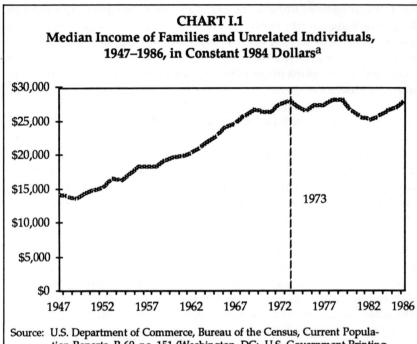

CHART I.1
Median Income of Families and Unrelated Individuals,
1947–1986, in Constant 1984 Dollars[a]

1973

Source: U.S. Department of Commerce, Bureau of the Census, Current Population Reports, P-60, no. 151 (Washington, DC: U.S. Government Printing
Office, 1984), table 11; and "At Last, There's More in the Family," *Wall
Street Journal,* 4 August 1987, p. 37.
[a]Numbers are deflated by the consumer price index.

With noticeable gains in retirement income, others wonder whether we
subsidize too many high-income retirees at the expense of others.

Improved income among the elderly and greater poverty among single
women and children may lead to struggles in the policy arena. These
strains will become more intense if the nation has overly optimistic income expectations when public funds are scarce. These strains feed into
the uncertainties expressed about future retirement income.

Financial Uncertainties—Increased volatility in the stock market also may
have added to anxieties. During the fourth quarter of 1987, which included
the October 19, 1987, stock market crash, directly held stock in private
trusteed pension portfolios fell from 40 percent to 36 percent of total assets.[7]

---

[7]Private-sector pension plans are either trusteed plans, in which the funds are directly invested by the pension trust, or insured plans, which are operated through an insurance
company. Quarterly data are currently available for trusteed plans only. Data on the investments of insured plans and state and local plans are available on an annual basis.

Private trusteed pension funds suffered net losses of $135 billion, or 10.4 percent of total assets, during the fourth quarter of 1987, the largest recorded quarterly capital loss over the five-year period since 1982 for which data were available.

Needless to say, gains made in the first three quarters of 1987 fully off-set the fourth-quarter losses, providing total 1987 earnings of $69 billion, a return of 6.4 percent. Even the direct stock holdings of private trusteed funds that represented most of the fourth-quarter loss showed a positive return of 9.2 percent for the year. Pension funds did not flee the stock market, although the decline in the stock market may have frightened many small investors.

In theory, participants in defined benefit plans should not be anxious about their benefits since these plans are invested for the long term. Furthermore, the investment risk in defined benefit plans generally rests with the employer since the pension promise is based on a basic benefit formula and not on investment returns. Many participants in defined contribution plans realize, however, that they could suffer loss of retirement income if their planned retirement coincides with a market crash. And more participants now have defined contribution plans.

The Changing Benefit Structure—For many years the majority of plan participants have been in defined benefit plans. These plans have traditionally provided the bulk of retirement income. While this is still true, the proportions have been changing. More participants have secondary defined contribution plans, and primary coverage under defined contribution plans has expanded as well. Research indicates that the movement toward defined contribution plans represents a long-run trend independent of shifts in firm size and industry (Gustman and Steinmeier, 1988; Clark, 1989). Several reasons are given for this change. Some say that government regulation has made defined benefit plans too costly (a topic considered in chapter VI for the case of small employers). Others note that employers are restructuring their benefits to prepare for the baby boom's retirement.

Younger workers react favorably to defined contribution plans because account balances showing a current cash value appear more meaningful than the promise of a monthly check at retirement for an unknown amount. Employers realize that to be cost effective, defined contribution plans must be considered an integral part of retirement income and not just a supplement to savings, because the baby boom's retirement will be costly. Primary defined contribution plans are one way to restructure the costs of retirement for the current work force.

The mix of total compensation, including wage and salary payments and voluntary and mandated benefits, also has been changing. Since

11

pensions are not the only employee benefit provided by employers, there are competing demands for the benefit dollar. Benefit contributions have grown for many years, and the composition of benefits has changed with that growth. According to U.S. Commerce Department data (1988), benefits made up 16 percent of total compensation costs in 1987 compared to just under 8 percent in 1960 (table I.2).[8] Voluntary benefits grew from somewhat over 4 percent of compensation in 1960 to 9 percent in 1987. About 56 percent of all benefits provided in 1987 were voluntary.

The shares of compensation going to voluntary retirement and health benefits both increased over that period. Health insurance contributions increased faster, however, through increases in coverage rates and premium

TABLE I.2

Employer Outlays for Employee Benefits, 1960–1987

Type of Benefit	1960	1970	1982	1984	1986	1987
	as a percentage of compensation[a]					
All Benefits	8.0%	10.7%	16.7%	16.8%	16.3%	16.1%
Mandatory	3.6	4.4	6.5	7.0	7.1	7.0
Voluntary	4.4	6.4	10.2	9.9	9.3	9.0
	as a percentage of voluntary benefits					
Pensions	65.8	61.3	54.8	51.6	49.3	47.9
Health[b]	25.9	31.3	41.4	44.8	46.6	48.0
Life Insurance	8.3	7.4	3.8	3.6	4.1	4.1

Source: EBRI tabulations from U.S. Department of Commerce, Bureau of Economic Analysis, *National Income and Product Accounts of the United States, 1929–1982, Statistical Tables* (Washington, DC: U.S. Government Printing Office, 1986); and *Survey of Current Business*, U.S. Department of Commerce, Bureau of Economic Analysis (Washington, DC: U.S. Government Printing Office), July issue, various years.

[a]Includes income from other labor income, which primarily includes directors' fees of $4 billion in 1987.

[b]Includes military medical insurance, which consists of payments for medical services for dependents of active-duty military personnel for medical care at nonmilitary facilities which totaled $1.1 billion in 1987.

Note: Percentages may not add to 100 percent due to rounding. These numbers do not include vacations, lunch periods, etc.—time paid for and not worked.

---

[8]These percentages are higher when time paid for but not worked (vacation time, holidays, personal days, lunch breaks, etc.) is included in the benefit portion of the compensation package.

costs. Consequently, payments for health care rose from nearly 26 percent of voluntary benefit expenditures in 1960 to 48 percent in 1987 (table I.2). By contrast, pension contributions made up 66 percent of voluntary benefit payments in 1960 and nearly 48 percent in 1987.

Recent data suggest that the share of compensation provided as benefits may have peaked in the early 1980s. In 1984, mandatory and voluntary benefits combined amounted to nearly 17 percent of total compensation. They edged off to 16 percent by 1987. Voluntary benefits peaked in 1982 at 10 percent of total compensation compared to 9 percent in 1987. By 1987, contributions to employer-sponsored pensions and health insurance plans were a smaller percentage of compensation than in the previous year.

Observers point to increasing future demands for the retirement dollar as medical care costs rise and benefits formerly provided on a relatively low-cost basis become more expensive. Employees face higher medical payments in the form of copayments and deductibles. While Social Security replacement rates are scheduled to edge off, retirees will face the additional costs of catastrophic coverage under Medicare. In addition, any new program to provide social insurance for long-term care could fall on retirees as well. Consequently, the demands on retirement income will be greater than ever before.

Other Sources of Uncertainty—An additional concern results from continued doubts about the stability of Social Security despite the steps taken by many politicians and policymakers to allay those fears. Although legislation enacted in 1983 ensured that the Social Security trust fund would be in actuarial balance for years to come, high payroll tax rates borne by younger workers have frightened some into believing that the system has started to crumble. Others want reforms to make the system more equitable or economically efficient.[9] Those proposals may feed the fears of some who suspect that the system is in jeopardy. The expected build-up of the trust fund in the 1990s, legislated under the 1983 Amendments, has added to the uncertainty because of its potential effect on the federal deficit and on financial markets. These issues will be examined more thoroughly in chapter VIII.

In this environment, some younger workers have ceased to believe that the retirement income system will be able to deliver to them when they retire, even though (or perhaps because) their parents and grandparents have received generous benefits. As a consequence, the old question about pension coverage has reemerged: is the pension coverage cup half empty or half full?

---

[9]For instance, see Boskin, 1986.

The best statistics show that 56 percent of nonfarm wage and salary workers were covered by a pension plan in 1983 (Andrews, 1985).[10] Other data, not strictly comparable,[11] show that the proportion of workers aged 25 to 64 participating in a pension plan edged off between 1979 and 1987 from 55.7 percent to 49.5 percent (chart I.2).

Nevertheless, the issue remains one of perspective. Optimistic analysts contend that more workers are covered by pensions than before. The more pessimistic view holds that retirees will need better pensions in the future. To fill the empty half of the pension cup, many look to small employers.

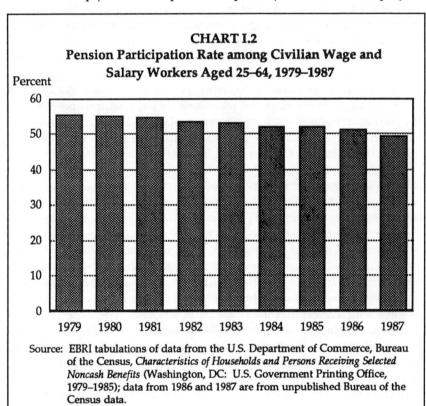

CHART I.2
Pension Participation Rate among Civilian Wage and Salary Workers Aged 25–64, 1979–1987

Source: EBRI tabulations of data from the U.S. Department of Commerce, Bureau of the Census, *Characteristics of Households and Persons Receiving Selected Noncash Benefits* (Washington, DC: U.S. Government Printing Office, 1979–1985); data from 1986 and 1987 are from unpublished Bureau of the Census data.

---

[10]These figures are from the Census Bureau's May 1983 Current Population Survey pension supplement funded by EBRI and the U.S. Department of Health and Human Services. New data will be forthcoming in 1989 from a similar survey conducted by the Census Bureau and funded by EBRI, the Social Security Administration, and four other federal and congressional organizations.

[11]These figures are based on responses for the previous year from the Census Bureau's March Current Population Survey income supplement.

Pensions and Small Employers

Faced by an uncertain future and fears for the security of the retirement income system, some policymakers hope to buttress the foundations of the system. Their focus turns to small employers, where they see both untapped resources and inequity as far as benefits are concerned. Small businesses employ the most workers without pension plans, it is argued, and those offering pensions only do so in the interest of owners and managers. Before analyzing the validity of these claims and developing an economic model of pension plan provision, the role of the small employer in the retirement income system needs to be understood.

Where do employees with pensions work? Data show that in 1983 workers with pension coverage tended to work in large firms; those without coverage were employed by small businesses (chart I.3). In particular, 80 percent of nonfarm employees with coverage worked for businesses with 100 or more employees. Conversely, 76 percent of workers without pension coverage worked for businesses with fewer than 100 workers. Such statistics spur policy interest in expanding the number of small-employer plans.

Pension coverage tends to be associated with workers who have a long-term commitment to the labor force. Since pensions are employment based, with benefits often related to years of plan participation, only workers with relatively long careers will accrue meaningful pension benefits at retirement. Very young workers are often not interested in pension coverage and are unlikely to be on any one job as long as five years early in their careers. Workers who have reached retirement age may already be receiving benefits or may continue on the job for such a short time that benefit accrual would be negligible.

Review of 1983 data shows that many uncovered employees are not prime-age workers (aged 25 through 64) who could accrue meaningful retirement benefits under a pension plan (chart I.4). Among uncovered employees, a sizable minority (46 percent) were less likely to accrue a meaningful pension from their current job: 30 percent were relatively young (under age 25), 3 percent were of retirement age (aged 65 and over), and 13 percent worked very limited hours (less than 1,000 annually).

Nonetheless, the majority of workers not covered by a pension plan (54 percent) were in those prime age groups who spent many hours on the job (1,000 hours or more annually)—nearly three-quarters worked full time (2,000 hours or more). Likewise, 65 percent of these prime-age "core" workers earned over $10,000 a year. The additional fact that 68 percent of "core" workers without pension coverage worked for small employers is of particular concern to policymakers.

15

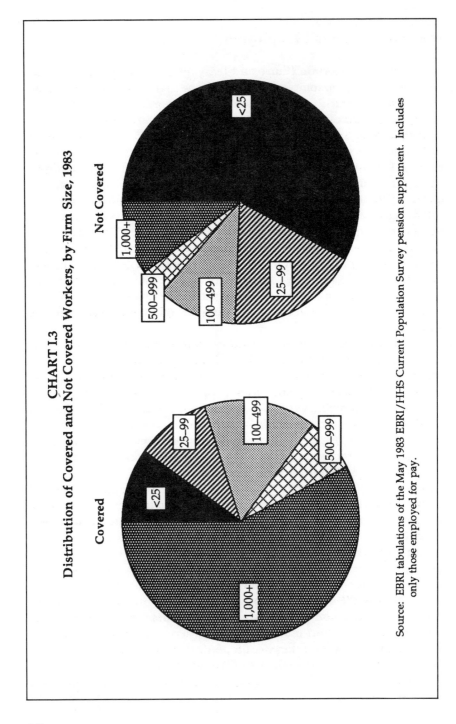

CHART I.3

Distribution of Covered and Not Covered Workers, by Firm Size, 1983

Covered

Not Covered

Source: EBRI tabulations of the May 1983 EBRI/HHS Current Population Survey pension supplement. Includes only those employed for pay.

CHART I.4
Nonfarm Workers by Coverage Status and Type of Employment, 1983

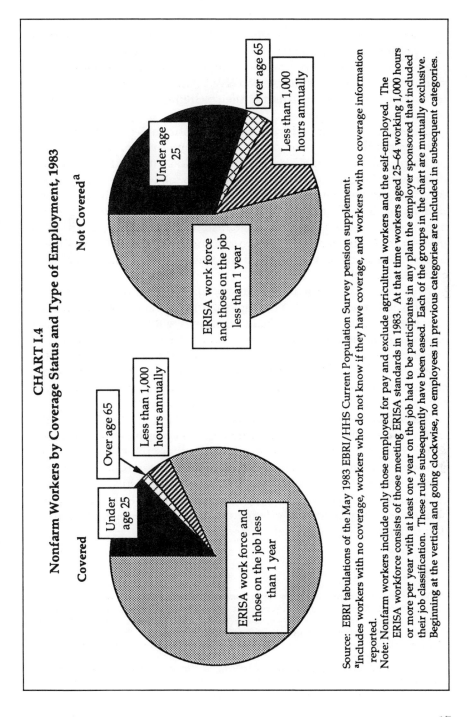

Source: EBRI tabulations of the May 1983 EBRI/HHS Current Population Survey pension supplement.
[a]Includes workers with no coverage, workers who do not know if they have coverage, and workers with no coverage information reported.
Note: Nonfarm workers include only those employed for pay and exclude agricultural workers and the self-employed. The ERISA workforce consists of those meeting ERISA standards in 1983. At that time workers aged 25–64 working 1,000 hours or more per year with at least one year on the job had to be participants in any plan the employer sponsored that included their job classification. These rules subsequently have been eased. Each of the groups in the chart are mutually exclusive. Beginning at the vertical and going clockwise, no employees in previous categories are included in subsequent categories.

17

There are many who believe that small businesses do not generally provide pension plans for their employees, and that when they establish a plan, it is intended for a minority of employees, which contributes to pension inequality. It is commonly perceived that small employers are able to manipulate pension plans for their self-interest, providing limited benefits to their workers.

These accusations are difficult to evaluate. Although private-sector pensions generally replace about 20 percent of preretirement income,[12] data on retirees show that the percentages vary widely (Grad, 1988). Some of the reasons for these variations are clear. Not all workers have pension coverage over their entire working lives and not all workers have the same number of jobs. In addition, not all workers have the same salary, and not all pension plans have the same benefit formulas. The diversity of the retirement income system reduces the uniformity of benefits. But the impact of small employers on the dispersion of benefits has yet to be addressed directly.

To some extent, legislation has limited the range of benefits that may be provided under ERISA. At the top end, rules govern contributions and benefits to ensure that highly paid employees will not receive pensions exceeding maximum allowable limits under plans that are qualified by the Internal Revenue Service. At the bottom end of the scale, the extent to which pension plans can reduce benefits based on integration with Social Security is controlled by legislation to ensure that vested workers will receive at least a minimum benefit from their plan.[13]

Special rules, reviewed in chapters VI and VII, have been enacted to ensure that small-business plans provide greater benefits to more of their employees. No one knows, however, whether these rules have promoted pension equity or deterred plan formation. Furthermore, research has not determined whether small-employer plans are in any way more "discriminatory" than those of large employers. One of the key questions to be addressed by this study is whether the factors influencing plan formation differ for large and small firms.

---

[12]While target replacement rates set by corporations for career employees are generally higher, many workers do not spend a full career with a single employer. Although the data are fragmented, it appears that actual workers receiving pensions replace around 20 percent of their preretirement earnings with income from pensions.

[13]Some employers coordinate their plans with Social Security benefits to provide pensions that more nearly equal the same target percentage of preretirement earnings for all employees. Social Security benefits are relatively higher in relation to salary among the less highly paid. The Tax Reform Act of 1986 changed the rules governing integration provisions. The legislation is still a topic of controversy.

Formulating Informed Policy

Despite projections that the retirement income system will continue to deliver benefits to future retirees, recent economic uncertainties have led to fears that the system cannot be sustained. Gains in total compensation have not been strong and benefits have not continued their earlier expansion. Changing benefit structures, costly health care premiums, and increasing stock market volatility have stimulated public interest in improving the retirement income system.

At the same time, many believe that pension plans in general, and small-business plans in particular, are over-regulated and that recent changes in pension policy have not contributed to the expansion of the system. As a result, legislation has been proposed to remove special small-employer regulations. Yet no studies have addressed what the balance between pension equity and plan formation should be. And pension "equity" may have different meanings for different observers.

Despite the long-standing interest in the potential of small businesses to increase pension coverage, no empirical analysis has been conducted to assess the efficacy of different policy proposals to expand the voluntary pension system. What is more, no research has evaluated the extent to which discriminatory plans are a public policy concern. As with any federal regulation, a balance must be struck between regulation that addresses fraud and abuse and regulation that burdens honest enterprise.

Studies show that the small-business sector accounts for the majority of workers without pensions. But to understand how legislation has affected and may affect small-employer plans, the relationship between small firms and the labor market must be understood. While some research has been conducted on wages and firm size,[14] few studies have analyzed the connection between firm size and pension benefits. Do pensions serve a business purpose, or are they simply tax-favored compensation for owners, managers, and employees? If pensions are a management tool, what factors influence their effectiveness and, hence, their availability?

Recent legislative proposals have concentrated on providing more voluntary incentives for pension plan sponsorship by small employers. Whether these proposals will work depends on the economics of pension plan provision. Chapter II explores the role of small businesses within the economy, providing the background to analyze the economic determinants of pension coverage. Drawing on this analysis, the effectiveness of policy proposals designed to foster pension plan growth among small employers will be evaluated, and the desirability of various proposals will be assessed within the broader context of social and economic considerations.

---

[14]For a review of this work, see chapter III.

II. Small Employers and the Economy

Introduction

Differences between small businesses and large businesses often appear intuitively obvious. Big business is identified with General Motors, IBM, and AT&T; small businesses include the neighborhood restaurant, the local garage, doctors, dentists, and lawyers. Yet, a more thoughtful appraisal of the situation indicates that distinctions between businesses of different sizes are more than a matter of scale. Small businesses engage in different activities, are run differently, and provide employment to different workers.

Business size can be defined in many ways—from annual sales to net assets to number of employees. Different definitions have been used within each of these categories. Perhaps the most widely accepted measure is based on the total number of workers employed by the firm. That definition is adopted here. Since pension provision is the focus of this study, a definition based on employees is most appropriate.

No cutoff unambiguously delineates businesses by employment size since employment forms a continuum ranging from large to small. In the interest of definitional consistency, the following terms will be used. *Small businesses* are those with fewer than 100 employees; *very small businesses* are those with fewer than 25 employees. *Medium-sized businesses* employ 100 to 500 workers. *Large businesses* have work forces of 500 or more employees; *very large businesses* have work forces of 1,000 or more. If a business operates in more than one location or work site (establishment), the total number of employees in all locations determines whether the business is large or small.

Although many employees work for large firms, the vast majority of all businesses are small in terms of their number of employees. According to the U.S. Small Business Administration, 93 percent of 2.6 million corporations filing income tax returns in 1979 had fewer than 50 employees (SBA, 1986).[1] Similarly, 98 percent of 1.3 million partnerships that filed returns had fewer than 50 employees. Virtually all of some 9.3 million sole proprietorships had fewer than 50 employees.

---

[1] The Internal Revenue Service (IRS) matched 1979 tax return information to records of employment by firm size for the Small Business Administration (the SBA/IRS match file). While these data are nearly a decade old, findings from this file remain valid as employment by firm size has not changed radically. A 1982 file has been prepared but findings from the updated version have not been published by the SBA. The 1979 file is one of the major data sets used in this book's analysis. See appendix A for a more complete description of these data.

Although each individual small business may have few workers, small business in the aggregate provides substantial employment opportunities in today's economy. In 1983, 45.5 percent of all private-sector civilian non-farm employees reported working for small companies, and 41.0 percent worked for large employers.[2] The remainder of the work force, 13.5 percent, worked for medium-sized firms.

Small businesses make a significant contribution to business activity, but their share of assets and sales is lower than their share of employment. According to the SBA (1986), small firms contributed 33 percent of total sales and held 22 percent of all business assets in 1979. Small firms also received 27 percent of net reported business income. By comparison, large firms reported 55 percent of sales, 65 percent of business assets, and 65 percent of net income.

Since business conditions are not static, and changes may influence the growth of pension plan provision, this chapter considers how the economy may be changing. Census data are tracked to determine whether employment in firms and establishments (plants or work sites) has shifted toward smaller entities. Chapters III and IV develop an economic theory of pension provision that suggests that the size of the economic unit is important.

This chapter looks at other economic changes that may be crucial to the future of pension coverage as well, including overall trends in unionization, self-employment, and the industrial composition of the economy. Finally, since improvements in productivity ultimately underlie long-run changes in compensation, trends in labor productivity are reviewed to provide a background against which to assess whether a slowdown in the economy would affect pension provision.

Within this macroeconomic framework, the industrial, financial, organizational, and labor force characteristics of large and small businesses are compared, highlighting areas of similarity and of divergence. Chapters III and IV draw upon this background to analyze how these factors motivate employers to sponsor a pension plan.

---

[2]These findings are based on the 1983 Current Population Survey (CPS) pension supplement that provides detailed information on demographic and employment characteristics of private-sector employees with and without pension coverage on their job. The survey, funded by EBRI and the U.S. Department of Health and Human Services and conducted by the U.S. Bureau of the Census, is one of the primary data sources used in this study. For a fuller description of the survey, see appendix A. The CPS data on coverage are roughly comparable to those from the 1979 SBA/IRS match file, which show that small employers employed 41 percent of the labor force and large businesses employed 47 percent. Because the SBA/IRS match does not report employment of nonprofit institutions, the SBA/IRS match file findings are not strictly comparable to those of the CPS pension supplement. Nonprofit institutions are more likely to be small employers. In addition, the CPS only reports one job per worker, while the SBA/IRS match counts employment in all jobs.

Shifts in Firm Size

Because pension policy is a long-term commitment, the role of small business in tomorrow's economy must be understood to forecast trends in pension coverage. Inasmuch as small businesses are less likely to have pension plans, a shift in the structure of employment toward small firms could lead to a lower pension coverage rate. One way to project future trends in coverage is to determine whether the employment profile of wage and salary workers has been shifting toward smaller firms.[3]

Many believe that such a shift has taken place. Certain changes in the structure of the economy make plausible the proposition that small firms have been increasing their employment share. These include contracting out by larger firms and the deregulation of the transportation and financial services sectors.

Nonetheless, alternative arguments suggest that large firms have not lost ground. One such argument holds that the rash of mergers and acquisitions in recent years has consolidated business holdings. In addition, a number of small high-tech companies have grown quite large.

Determining whether small business has become more dominant appears to be a simple statistical exercise. Nonetheless, conceptional issues and data problems combine to forestall an easy answer. From a public policy perspective, a number of snapshots of the small-business share of employment taken at different points in time are needed to assess whether its share has grown. The underlying distribution of employment by firm size is the key for research that seeks to determine future trends in pension coverage.

Unfortunately, consistent data have not been collected over a long enough period to determine whether the pattern of employment has changed significantly in recent decades.[4] The best available data indicate

---

[3]The discussion and data in this section exclude the self-employed, who are of lesser interest to policymakers since they can individually establish their own plans as employers.
[4]Some data, such as the Census Bureau's County Business Patterns data, are collected on establishments (plants or work sites—the building blocks of the firm) but not on entire firms. Other data that provide information on firm size, such as the Census Bureau's Enterprise Survey, have only recently expanded their sample to nationwide industry groupings. The SBA's United States Enterprise Establishment and Microdata file provides data on *changes* in employment by firm size but does not compare its data with other national figures on total *employment* to ensure that they are consistent. Without benchmarking, it is impossible to weight the file appropriately. As a consequence, changes in employment in industries that are more completely surveyed (such as manufacturing) may appear more important than changes in employment that are less completely surveyed (such as services). And shifts in the relative representation of those industries in the file over the years may lead to spurious changes in employment growth. The use of that file to describe changes in employment is discussed later. While the SBA's file that matches employment data with IRS tax returns for 1979 was recently updated to 1982, that file was not available for comparative analysis.

that the profile of employment has not shifted toward smaller firms. The employment share of small firms was almost 46 percent in both 1979 and 1983.[5] Between those years, the employment share of very large firms edged off slightly while medium-sized firms picked up employment (table II.1). Any shift toward smaller firms ought to have been heightened during this period since employment in large manufacturing firms was disrupted by layoffs after the 1982 recession (Andrews, 1985).

The stability in employment shares in the aggregate, however, masks significant shifts in firm size within industries. Employment in very large manufacturing firms dipped from nearly 58 percent of the manufacturing work force in 1979 to 53 percent in 1983. In the case of durables manufacturing, very large firms lost 1.3 million workers as a result of significant layoffs of auto and steel workers. As a consequence, the percentage of manufacturing employees in small firms expanded somewhat from 22 percent of employment in 1979 to 25 percent in 1983.

Shifts to larger firms in the service-producing industries fully offset the decline in the employment share of large manufacturers. Employment in very large retail trade firms increased from 29 percent in 1979 to 32 percent in 1983, while the share of small firms fell from 60 percent to 54 percent. Similarly, very-large-firm employment in finance, insurance, and real estate increased from 40 percent in 1979 to 44 percent in 1983, while small-firm employment dropped from 42 percent to 34 percent. This trend was also apparent in services—very-large-firm employment grew from 18 percent in 1979 to nearly 20 percent in 1983 while small-firm employment decreased from 62 percent to 59 percent.

Based solely on firm size, pension coverage in manufacturing would be expected to decline while coverage would increase in other areas. The stability in the share of small-firm employment in the aggregate may mask significant changes in pension coverage taking place in different sectors of the economy.

The Shift to Smaller Establishments—Changes in establishment size may also be important in terms of pension policy if smaller work sites, like smaller firms, are less likely to provide a pension.

While employment by firm size remained constant overall between 1979 and 1983, employment in firms of all sizes was redirected toward smaller establishments or work-site locations.[6] This change may be one reason for the popular opinion that small firms are becoming more predominant.

---

[5]These findings are based on the May CPS pension supplements for 1979 and 1983. Work by Hamilton and Medoff, 1988, supports this analysis.
[6]The firm, as the primary business entity, may control more than one establishment consisting of one or more plants or work sites.

TABLE II.1
Distribution of Employment, by Industry and Firm Size, 1979 and 1983

Industry	Total		<25		25–99		100–499		500–999		1,000 +	
	1979	1983	1979	1983	1979	1983	1979	1983	1979	1983	1979	1983
Total	100.0%	100.0%	30.6%	31.4%	15.0%	14.2%	12.6%	13.5%	4.8%	5.3%	36.9%	35.7%
Manufacturing	100.0	100.0	9.0	12.4	13.0	12.6	14.9	15.4	5.5	6.1	57.6	53.5
Services	100.0	100.0	47.6	45.2	14.3	13.6	13.3	14.6	6.5	6.9	18.4	19.7
Wholesale Trade	100.0	100.0	32.8	36.2	22.5	22.1	17.7	15.8	4.8	3.5	22.3	22.4
Retail Trade	100.0	100.0	42.8	39.6	17.0	14.5	8.5	10.1	2.9	3.8	28.9	32.1
Transportation	100.0	100.0	23.5	22.3	13.6	12.4	8.5	16.0	4.4	3.9	50.0	45.4
Communications and Public Utilities	100.0	100.0	5.2	4.9	7.7	9.9	6.8	8.7	2.6	3.1	77.7	73.5
Mining	100.0	100.0	6.7	12.2	9.2	7.6	12.1	13.0	6.3	2.4	65.7	64.7
Construction	100.0	100.0	55.6	58.4	20.1	20.2	12.8	9.7	2.7	2.3	8.8	9.6
Finance, Insurance, and Real Estate	100.0	100.0	26.8	20.9	14.9	13.5	13.4	14.9	5.1	6.5	39.7	44.3

Source: EBRI tabulations of May 1979 and May 1983 Current Population Survey pension supplements.
Note: Percentages may not add to 100 percent due to rounding.

Even very large employers may have plants or work sites at which a relatively small number of workers are employed. Between 1979 and 1983, the percentage of nonfarm employment in large establishments declined from 19 percent to 17 percent. At the same time, very small establishments grew from 40 percent to 42 percent of the labor force.

Manufacturing businesses made a sizable shift toward smaller plants between 1979 and 1983 (table II.2). In 1979, 51 percent of all employees at very large firms worked in plants with 1,000 or more workers. In 1983, 46 percent of workers in very large businesses were in plants with 1,000 or more workers. Both durable and nondurable goods manufacturing employment moved toward smaller establishments. In durable goods manufacturing, the reduction of plant sizes was dramatic in firms employing 500 to 1,000 workers. A higher proportion of workers were in plants employing 100 to 500 workers (52 percent in 1983, compared to 40 percent in 1979), and a lower percentage were in plants with 500 to 1,000 workers (35 percent, compared to 52 percent).[7]

More employees of larger service providers (including finance, insurance, and real estate as well as services) also operated at smaller work sites. Unlike manufacturing, these shifts were not a result of the 1982 recession, since employment in these industries increased strongly between 1979 and 1983. Among very large firms in finance, insurance, and real estate, the share of employment in very large establishments fell from 25 percent to 22 percent. In 1979, 53 percent of all service-sector workers in very large firms worked in establishments with 1,000 or more workers. By 1983, that percentage had dropped to 46 percent.

In wholesale trade, smaller firms moved toward even smaller establishments. In 1979, 18 percent of the employees in firms with 25 to 100 employees worked in smaller establishments. By 1983, that ratio rose to 28 percent. Similarly, in 1979 54 percent of workers in firms with 100 to 500 employees worked in smaller establishments, compared to 63 percent in 1983.

The shift toward smaller establishments may have been influenced by changing economic conditions. In recent years, some companies have acquired smaller subsidiaries in completely new lines of business. Other companies have decentralized their operations, running corporate departments as independent profit centers. Smaller plant sizes may also have been one of the results of geographic decentralization. Employment in the South and the West has grown relative to that in the North and the Midwest, providing employers cheaper production facilities and lower-cost

---

[7]Some of this shift may have been a result of layoffs in plants employing approximately 500 workers.

labor. Furthermore, many corporations have shifted their operations from cities to suburban areas and possibly toward smaller establishments as well.

The finding that establishments have become smaller raises many questions about the future. A movement toward smaller plant sizes will tend to reduce pension coverage overall if pensions are less prevalent in firms with smaller establishments. To date, research has not related pension coverage to the size of the plant or work site. The impact of establishment size on pension coverage is discussed in chapter V.

Small Firms and New Jobs—Although the data indicate that the small-firm share of employment did not expand between 1979 and 1983, the role of small employers in job creation continues to excite controversy.[8] Job creation statistics have been used to imply that employment has moved toward small firms, although these figures do not necessarily provide a clear measure of the shift in the distribution of employment.[9]

Research on job creation has generally been based on a Dun & Bradstreet data base called the Dun's Market Identifiers (DMI).[10] The two most prominent users of this data base are David Birch and researchers associated with the SBA.[11] Birch's initial analysis in 1979 reported that small businesses accounted for 65 percent of all net new jobs created between 1974 and 1976 (Harris, 1985). Other researchers have disputed his findings. Using the SBA data, Armington (1983) stated that only 51 percent of job growth between 1976 and 1980 stemmed from small businesses, a figure more in harmony with the Census Bureau statistics cited earlier on the percentage share of small-business employment. Armington and Odle (1982) indicated that most growth in small businesses was generated by the expansion of a minority of firms.

---

[8]For instance, see Hamilton and Medoff, 1988, and Wessel and Brown, 1988.

[9]The term "job creation" is used to mean the growth in employment over two time periods (and the distribution of that growth by size of firm). Employment growth reflects net employment changes from the creation and demise of businesses as well as their expansion and contraction.

[10]The Dun's Market Identifiers (DMI) file includes 6 million records of a data base compiled by Dun & Bradstreet representing over 9 million businesses to support their credit rating service. The full data base is compiled and updated as businesses form, shut down, contract, and grow. New businesses are included when credit ratings are applied for, and business deaths are recorded upon bankruptcy. Updated information from ongoing firms is collected directly from employers by Dun & Bradstreet staff.

[11]Their use of the data is very different. Birch makes as few changes to the file as possible. He excludes businesses with incomplete records and adjusts for overseas employment. He estimates business starts from figures on new incorporations after excluding businesses that simply change their legal form, taking the view that the DMI data should be used as a sample and not be weighted to represent the universe. The SBA does extensive editing to ensure that it has appropriately categorized establishments and firms. The SBA has also compared its employment growth rates to BLS estimates, although it has not compared its employment levels with those of the BLS.

TABLE II.2
Distribution of Employment, by Firm Size, Establishment Size, and Industry, 1979 and 1983

Establishment Size and Industry	Firm Size									
	<25		25–99		100–499		500–999		1,000+	
	1979	1983	1979	1983	1979	1983	1979	1983	1979	1983
Manufacturing	100.0%	100.0%	100.0%	100.0%	100.0%	100.0%	100.0%	100.0%	100.0%	100.0%
<25	100.0	100.0	6.6	7.0	3.2	3.9	a	a	3.1	3.6
25–99			93.5	93.0	12.1	17.2	a	13.5	5.8	6.4
100–499					84.7	79.0	41.1	49.9	24.3	27.2
500–999							49.1	32.6	15.6	16.8
1,000+									51.2	46.1
Durables Manufacturing	100.0%	100.0%	100.0%	100.0%	100.0%	100.0%	100.0%	100.0%	100.0%	100.0%
<25	100.0	100.0	8.1	8.5	a	a	a	a	2.5	2.7
25–99			91.9	91.6	11.6	16.6	a	a	4.7	5.2
100–499					85.2	80.3	40.0	51.9	20.1	22.7
500–999							52.4	35.3	15.6	16.5
1,000+									57.1	53.0
Nondurables Manufacturing	100.0%	100.0%	100.0%	100.0%	100.0%	100.0%	100.0%	100.0%	100.0%	100.0%
<25	100.0	100.0	a	a	a	a	a	a	4.4	5.2
25–99			95.3	95.0	12.8	17.8	a	18.4	8.2	8.3
100–499					84.0	77.6	42.3	47.2	32.8	34.6
500–999							45.0	29.0	15.6	17.4
1,000+									39.0	34.5

Firm size	1	2	3	4	5	6	7	8	9	10
Wholesale	100.0%	100.0%	100.0%	100.0%	100.0%	100.0%	100.0%	100.0%	100.0%	100.0%
<25	100.0	100.0	28.5	24.3	31.7	a	a	a	33.5	30.9
25–99			71.5	29.5	31.6	a	a	a	29.4	25.0
100–499				46.3	36.8	a	a	a	25.1	26.9
500–999						a	a	a	a	a
1,000 +						a	a	a	a	a
Service	100.0%	100.0%	100.0%	100.0%	100.0%	100.0%	100.0%	100.0%	100.0%	100.0%
<25	100.0	16.9	17.1	11.5	16.0	a	a	a	11.1	11.9
25–99		83.1	82.9	10.5	12.1	a	7.8	a	11.1	12.4
100–499				78.1	71.9	16.1	9.3	a	15.8	18.0
500–999						a	17.3	a	8.6	11.2
1,000 +						70.2	65.6	a	53.3	46.5
Finance, Insurance, and Real Estate	100.0%	100.0%	100.0%	100.0%	100.0%	100.0%	100.0%	100.0%	100.0%	100.0%
<25	100.0	27.4	33.9	32.3	31.6	a	a	a	22.2	24.6
25–99		72.7	66.1	25.4	37.4	a	a	a	22.8	20.3
100–499				42.3	31.0	37.1	32.9	a	18.3	19.9
500–999						a	a	a	12.0	13.2
1,000 +						a	a	a	24.7	22.0

Source: EBRI tabulations of the May 1979 and May 1983 Current Population Survey pension supplements.
aLess than 75,000.
Note: Percentages may not add to 100 percent due to rounding.

Harris (1985) stated that the activities of large firms determine the impact of small firms on employment growth. In other words, if large firms contract, small firms appear more important. Using the SBA data, Kirchoff and Phillips (1987) supported Harris' hypothesis, tracking changes in employment over two-year intervals. The share of employment generated by small firms ranged from 38 percent between 1978 and 1980 to 100 percent between 1980 and 1982. These swings suggest a strong cyclical component to employment growth. In cyclical downturns, layoffs in large firms reduced the share of employment growth generated by large employers and inflated the share allocated to small employers.[12]

The cyclical volatility of small firms may help explain why they are less likely to sponsor a pension plan—a long-term commitment. Thus, cyclical movements may suggest a structural reason for differences in the behavior of large and small firms.

The SBA data also suggest that small firms may have provided more than their share of net new jobs since 1983, the last year for which comparable Census Bureau data on firm size were available. This shift could be an important indicator of changes in pension provision if it reflects a trend in the share of small-firm employment rather than a cyclical gain.[13]

How the Economy Has Been Changing

Changes in the economy can have a substantial impact on the future of pension coverage for small businesses. Earlier research has identified a number of economic factors that are related to pension coverage (Andrews, 1985). Pension coverage is higher among union members and lower among the self-employed. Pension plans tend to be less prevalent in the service sector—although that finding is subject to some further caveats. In addition, changes in productivity can lead to changes in compensation and, hence, in pension coverage. Pension contributions are, after all, only one cost of compensation faced by employers. To judge the course of pension coverage, future trends in these economic variables need to be evaluated.[14]

Self-Employment—The percentage of the work force that is self-employed in an unincorporated business has grown steadily. According to the SBA

---

[12]Another theory of small-firm employment growth suggests that even if the size of distribution of firms remains unchanged, small establishments appear to account for a disproportionate share of employment growth (Leonard, 1986). In other words, on average, small firms are expected to grow.

[13]Confirmation will be forthcoming after the May 1988 CPS benefits supplement becomes available in 1989. EBRI is scheduled to provide extensive analysis of these data.

[14]For a future-oriented look at pension coverage, see Andrews and Mitchell, 1986.

(1986), self-employed entrepreneurs grew from 6.3 percent of the civilian labor force in 1970 to 6.5 percent in 1980 and 6.9 percent in 1984 (chart II.1). The SBA notes that a number of factors may be responsible for the increasing incidence of self-employment, including:

> economic conditions, the availability of opportunities for wage and salary employment, the effects of the tax code on business formation, identification by entrepreneurs of unexploited opportunities, workers' dissatisfaction with wage-and-salary jobs, and entrepreneurs' desire to supplement other income.

Union Membership—The contraction of union membership has been one of the strongest labor force trends observed in recent years—competing only with the trends toward increased female labor force participation and earlier retirement. The percentage of union members declined from 30 percent of nonfarm workers in 1970 to 17 percent in 1987 (table II.3).[15] While the decline in unionization is not entirely understood, it has been affected by the shift toward services and away from manufacturing.

The Growth of Services—The shift toward services has been gradual but persistent. In 1970, services accounted for 16 percent of employment (chart II.2), rising to 24 percent of the work force by 1985. Service employment is estimated to reach 25 percent by the year 2000 (Personick, 1987). Services include business, personal, and professional services.

By contrast, the broader category—service-producing industries—also includes transportation, utilities, trade, finance, insurance, and real estate. In 1970, employment in service-producing industries accounted for 67 percent of the work force. Employment in service-producing industries is projected to grow to 71 percent of employment by the year 2000. This shift does not necessarily mean, however, that small-firm employment will expand, since firms producing services may be becoming larger.

Trends in Labor Productivity—The future expansion of employer-sponsored pensions will be affected by gains in service-sector productivity and productivity in other industries.

Kendrick (1985) has estimated productivity trends since 1948 for goods-producing industries and service-producing industries including trade, finance and insurance, real estate, and basic services. Output per labor hour in the service-producing sector increased at an average annual rate of 1.9 percent between 1948 and 1981, compared to a 2.8 percent increase in output per labor hour in the goods-producing sector. Labor productivity growth diminished over the four subperiods studied—1948–66,

---

[15]These figures are not strictly comparable, but the trend is well-enough known to mitigate this objection.

31

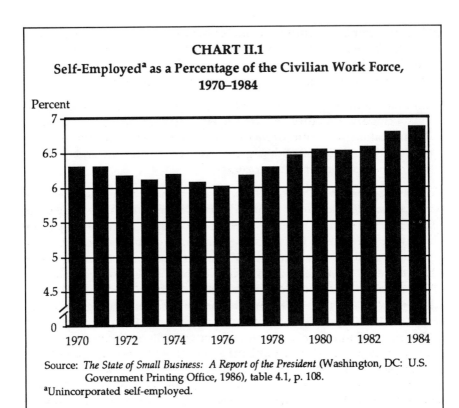

CHART II.1

Self-Employed[a] as a Percentage of the Civilian Work Force, 1970–1984

Percent

Source: *The State of Small Business: A Report of the President* (Washington, DC: U.S. Government Printing Office, 1986), table 4.1, p. 108.

[a]Unincorporated self-employed.

1966–73, 1973–79, and 1979–81. Labor productivity in basic services was the lowest of all the industries studied, averaging less than 1 percent over the period as a whole and dipping to zero between 1973 and 1979. Most other studies show the same pattern—declining overall productivity growth since 1948, with a considerable slowdown after 1966 and slower productivity increases in services than in manufacturing (chart II.3).

Wolfe (1985) reviews studies which seek to identify the sources of labor productivity slowdown. The sources of the decline that he lists include: (1) decline in capital formation; (2) change in the composition of the labor force; (3) dramatic increase in energy prices; (4) decline in research and development expenditures; (5) shift in the composition of output; and (6) effects of government regulation and cyclical factors.

Empirical findings on compositional shifts vary. Nordhaus (1972) reports that of a 1.17 percentage-point drop in productivity between 1948–65 and 1965–71, 0.90 points were attributable to the change in the composition of output. Kutscher, Mark, and Norsworthy (1977) conclude

TABLE II.3
Membership in U.S. Labor Organizations

Year	Total Employees[a] (thousands)	Union Membership (thousands)	Percentage
1970	70,880	21,248	30.0%
1971	71,214	21,327	29.9
1972	73,675	21,657	29.4
1973	76,790	22,276	29.0
1974	78,265	22,809	29.1
1975	77,364	22,361	28.9
1976	80,048	22,662	28.3
1977	82,423	22,456	27.2
1978	86,697	22,757	26.2
1979	89,886	22,579	25.1
1980	90,657	22,366	24.7
1983	88,290	17,717	20.0
1984	92,194	17,340	18.8
1985	94,521	16,996	18.0
1986	96,903	16,975	17.5
1987	99,303	16,913	17.0
1988	101,407	17,002	16.8

Source: Courtney D. Gifford, ed., *Directory of U.S. Labor Organizations: 1982–83 Edition* (Washington, DC: Bureau of National Affairs, 1982), p. 1, published in F. Ray Marshall, Vernon M. Briggs, Jr., and Allan G. King, *Labor Economics: Wages, Employment, Trade Unionism, and Public Policy,* fifth ed. (Homewood, IL: Richard D. Irwin, Inc., 1984), p. 118. Later data were gathered by the U.S. Department of Labor and represent a revised report of earlier released data.

[a]Total employees are those in nonagricultural establishments for 1970–1980, excluding Canadian members and members of single-firm labor organizations. For 1983–1987, the totals reflect all wage and salary workers.

that the shift in employment toward services decreased overall productivity growth by only 0.1 percent per year out of a 1.5 percent overall productivity decline between 1947–66 and 1967–73. Denison (1973) finds that the shift to services had a negligible effect on the productivity slowdown. Thurow (1979) attributes 45 percent to 50 percent of the decline in productivity growth between 1965–72 and 1972–77 to the shift toward low-productivity sectors.

The preponderance of evidence suggests that at least some of the slowdown in U.S. productivity was linked to the increasing share of service-

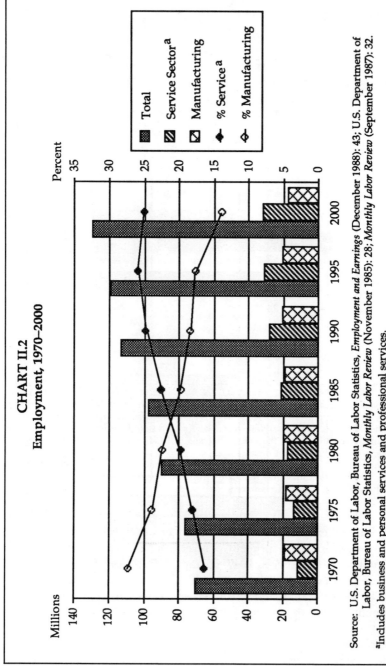

CHART II.2
Employment, 1970–2000

Legend:
- ▨ Total
- ▧ Service Sector[a]
- ▨ Manufacturing
- ◆ % Service[a]
- ◇ % Manufacturing

Source: U.S. Department of Labor, Bureau of Labor Statistics, *Employment and Earnings* (December 1988): 43; U.S. Department of Labor, Bureau of Labor Statistics, *Monthly Labor Review* (November 1985): 28; *Monthly Labor Review* (September 1987): 32.

[a]Includes business and personal services and professional services.

Note: Total employed number for 1995 excludes public electric utilities and service; number for the year 2000 excludes Standard Industrial Classifications 074,5,8 (agricultural services) and 99 (nonclassifiable establishments).

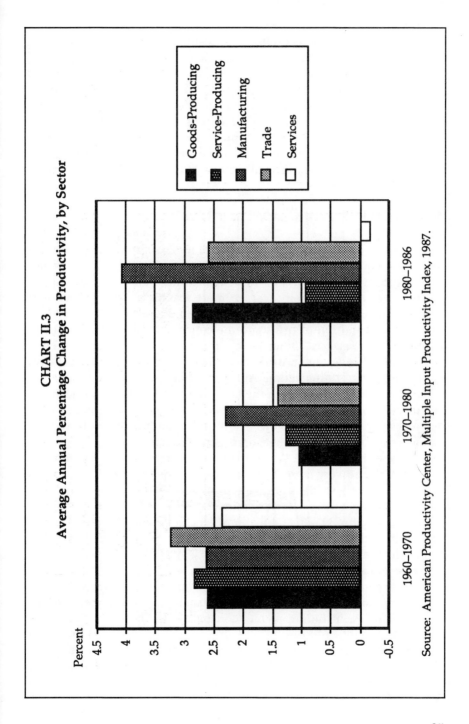

CHART II.3

Average Annual Percentage Change in Productivity, by Sector

Percent

Legend:
- Goods-Producing
- Service-Producing
- Manufacturing
- Trade
- Services

1960–1970 1970–1980 1980–1986

Source: American Productivity Center, Multiple Input Productivity Index, 1987.

sector output. Wolfe indicates that compositional shifts may account for 20 percent to 25 percent of the productivity slowdown.

Pension coverage is unlikely to expand if productivity does not improve. Productivity gains from capital improvements cannot be expected to be as important to services as they have been to manufacturing. Consequently, increased labor productivity must come from improvements in the labor force and from innovative ways to improve production. While these trends are important for the future, to understand current pension coverage we need to know how large and small firms differ in terms of their output, capital, and work forces.

What Do Small Businesses Look Like?

In terms of their participation in the economy, large and small businesses play equally important roles in the employment market, although large companies sell, earn, and own significantly more. To develop an economic theory of pension coverage, more specific differences between large and small employers must be understood. These factors include the industrial distribution of firms and the concentration of small-business employment in services. Other factors that vary by firm size are the degree of capital investment, differences in ownership and management, and the degree of unionization. Another difference of considerable importance is the composition of the labor force. While no single element explains why pension plans are more prevalent in larger companies, later chapters show that each one adds to our understanding of how those conditions relate to employer-sponsored pension plans.

Industry—Differences in the composition of employment by industry in very small and very large firms are striking. In 1983, only 10 percent of workers in very small firms worked in manufacturing (table II.4). By contrast, manufacturing was the dominant industry for very large employers, accounting for 39 percent of all workers. Employment in services, often considered the mainstay of small-business activity, provided 38 percent of all employment opportunities in very small firms. Only 15 percent of employees in very large firms worked in services.

A broad generalization that small-firm employees work in services is misleading, however, since 66 percent of small-firm employees work in other industries, including manufacturing, trade, transportation, communications, public utilities, and construction. However, small firms also employ more people in service-producing industries, such as wholesale and retail trade, with nearly one-third of all small-firm employees in trade compared to just over one-fifth of employees working for very large firms.

36

Capital Intensity—The relationship between the number of employees and the plant and equipment required for a business may signal differences in production requirements that also may lead to differences in pension coverage. Capital intensity (the ratio of capital to labor) is measured by the value of plant and equipment per worker employed by the firm. Manufacturing industries are typically more capital intensive, and service industries are more labor intensive.

A capital-labor ratio calculated for corporations in 1979[16] shows that depreciable assets per employee[17] averaged less than $9,000 for very small firms and nearly $28,000 per employee in very large companies (table II.5).[18] Depreciable assets per employee in manufacturing companies averaged around $7,700 for very small firms and over $18,000 for very large firms. Similarly, in service-sector firms, depreciable assets per employee averaged $7,000 in small firms and over $10,000 in very large firms. In other words, a pattern of greater capitalization for larger firms also holds in most industries.[19]

Corporate Structure—Small businesses are also less likely to be corporate entities. According to the SBA (1986), 63 percent of all employees in firms with one to nine employees worked for corporations in 1979, compared to 84 percent of employees in firms with 20 through 99 employees and virtually all employees in firms with 100 or more workers. These figures suggest that practically all large firms have an operating structure in which ownership and management are separate.

While some small corporations, even some that are closely held,[20] may have stockholder interests that are separate from management, many are likely to be subject to owner control. Despite their size, large partnerships are more likely than corporations to have a direct ownership interest in management. These differences in decision making can affect both the production process and the structure of compensation. One hypothesis is that pension plans in owner-managed businesses are more likely to be provided for the benefit of the owner rather than for the employees. Chapter V investigates some of these issues.

---

[16]These figures are based on the the SBA/IRS match file. See footnote 1, this chapter, and appendix A for a description of these data.

[17]Restricting the analysis to depreciable assets, essentially plant and equipment, removes nondepreciable assets such as land from the calculation. Differences in land values do not necessarily contribute to differences in workers' skills or productivity on the job.

[18]Firms with one to four employees appear to be a special case with higher values than other very small firms, perhaps because minimum equipment outlays are needed.

[19]Greater capitalization per worker with increasing firm size is not evident in finance and real estate.

[20]In closely held corporations most voting stock is held by a relatively small number of shareholders.

TABLE II.4
Distribution of Employment, by Firm Size and Industry, 1983

Industry	Firm Size				
	<25	25–99	100–499	500–999	1,000+
Total	19,197,786	8,662,312	8,289,721	3,242,154	21,831,651
Percentage	100.0%	100.0%	100.0%	100.0%	100.0%
Manufacturing	10.4%	23.3%	29.8%	30.0%	39.2%
Services[a]	38.4	25.7	28.8	34.9	14.7
Wholesale Trade	6.5	8.8	6.6	3.7	3.6
Retail Trade	25.3	20.5	14.9	14.5	18.0
Transportation	2.4	2.9	3.9	2.5	4.2
Communications	[b]	1.5	1.4	0.9	4.2
Public Utilities	[b]	1.0	0.8	1.0	2.9
Mining	[b]	0.6	1.1	0.5	2.1
Construction	11.0	8.4	4.2	2.5	1.6
Finance, Insurance, and Real Estate	5.1	7.4	8.5	9.4	9.6

Source: EBRI tabulations of the May 1983 EBRI/HHS Current Population Survey pension supplement.
[a]Includes business, personal, and professional services.
[b]Less than 0.5 percent.
Note: Percentages may not add to 100 percent due to rounding.

Unionization—Unionization also affects the operational structure of businesses and is far more prevalent in large companies. Among nonfarm private-sector employees, 31 percent of workers in very large firms in 1983 were unionized compared to less than 5 percent of workers in very small firms. Lower rates of unionization among small-firm workers are also found within different industries. Thirty-six percent of employees in large manufacturing firms were unionized, compared to only 20 percent in manufacturing firms with fewer than 500 employees. Similarly, 16 percent of workers in large service firms are unionized, compared to only 6 percent in these firms with fewer than 500 workers. While the service sector is less unionized than manufacturing, firm size affects union organizing across the board.

Types of Workers—The production activities, extent of capital intensity, and structural organization of a business may be instrumental in determining whether the business offers pension benefits to its employees. The composition of the labor force is equally important, for this will affect

TABLE II.5
Depreciable Assets per Employee,
by Firm[a] Size and Industry, 1979

Industry	Total[b]	< 20	20–99	100–499	500–999[b]	1,000 +[b]
			Firm Size			
Total	$12,955	$ 8,800	$ 7,048	$ 9,936	$14,091	$27,840
Manufacturing	11,034	7,656	6,349	7,980	10,511	18,391
Service Sector	10,904	7,065	5,811	4,591	6,370	10,323
Trade	5,061	4,676	2,936	9,731	5,236	8,027
Transportation and Utilities	31,457	26,972	26,900	42,478	77,512	145,351
Mining	40,344	32,038	24,699	56,269	70,003	69,932
Construction	7,519	6,275	4,702	5,358	8,952	8,901
Finance, Insurance, and Real Estate	41,534	27,065	18,570	17,062	15,972	12,758
Agriculture, Forestry, and Fishing	26,110	14,750	8,394	7,208	15,765	16,598

Source: EBRI compilation of 1979 Small Business Administration/Internal Revenue Service match file tabulations.

[a]Numbers are only for corporations.

[b]Total, 500–999, and 1,000 + columns are weighted averages. Other columns are averages of smaller, weighted groups.

which workers will benefit from—or even want—pension coverage. Understanding how employees of small businesses differ from those of larger concerns is an important step toward understanding patterns of pension provision.

Very small firms generally use a different type of work force than larger firms. They hire more teenagers and more "retirees" (those aged 65 or older) (table II.6). While very-small firm employment accounts for somewhat less than one-third of the work force, 57 percent of working teenagers (under age 18) and 56 percent of workers aged 65 and over are hired by very small firms. In contrast, very large firms account for somewhat over one-third of the work force but hire only 22 percent of working teenagers (under age 18) and 16 percent of workers aged 65 and over.

Very small businesses are more likely to hire individuals who limit their hours and are less attached to the labor force. In particular, 67 percent of workers with fewer than 500 hours on the job annually and 53 percent

TABLE II.6
Characteristics of the Work Force, by Firm Size, 1983

		Firm Size			
	Total	<25	25–99	100–499	500–999	1,000+
Age of Employee (years)						
16–17	100.0%	57.3%	10.9%	7.1%	2.5%	22.3%
18–24	100.0	37.3	15.8	13.4	4.8	28.7
25–44	100.0	27.7	13.9	14.3	5.5	38.6
45–64	100.0	29.4	13.7	12.8	5.8	38.3
65+	100.0	56.3	12.4	12.4	3.0	15.9
Hours Worked per Year						
1–499	100.0	67.0	9.9	8.7	1.4	13.0
500–999	100.0	53.2	12.1	9.3	5.0	20.5
1,000–1,999	100.0	36.9	14.7	13.4	4.7	30.4
2,000+	100.0	25.2	14.4	14.3	5.8	40.3

Average Tenure 6.6 yrs. 4.7 yrs. 5.3 yrs. 6.0 yrs. 6.8 yrs. 8.9 yrs.

Source: EBRI tabulations of May 1983 EBRI/HHS Current Population Survey pension supplement.
Note: Percentages may not add to 100 percent due to rounding.

of those with 500 to 1,000 hours are employed by very small firms. Part-time workers may be called in for specific tasks or for seasonal and peak-load employment.

In contrast, large firms tend to hire workers with more stable patterns of employment. Employees who work full-year, full-time schedules are generally permanent workers. Those working 2,000 hours or more a year account for 57 percent of total employment in very small firms, compared to 75 percent of employees in firms of other sizes.

Job tenure in all industries generally is higher in large firms. Employee job tenure averaged 4.7 years in very small firms, compared to 8.9 years in very large firms in 1983. Twenty-two percent of all workers in small firms of 25 through 99 employees had less than one year of tenure. In contrast, 12 percent of workers in very large firms had less than one year of tenure on the job. Thirty-six percent of employees working for very large firms were on the job for 10 or more years, whereas only 16 percent of workers in small firms had that length of tenure. These findings, in part, reflect industrial differences. Service-sector workers had fewer years on the job than manufacturing workers (4.9 years of tenure on average versus 9.2 years, respectively). Nevertheless, differences in tenure by firm size are found in all industries.

Workers in large firms are concentrated in occupations different from those of workers in small firms. Employees in professional and technical occupations are more prevalent in large firms (table II.7). Sixteen percent of employees in very large businesses were professional or technical staff, compared to only 9 percent in very small firms. Larger firms also had relatively more administrative and clerical staff. Employees of very small firms are more likely to have service jobs and are more likely to be construction workers, compared to employees of larger firms. In contrast, very large firms employ relatively more production and craft workers.

The proportion of managers within a firm also varies by size. Looking only at wage and salary workers, very small firms are less management intensive than large firms. Nine percent of nonfarm wage and salary workers are managers in very small firms, compared to an 11 percent ratio in large companies. These statistics exclude self-employed managers, however. Haber, Lamas, and Lichtenstein (1987) indicate that nearly 22 percent of all sole proprietorships had more than one worker (including the

TABLE II.7
Distribution of Occupations, by Firm Size, 1983[a]

Occupation	Firm Size				
	< 25	25–99	100–499	500–999	1,000 +
Total	100.0%	100.0%	100.0%	100.0%	100.0%
Managerial	9.3	11.7	12.8	10.9	11.6
Professional	7.6	8.4	11.2	13.6	11.1
Technical	1.8	2.5	3.7	5.6	4.7
Sales	15.5	12.8	11.5	10.9	12.2
Administrative and Clerical	15.9	15.8	17.2	19.5	19.8
Service	19.9	14.3	11.7	13.5	7.7
Construction Trades	6.3	4.5	3.0	1.1	1.9
Other Production and Craft	18.3	25.1	24.6	22.3	26.8
Operatives and Laborers	5.3	4.9	4.4	2.6	4.3

Source: EBRI tabulations of the May 1983 EBRI/HHS Current Population Survey pension supplement.
[a]Does not include all occupations; "other occupations" are excluded.

owner and unpaid family workers.)[21] Using an estimate of self-employed entrepreneurs who hire their own workers, the number of managers involved with very small firms is doubled, raising the percentage of managerial workers in very small firms to 18 percent.

Thus, if self-employed managers are counted, very small firms are more management intensive than very large firms. In terms of the production process, this difference may be deceptive if very-small-firm owners perform nonmanagerial duties themselves. Nevertheless, the management-intensive structure of very small firms may lead to differences in decision making by firm size and affect the provision of wages and benefits. This point will be discussed further in chapter III, which relates compensation to business size.

Summary and Conclusions

Despite a number of highly publicized studies, small firms have not rapidly increased their share of the work force over the past decade. A shift to smaller establishments is evident, however, as firms now operate smaller plants. Between 1979 and 1983, the size of work sites diminished while the size distribution of companies stayed the same. Of course, if new job opportunities are provided by small businesses in proportion to their current share of employment, small businesses will continue to supply the lion's share of all new jobs. If firm size is stable, pension coverage is not likely to decline. Pension coverage rates may edge off in manufacturing, however, and gain in services as shifts in firm size within industries take place. The effect of establishment-size shifts on pension coverage will be investigated in later chapters.

Another trend that could impact pension coverage is the slowdown of productivity growth that has taken place over the past two decades. Service-sector employment also has expanded during this time. The continued expansion of the service sector in combination with low rates of productivity growth could have negative implications for pension coverage. Similarly, the shift away from unions does not augur well for pension coverage, unless unions step up their organizing in small firms.

More generally, the role of small employers in the economy needs to be understood to assess their provision of wages and benefits. While small firms are major employers, they are not simply smaller versions of larger

---

[21]Their analysis is based on data from the Census Bureau's Survey of Income and Program Participation (SIPP), which interviews the same households over an 18-month period. This is also one of the primary data sets used in subsequent analysis. For a description of the data used, see appendix A.

enterprises. Small businesses differ from larger firms in their production activities and in their work force. In particular, their employment is more highly concentrated in services and service-related industries. Small firms are less highly capitalized, in part because of their different industrial mix. But even within industries, smaller firms are less capital intensive. These factors will be reconsidered in the development of an economic theory of pension provision.

The work force employed by very small firms provides a striking contrast to that of other employers. It includes many more teenagers and retirees, more part-time help, and fewer unionized workers. Employees working for small businesses tend to remain with their firm for fewer years. Small-firm employees are less likely to be in professional or technical occupations and clerical jobs. They are more likely to be construction workers. The occupational structure of small business generally follows differences in industry. Of greater interest is the fact that very small firms are more management intensive than others.

The question in terms of pension policy is how, and whether, these differences affect the employee benefits provided. In particular, do the production process and the types of workers employed influence employers to sponsor pension plans? The next chapter begins to investigate some of these issues by analyzing how wages and benefits are set in companies of different sizes.

III. Wages, Benefits, and Small Employers

Introduction

To learn why small businesses sponsor pension plans requires an examination of the broader issues related to employee compensation. To that end, this chapter first tracks the way in which weakened productivity growth has translated into slower compensation gains. Against this macroeconomic background, national data are presented showing that most workers in large firms earn higher wages and salaries, and receive better benefits, than workers in small firms. Studies are reviewed that investigate whether wage-rate differentials for firms of different sizes are a result of differences in the quality of the work force or differences in the work place. Other theories are examined that suggest that larger firms must pay higher wages than smaller companies if they want to manage their work force effectively. The same argument is considered as an explanation for the better benefit packages generally provided by larger employers.

Before developing an economic theory of pension provision, this chapter reviews studies that analyze the connection between wage and benefit payments. An academic debate is under way about how employers view the employment relationship. Do most firms hire workers for the long term, or are workers provided little guarantee of job security? The resolution of this debate has clear implications for pension policy. If some firms provide long-term employment opportunities and use pensions to encourage workers to live up to their potential, the structure of the pension plan is important to the employer. This chapter presents research findings that test competing theories of the employment relationship to provide a framework for analyzing the economics of plan sponsorship.

Trends in Wages and Compensation

Productivity gains and real wage growth have not been robust in recent years. Real average hourly earnings grew at a 1.9 percent compound annual rate between 1952 and 1972 and declined by 0.2 percent annually between 1972 and 1985 (chart III.1). Similarly, real hourly compensation grew at a 2.6 percent annual rate between 1952 and 1972 (with large gains during the early years), but slackened to 0.8 percent per annum between 1972 and 1985. The effect of the business cycle on wages intensified in the early 1970s, with average wages and compensation undergoing pronounced fluctuations thereafter.

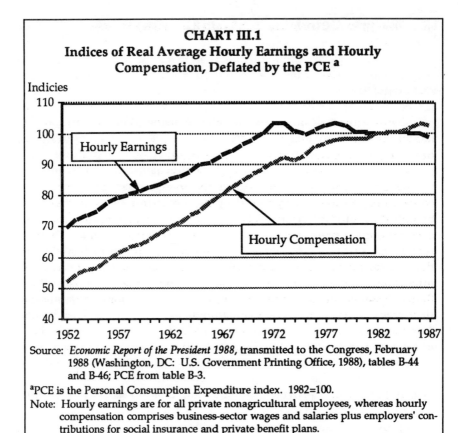

CHART III.1
Indices of Real Average Hourly Earnings and Hourly Compensation, Deflated by the PCE [a]

Indicies

Hourly Earnings

Hourly Compensation

1952   1957   1962   1967   1972   1977   1982   1987

Source: *Economic Report of the President 1988*, transmitted to the Congress, February 1988 (Washington, DC: U.S. Government Printing Office, 1988), tables B-44 and B-46; PCE from table B-3.

[a]PCE is the Personal Consumption Expenditure index. 1982=100.

Note: Hourly earnings are for all private nonagricultural employees, whereas hourly compensation comprises business-sector wages and salaries plus employers' contributions for social insurance and private benefit plans.

Slower compensation gains could result from sluggish economic conditions, differences in the composition of the labor force, or changes in the relative demand for different products. Kosters and Ross (1987) report that real hourly wage rates increased by 2 cents (in 1977 dollars) between 1972 and 1985. Disaggregating the sources of that increase to account for the independent effect of other factors, they estimate that the change in employment shares by industry alone led to a decline in real hourly wages of 15 cents. The shift toward greater female employment and toward a younger labor force caused an additional decline of 16 cents. At the same time, other labor market influences tended to raise real wages. Changes in average weekly hours increased average hourly earnings by 5 cents, while improvements in education accounted for a 33 cent increase in wages. In the absence of all these changes, real wages would have declined by 5 cents.[1]

Structural shifts in employment may not provide the full explanation for the modest wage-rate gains reported. Until the mid-1980s, benefits represented an increasing share of compensation (chart III.2). In particular, coverage under employer-sponsored pension and health insurance plans grew rapidly throughout the 1970s. More recently, pension and health insurance coverage rates have leveled off. The double impact of declining productivity growth and increasing health care costs may have further restricted wage gains to keep total compensation costs in line.[2]

Although real wages have stagnated, employment did not become more concentrated in low-wage jobs during the 1970s and 1980s. Earlier work by Bluestone and Harrison (1986) positing such a shift toward low-wage occupations has been largely discredited on technical grounds. Their research spanned years that were particularly sensitive to cyclical fluctuations in earnings, and overadjusted nominal wage rates for increases in inflation.[3] Using different time periods and an alternative measure of inflation lessened the apparent shift toward low-wage jobs.[4] Nonetheless, since recent wage gains have provided only modest improvements in the living standards of most families, pay differences among workers have become more noticeable. One frequently cited source of wage dispersion is the difference in wages paid by large and small employers.

Wage Payments in Small Firms

Employees at small firms earn less than workers in large firms in most industries and occupations. Wages in two job categories are of particular interest for issues related to pension policy—wages in the service sector and managerial salaries. Service-sector jobs often are assumed to pay poorly and provide few benefits. The relationship between managerial compensation and pension provision has been a recurrent theme with regard to pension equity. This section examines salary differences by firm size

---

[1]The difference between this decline and the actual 2 cent increase indicates that factors other than those measured also influenced wage gains.

[2]Many economists consider that there may be a long-run tradeoff between wages and benefits even if there are not yearly tradeoffs for any one individual worker. Researchers generally consider that there is a long-run tradeoff between Social Security payments and wages (Hammermesh, 1979; Hagens and Hambor, 1980; Halpern and Munnell, 1980; Dye, 1984).

[3]The consumer price index (CPI) weighted the run-up in housing prices too heavily at the time, although the problem has now been corrected.

[4]The other index used that weighted housing costs appropriately was the U.S. Commerce Department's Personal Consumption Expenditures deflator. For a detailed discussion of these points, see Kosters and Ross, 1987.

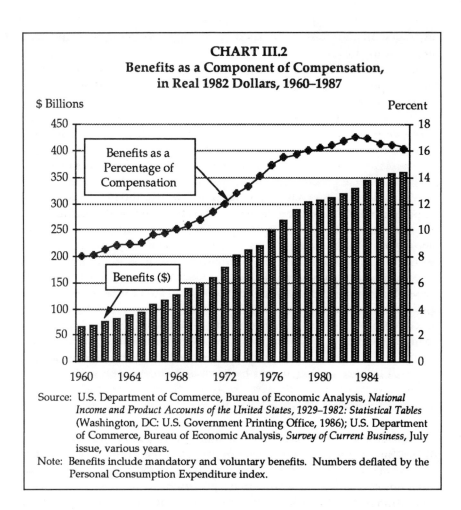

CHART III.2
Benefits as a Component of Compensation,
in Real 1982 Dollars, 1960–1987

$ Billions   Percent

Benefits as a Percentage of Compensation

Benefits ($)

1960   1964   1968   1972   1976   1980   1984

Source: U.S. Department of Commerce, Bureau of Economic Analysis, *National Income and Product Accounts of the United States, 1929–1982: Statistical Tables* (Washington, DC: U.S. Government Printing Office, 1986); U.S. Department of Commerce, Bureau of Economic Analysis, *Survey of Current Business,* July issue, various years.

Note: Benefits include mandatory and voluntary benefits. Numbers deflated by the Personal Consumption Expenditure index.

for a range of job classifications, analyzing wage and salary patterns more broadly and their relationship to pension coverage.

Differences in Wages and Salaries by Firm Size—The average earnings of workers employed by small firms in 1983 was $11,300 annually, which contrasts starkly with the $20,200 average annual earnings of workers in very large firms.[5] Differences in earnings by firm size are persistent despite industrial variations. Employees of small firms generally earned less than those of large firms in service-producing industries[6] and in goods-producing

_____

[5]Earnings are estimated using the May 1983 EBRI/HHS Current Population Survey pension supplement. See appendix A for a complete description of these data.

[6]The service-producing industries are composed of transportation, communications, public utilities, trade, finance, insurance, real estate, and services.

48

industries[7] (chart III.3). Average wages decreased with firm size across the board in manufacturing and services but not in construction and trade. Compensation patterns in services and trade are of particular interest for pension policy, as these industries are often presumed to have the lowest rates of pension coverage.

Differences in earnings by occupation generally mirrored industrial patterns, with employees in large firms having higher earnings (chart III.4). On the upper end of the wage scale, professionals in very large firms earned $28,000 annually while those in very small firms earned $16,000. Similarly, administrative and clerical workers earned $15,800 in very large firms and $9,900 in very small firms. Workers in some service-related occupations were paid more in medium-sized firms, however, with the earnings of retail sales workers highest in firms employing 100 to 250 persons. The average earnings of certain specialized professional and technical occupations were highest for employees of small firms. Computer scientists, natural scientists, some health professionals (including physicians), and attorneys earned more in very small firms than similar professionals in larger companies.

If professionals in these occupations can be more productive in smaller settings, more capable individuals may gravitate to smaller offices and professional practices. This tendency could reinforce the impression held by some policymakers that doctors and lawyers, compared to other small-business owners, are particularly likely to sponsor pension plans with little regard for their employees. The relationship between higher earnings and pension coverage is discussed in chapter IV.

Salaried managers earn more in large corporations than in smaller firms. But managerial pay in very small firms may be underestimated if owners of unincorporated businesses, who may collect higher salaries than their employees, are not included. According to a survey of executive compensation that included owner-managers of firms, companies with higher sales revenue[8] report paying top managers[9] more, on average, than companies with lower sales (Brown, 1988).

But even surveys that include the self-employed may not present a fair picture of managerial pay in very small companies if the business income of self-employed individuals is underreported. According to Haber, Lamas, and Lichtenstein (1987), "underreporting by business owners in survey data is a well-known phenomenon." They noted that 14 percent of owners

---

[7]The goods-producing industries are composed of manufacturing, mining, and construction.
[8]Revenue can be used as an alternative definition of firm size. The revenue categories ranged from $1 million or less to $10 million or more in receipts.
[9]The managers included were chief executive officers, chief operating officers, chief financial officers, and chief marketing officers.

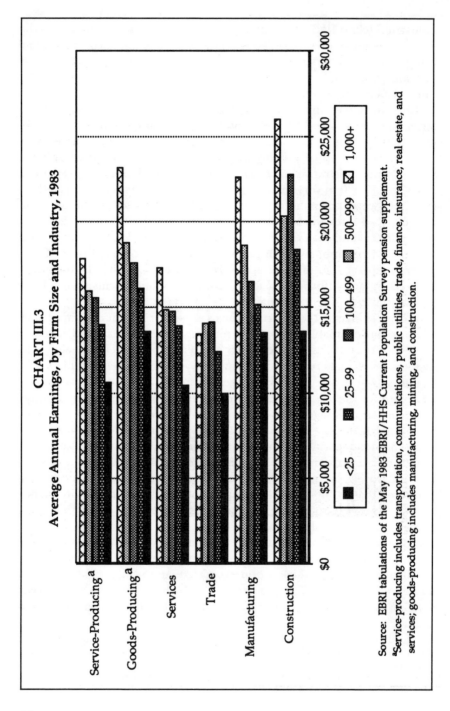

CHART III.3
Average Annual Earnings, by Firm Size and Industry, 1983

■ <25 ▨ 25–99 ▨ 100–499 ▨ 500–999 ⊠ 1,000+

Source: EBRI tabulations of the May 1983 EBRI/HHS Current Population Survey pension supplement.

[a]Service-producing includes transportation, communications, public utilities, trade, finance, insurance, real estate, and services; goods-producing includes manufacturing, mining, and construction.

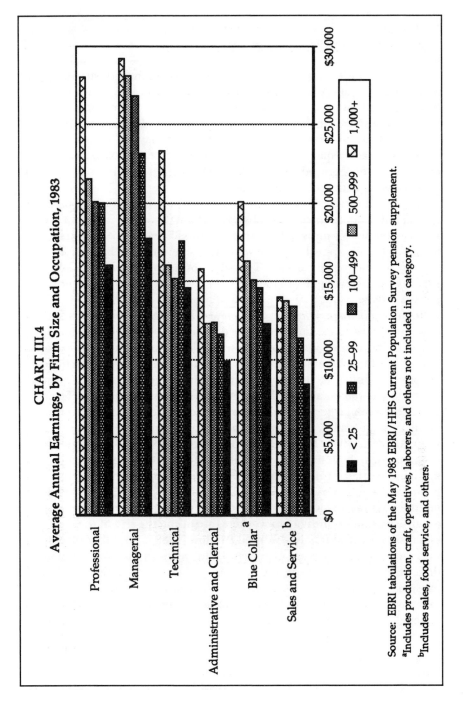

CHART III.4

Average Annual Earnings, by Firm Size and Occupation, 1983

Legend: ■ <25 ▨ 25–99 ▨ 100–499 ▨ 500–999 ▨ 1,000+

Occupations: Professional, Managerial, Technical, Administrative and Clerical, Blue Collar [a], Sales and Service [b]

Source: EBRI tabulations of the May 1983 EBRI/HHS Current Population Survey pension supplement.

[a]Includes production, craft, operatives, laborers, and others not included in a category.

[b]Includes sales, food service, and others.

of unincorporated businesses with three or more employees reported having no earnings in 1984, a higher rate than actual business losses would warrant.[10]

Further, a study on entrepreneurs in the petroleum industry indicates that owner-managers also exercise control over how much they are paid (Cooley and Edwards, 1985). Business owners may forgo compensation in the early stages of their firms' development and raise their own pay later. Similarly, owners reaching retirement age may cap their salaries to build up greater equity in their firm while deferring taxes. As a result, the meaning of reported earnings for small-business owners who set their own wages is extremely ambiguous.

The complicated structure of owner-manager compensation takes on special importance, since some observers claim that small employers sponsor pension plans simply to limit their personal income tax liabilities. This theory is initially appealing in view of the discretion small business owners have to set their own salaries. The situation is more complicated, however, as the assessment in chapter V of the practices of small-business owners will show.

Research Findings: Why Large Employers Pay More—Numerous studies have attempted to explain why wage differentials by firm size are so pervasive. Using statistical methods, these studies have sought to measure the degree to which factors such as industry, unionization, and working conditions have influenced the wages paid in different-sized firms. The earliest studies, based on average industry wage rates, showed that differences in pay between large and small firms reflected more than differences in industry wage scales, confirming the findings presented above (Rosen, 1979; Masters, 1969; Haworth and Reuther, 1978; and Pugel, 1980).

Later research analyzed the extent to which differences in factors that influence worker productivity led to differences in earnings by firm size. Productivity is generally considered to increase with greater investment in education and work experience (Mincer, 1974). In an analysis based on information on individual workers, including the size of the firm and establishment at which they worked, Mellow (1982) found that employees with more education, work experience, and years on the job earned more than other workers. Unionized workers (and those in unionized industries) also earned more. Nevertheless, after accounting for all these factors, wages were 23 percent higher among workers in very large firms and in very large plants compared to those working for very small businesses.

---

[10]Haber, Lamas, and Lichtenstein use the Census Bureau's Survey of Income and Program Participation (SIPP) for their analysis.

Researchers tried to provide other explanations to account for the persistence of wage differentials by firm size. One theory suggested that superior on-the-job performance was easily observed by supervisors, but could not be measured by the less specific methods employed by researchers (Stafford, 1980). Another argument suggested that better workers were attracted to larger firms (Oi, 1983; Oi and Rasian, 1985). To avoid making direct comparisons between different workers with different (unobserved) skills, Brown and Medoff (1986) tracked the pay of the same workers moving between firms of different sizes. While the pay differential between employees working for large and small businesses was reduced, identical workers in large firms still earned more than they would in small firms.

Another theory held that union bargaining increased wages by granting a monopoly rent, and that unions induced workers to work harder by raising their wages (Oi, 1985). Studies such as Mellow's (1982) found, however, that large firms paid more even after controlling for the effect of unionization. Another hypothesis was that large firms paid higher wages to avoid unionization (Oi, 1983). Finding that the difference in wages among large and small employers was not weaker in sectors in which unionization was weak, Brown and Medoff (1986) concluded that wage differentials by firm size were not caused by union avoidance.

Another theory used to justify lower pay within smaller firms is "compensating differentials." This theory states that workers in dangerous jobs will demand higher wages, and workers in safe, pleasant jobs will require less pay. By extension, workers in small firms will accept lower wages because they prefer the small-firm environment. Oi (1985) suggested that workers in large firms are more likely to work longer hours and undesirable shift schedules. Stafford (1980) indicated that highly structured assembly line jobs may be less attractive than jobs in smaller work groups with more relaxed work settings and greater opportunities for personal autonomy. He also suggested that small employers may be able to cater to their workers' tastes and ensure a homogeneous and harmonious work force. Studies measuring specific attributes of particular jobs, however, have not found that employees in large firms face less desirable working conditions (Dunn, 1984; Kwoka, 1980). In particular, empirical work by Brown and Medoff (1986) suggested that the difference in wage rates by firm size cannot be attributed to work place amenities.

While many of these theories partly explain why employees of small companies earn less on average than workers in major corporations, a wage differential still remains. Consequently, researchers have searched for an alternative explanation for the persistence of wage differentials by firm size.

Research has considered whether the ability of employers and managers to evaluate worker productivity in large and small organizations may differ. The basic premise of this theory is that managers of small firms are able to monitor the performance of their workers more easily than managers of larger companies. One version of the theory suggests that large firms have to pay top wages to all their workers because they monitor job performance imprecisely (Brown and Medoff, 1986). Another version suggests that some employers must provide additional incentives to ensure that their employees are not shirking work. In that case, higher-paid workers will work harder to keep their job since they face a greater financial loss if they lose their job than they would if they were paid less (Bulow and Summers, 1986). At least some empirical tests are consistent with monitoring theory (Brown and Medoff, 1986).

Yet, as chapter II indicates, the ratio of management to workers is essentially the same for all firms except for very small employers. Consequently, the concept that managers in large companies find individual performance difficult to evaluate demands greater scrutiny. Leonard (1987), for one, rejects monitoring theory for this reason. But more complex explanations seem plausible. In particular, the evaluation of the performance of a combination of productive units (each made up of a group of employees) may be more difficult in a large firm than the direct evaluation of job performance in a smaller operation. Operational complexity means that management may be less able to distinguish the contribution of any one worker or group of workers. Oi (1985) has suggested that team performance on the job makes the evaluation of individual productivity more difficult. Large employers also may have difficulty developing company-wide pay scales that are appropriate for different groups of workers.

Under a broader definition of supervisory control, more large firms may encourage their employees to stay on the job longer to build up a corporate memory of success and failure as insurance against the repetition of costly mistakes. Employees on the job for an extended time will have a working knowledge of the potential pitfalls of the job and will be able to work together more effectively. If higher wages are paid for firm-specific knowledge (job skills and information connected to the particular business), employees would find it financially advantageous to remain with the firm. They would be less likely to earn as much at another company.

Benefits in Small Firms

Not only do small employers pay lower wages across the board, they also provide fewer benefits. For that reason, most workers without pension or health insurance coverage are employed by small firms. Consequently, it is instructive to identify how much large and small firms differ in their provision of employee benefits.

Differences in Benefits by Establishment Size—Paid vacations and health insurance were the most widespread benefits provided by small and large establishments alike.[11] Almost all full-time employees of medium-sized and large establishments were granted paid vacations in 1985, as were 81 percent of full-time workers in small firms (table III.1). Health insurance was provided to 96 percent of all full-time employees of medium-sized and large establishments, compared to 75 percent of full-time workers in small companies. Paid sick leave, employee discounts, and long-term disability insurance were offered less frequently. Full-time employees of small businesses were at least 30 percent less likely than employees of large companies to have these benefits. Other job enhancements, such as paid lunch breaks and child care, were more likely to be offered to workers in small firms. Differences in pension and retirement plan participation rates by establishment size are substantial. Ninety-one percent of all full-time employees in medium-sized and large establishments participated in a retirement plan in 1985. Only 43 percent of full-time workers in small firms were plan participants.[12]

Large and small establishments also provide different types of retirement plans. Of the 91 percent of full-time employees in medium-sized and large establishments participating in retirement plans, 80 percent were

---

[11]Two roughly comparable sources of data provide information on the percentage of full-time employees participating in a wide variety of benefit programs in 1985. The National Federation of Independent Business (NFIB) surveyed approximately 1,400 of its members, primarily small employers, about the benefits they provided (Dennis, 1985). These data, used extensively in chapters V and VI, are described in detail in appendix A. NFIB members are probably relatively established employers, by virtue of their membership in a trade association, and may provide more liberal benefits than other small firms. The Bureau of Labor Statistics (BLS) surveys employers operating large and medium-sized establishments about the benefits they provided their employees. This survey was conducted annually up to 1986 and is now conducted biennially (U.S. Department of Labor, 1986). Data from 1985 are used to provide comparative findings to the NFIB small-employer survey. The BLS defines an establishment as an economic unit that produces goods and services, a central administration office, or an auxiliary unit providing support service to a company. In manufacturing industries, the establishment is usually a single physical location. In nonmanufacturing industries, all locations of an individual company within a Metropolitan Statistical Area or within a nonmetropolitan county are usually considered an establishment. Thus, the definition is somewhat of a hybrid. See chapter II for a general discussion of the relationship between firm size and establishment size.

[12]These pension participation rates can be compared to rates estimated from other sources. The May 1983 EBRI/HHS Current Population Survey pension supplement indicates that only 28 percent of full-time employees in small firms were covered by a pension plan. Analysis of the 1979 SBA/IRS match file suggests that only 21 percent of corporations with fewer than 100 workers took a pension deduction.

TABLE III.1
Percentage of Full-Time Employees Participating in Employee Benefit Programs, Medium-Sized and Large Establishments and Small Firms, 1985

Benefit Program	Employees[a] in Medium-Sized and Large Establishments[b]	Employees in Small Firms[c]
Retirement	91%	43%
Health Insurance	96[d]	75
Life Insurance	96	59
Vacations	99	81
Paid Lunch Break	10	19
Sick Leave	67	46
Long-Term Disability Insurance	48	26
Child Care	1	4
Educational Assistance	76	23
Employee Discounts	57	35

Source: Small-firm data from EBRI tabulations of National Federation of Independent Business survey data. Medium-sized- and large-firm data from U.S. Department of Labor, Bureau of Labor Statistics, *Employee Benefits in Medium and Large Firms, 1985* (Washington, DC: U.S. Government Printing Office, 1986).

[a]Participants are workers covered by paid time off, insurance, retirement, or capital accumulation plan. Employees subject to a minimum service requirement before they are eligible for a benefit are counted as participants even if they have not met the requirement at the time of the survey. If employees are required to pay part of the cost of a benefit, only those who elect the coverage and pay their share are counted as participants. Benefits for which the employee must pay the full premium are outside the scope of the survey. Only current employees are counted as participants; retirees are excluded.

[b]Medium-sized and large establishments are those firms with at least 100 or 250 employees, depending on the industry. An establishment is defined as an economic unit that produced goods or services, a central administrative office, or an auxiliary unit providing support services to a company. In manufacturing industries, the establishment is usually a single physical location. In nonmanufacturing industries, all locations of an individual company within a Metropolitan Statistical Area (MSA) or within a nonmetropolitan county are usually considered an establishment.

[c]Small firms are those with fewer than 100 employees.

[d]Includes 0.7 percent of employees in plans that did not offer family coverage.

in defined benefit plans and 41 percent in defined contribution plans (with some firms providing both types of plans). Defined contribution plans, including both money-purchase and profit sharing plans, are favored by small employers. Such plans were provided to 62 percent of small-firm workers covered by a pension. Nearly two-thirds of all defined contribution plan participants were covered by profit sharing plans.

Contributions to profit sharing plans may vary according to the employer's profits and, hence, ability to pay, which contributes to their popularity among small employers. Only 32 percent of full-time participants were included in a traditional single-employer defined benefit plan. Another 6 percent were included in a multiemployer plan covering more than one employer, probably as a result of a collective bargaining agreement with a union.

Research Findings: Some Employees Receive Fewer Benefits—Why do smaller employers provide fewer benefits and pay lower wages? In contrast to the many studies on differences in wages by firm size, relatively little research has addressed the question of benefits directly. Nevertheless, some of the arguments related to differences in wages may be directly applicable to differences in benefits. Studies have shown that workers with more education, experience, and years on the job are more likely to be covered by a pension plan than other workers (Andrews, 1985). Yet even after these factors are taken into account, workers in large firms still have better coverage. These findings parallel the findings on differences in wages by firm size.

The greater prevalence of benefits in large firms may be linked to the greater difficulty large firms have monitoring the job performance of their workers. Pension plans could encourage superior job performance since the loss of pension benefits may be substantial for a worker who is terminated before vesting. Similarly, even vested benefits accrued under defined benefit plans with final-pay formulas are lower for job changers than for employees who stay with the firm. Thus, pension plans amplify the potential loss workers face if they are dismissed and, presumably, encourage those who stay to perform diligently. Lazear (1981, 1983) proposed this type of argument to explain why employers sponsor pension plans, but did not directly link it to differences in plan sponsorship by firm size. Nonetheless, these kinds of management needs may provide large employers with particularly strong incentives to sponsor pension plans.

Other research has focused on the different incentives provided by defined benefit and defined contribution plans (Mitchell and Luzadis, 1987; Clark, Gohmann, and McDermed, 1988). While the findings of these studies are not conclusive, defined benefit plans are generally considered to have characteristics that link them to management needs to improve supervisory control—in particular the ability to provide more generous benefit accruals with additional years of service, which encourages longer job tenure. This reasoning provides a partial rationale for large firms to have defined benefit plans while small employers would have defined contribution plans or no plan at all. This research goes beyond the direct issue of differences in benefit provision by firm size, however, and relates to a more fundamental concept—the nature of the labor contract.

The Relationship between Wages and Pensions

Without an explicit reason to provide a pension plan based on the management needs of the firm, small employers would sponsor a plan only if they and their workers wanted one. Recent research on compensation, focusing on the relationship between wages and benefits, has led to competing theories of the labor market: in one case, firms hire workers on a year-to-year basis and, in the other, firms hope to have a continuing relationship with their employees. As chapter IV shows, the way in which small firms approach the labor market influences their decision to sponsor a pension plan.

Researchers initially assumed that employers divided compensation between wages and benefits by exchanging wage payments for pension contributions. This theory presumed that an individual worker's total compensation (wage and benefit payments) in each and every year would equal that worker's annual contribution to the company's output. Employers would not care whether they paid cash wages or made a pension contribution so long as their total compensation costs remained the same. Consequently, only workers who wanted some of their income deferred would be covered by a pension plan. Benefits provided by multiemployer plans have been said to confirm this theory since employers bargain for a total cents-per-hour package rather than for specific pension or wage rate changes.

Based on this theory, researchers tried to measure the extent to which workers traded pension contributions for wages. The results of early studies were mixed: evidence of wage-pension tradeoffs was found in only a small percentage of cases (Ehrenberg, 1980; Schiller and Weiss, 1980; Smith, 1981). A later study, using a unique data set designed to avoid many of the statistical problems of earlier efforts, also could not identify wage-pension tradeoffs (Smith and Ehrenberg, 1983).

By this time, this initial theory of wage and pension determination was being called into question. Evidence that many employees are on the job for many years (Hall, 1982) led a number of researchers to suspect that employers hired their workers for more than one year at a time, even though no explicit contract was signed guaranteeing a longer term of employment. One of the first researchers to consider an alternative wage-setting model, Lazear (1979) hypothesized that employers used mandatory retirement to terminate employees at the point at which the value of the output they produced for the firm equaled all the compensation paid them during their career.

In particular, wages do not have to equal the value of employee output in each and every year. If both the employer and the employee expect the employment relationship to last for many years, the employee can be paid relatively less in early years of employment and relatively more in later years. This tilting of the compensation profile may be achieved by delaying raises or by providing pension benefits. It may be accomplished through vesting standards, increased pension accruals, and benefit entitlement at retirement age. Benefits will be set to convince workers that job changes do not pay.

A number of studies have attempted to determine whether compensation is set on a year-to-year basis or over a longer time horizon.[13] Perhaps the simplest evidence is offered by Kotlikoff and Wise (1985), who note that with vesting provisions, workers automatically are entitled to large real gains in compensation (albeit deferred until retirement age) when they become fully vested. This gain was particularly notable under 10-year vesting.[14] They stated that the presence of large gains in total compensation in certain years resulting from pension vesting schedules indicated that workers were not paid their productive worth in each and every year of employment.

Compensation and Small Employers

Based on the following theoretical premises, small firms would be more likely to hire and pay their workers on a year-to-year basis and not encourage a long-lasting employment relationship. First, small companies pay lower wages and employ more short-tenured unskilled workers. Second, workers in jobs requiring little skill are easily replaced because they do not become appreciably more productive with continued employment. Thus, employers in small firms would have no incentive, under this hypothesis, to structure their compensation package to encourage tenure. As a consequence, small employers would provide pensions only if they themselves, their workers, or their managers desired a pension. If a plan

---

[13]Mitchell and Pozzebon, 1987, reviewed these studies and found that the hypothesis that compensation was set over a longer time horizon was supported in several cases although, in general, the evidence was inconclusive (Lazear, 1979; Ehrenberg, 1980; Lazear, 1983; Kotlikoff and Wise, 1985). Their own work supports the hypothesis that employers hire and pay workers with a longer time horizon in mind. By contrast, Clark and McDermed, 1986, find that their analysis of earnings prior to retirement is consistent with year-by-year wage setting.

[14]The 1986 Tax Reform Act generally substituted a five-year vesting standard for the 10-year schedule required in 1974. (Further discussion of this point can be found in chapter VII.) Nonetheless, compensation under five-year vesting will exhibit the same general patterns that were found under the earlier standard.

were provided, it would tend to be a defined contribution plan that did not tilt benefit accruals as much as defined benefit plans do toward older, long-tenured workers.[15]

Typical small-employer plans do provide fewer incentives for continued employment. Since small plans have shorter vesting periods which, thus, limits the extent to which pension accruals can be deferred, workers in these plans give up little financially by changing jobs. Thirteen percent of participants in very small plans had immediate vesting, compared to 4 percent of those in very large plans (table III.2) (Kotlikoff and Smith, 1983).[16] Only 21 percent of very small plans had 10-year cliff vesting schedules (benefit entitlement starting in the tenth year), compared to 80 percent of very large plans.

Since small employers prefer defined contribution plans, most vested workers in small firms will not forfeit future benefits if they change jobs

TABLE III.2

Percentage of Participants in Private Defined Benefit and Defined Contribution Plans, by Vesting Schedule and Number of Plan Participants, Original ERISA Filing,[a] 1977

Number of Plan Participants	Cliff Vesting			Graduated Vesting: Fully Vested after	
	Immediate	10-year	Other	10 years	Other
1–24	13%	21%	8%	34%	25%
25–49	6	48	4	29	13
50–99	2	67	3	16	12
100–999	7	70	5	5	12
1,000 +	4	80	6	3	7

Source: EBRI tabulations based on Laurence J. Kotlikoff and Daniel J. Smith, *Pensions in the American Economy* (Chicago: The University of Chicago Press, 1983), table 4.3.4, p. 185.
[a]These findings are based on the National Bureau of Economic Research/U.S.Department of Labor EBS-1 subsample, excluding responses not classified by Kotlikoff and Smith.

---

[15]If employees are hired for the long term and their compensation is set accordingly, defined benefit plans will tilt compensation toward later years of employment because of the way in which actuarial accruals are made.

[16]These figures represent plans at the time the Employee Retirement Income Security Act of 1974 (ERISA) was enacted. More recent data are not available. Other evidence has not indicated significant changes in vesting since that time.

(apart from the fact that contributions stop). Preretirement cashouts from defined contribution plans can be reinvested to provide the same retirement income that the worker would have had without changing jobs (EBRI, 1987).[17] By contrast, most job changers under defined benefit plans suffer a reduction in benefits (based on comparable periods of service) compared to workers who stay with the firm. Based on this evidence, small firms ought to be more likely to exhibit explicit short-term wage-pension tradeoffs, with pension contributions directly reducing cash wages. Such pensions would not be intended to raise worker productivity by encouraging continued employment with the firm.

Nevertheless, despite this plausible scenario, some small companies may need to retain workers with experience on the job. Such firms would also hire employees under the presumption of continued employment. Small employers concerned about employee retention would use deferred compensation in the same way as large employers, as a reward for longevity. If long-term employment were encouraged, a defined benefit pension plan, or a defined contribution plan with delayed vesting, would provide an additional incentive for workers to stay with the firm.

Empirical Evidence Regarding Wages and Pensions in Small Firms—Evidence of a tradeoff between wage and pension payments in small firms would support the hypothesis that compensation was not set to encourage continued employment and that pensions were not part of the firm's personnel policy. Recent research suggests, however, that small firms also may sponsor pensions to achieve long-run objectives.[18]

If compensation is set annually, and job tenure is not encouraged by wage or benefit policies, the wages of workers without pensions would be expected to grow faster than the wages of workers with pensions, or workers with pension plans would initially be paid lower wages. Pension payments would make up the difference in compensation for plan participants. Even after accounting for differences in education, industry, and overall work experience, however, pension plan participants were not paid less, and their salaries kept up with those of nonparticipants (Andrews, 1989c). Furthermore, pension plan participants with more years on the

---

[17]Retirement income losses do occur, of course, if workers decide to use the preretirement distribution for current consumption.

[18]See Andrews, 1989c. This research uses two data bases—the May 1983 CPS pension supplement and the 1984 Survey of Income and Program Participation (SIPP)—to analyze the compensation patterns of men aged 25 to 64 working for a year or more in firms with fewer than 100 employees. (The analytic complications created by the less stable work patterns of younger workers, retirees, and women are avoided.) The SIPP and CPS pension supplement data are described in detail in appendix A.

job made greater actual wage gains than other workers with similar job tenure.

These findings suggest that small employers who provide pension plans encourage their workers to stay on the job for more than a year at a time and set their compensation packages accordingly. Furthermore, since workers make greater wage gains in jobs with pension plans, the knowledge they gain on the job must make them more valuable to the firm. These arguments suggest that small employers also provide pension plans to improve their company's productivity though worker retention.

Summary and Conclusions

Wage payments have stagnated since the 1970s, and compensation has grown slowly. These trends are consistent with declining pension coverage rates. Small employers have not gained an increasing share of the labor market, and differences in wage payments and benefits offered by large and small employers probably have remained the same. Small businesses pay less than large employers and are less likely to provide employee benefits.

Differences in the wages and benefits paid by large and small employers in part reflect differences in the composition of their work forces. Nonetheless, even after accounting for differences in worker productivity, large firms pay more. Recent research suggests that this pay differential is intended to keep employees from shirking on the job because worker productivity in large firms cannot be adequately monitored. Pension plans provided by large employers also may be used for the same purpose.

Yet this is not the only rationale possible for pension plan provision. If it were, all large firms would provide pensions and small firms would not. Consequently, we need to know more about how compensation is set to understand why small employers provide pension plans. Two theories have been proposed. One assumes that wages are set annually in a competitive market. In that case, employers are equally willing to pay for benefits or wages as long as the total costs of compensation do not increase. A second theory suggests that employers hire their work force for a longer period of time and encourage longer tenure with the firm. These employers find that worker productivity will improve with continued employment. In that case, annual tradeoffs between wages and benefits need not take place because the firm's compensation policies set payments over a longer time horizon.

Small employers with pension plans probably do not have year-to-year hiring practices. Wage gains made by plan participants in small firms suggest that increased job tenure enhances worker productivity. This information sets the stage for the development of a theory of pension plan provision. If small employers provide pensions to workers who become more valuable to the firm over time, pensions are an important management tool for the small companies that offer them. In that case, differences in the production processes of small firms may be the key to understanding why some employers offer pensions while others do not.

IV. Small Employers and Pensions

Introduction

If small businesses expect their employees to have a continuing relationship with the firm, pension plans can be used to reward workers who stay with the firm longer. In that case, the small-business pension plan, as a component of personnel policy, would be established according to the management needs of the firm. Based on that premise, this chapter examines how characteristics of the employer's work place and work force are related to pension coverage. For the time being, these arguments do not take into consideration the effects of government regulation, which are considered in detail in chapters VI and VII.

First, the data speak for themselves. Chapter II demonstrated that the mix of goods and services produced differs by firm size and that the work forces of large and small employers differ as well. Small businesses are more concentrated in service-related industries, and their production is less capital intensive. Workers in small firms are younger and less unionized, and they spend fewer years on the job. This chapter investigates similar criteria for businesses with pension plans and those without plans to determine whether these factors may be related to plan provision.

The reasons small employers themselves give for plan provision are then reviewed. Between 1980 and 1988, a number of researchers have approached owners and managers of small firms asking them to respond to questions about the costs and benefits of plan provision. These responses provide important insights into the decision to sponsor a plan. Three general influences are reported—those related to the operation of the business, those related to the work force, and those related to the personal finances of owners and managers.

Building on these responses and on the statistical findings reported earlier, an economic theory of pension coverage is constructed using a cost-benefit approach to explain why some small employers provide pension plans while others do not. These arguments implicitly incorporate the responses made by small business owners and integrate the research findings presented in chapter III. Two complementary theories of pension provision are highlighted: (1) pensions help large employers monitor the performance of their workers; and (2) pensions further long-term employment relationships. Differences in the production requirements of pension plan sponsors and differences in their work forces are shown to influence whether plan sponsorship is a cost-effective business decision.

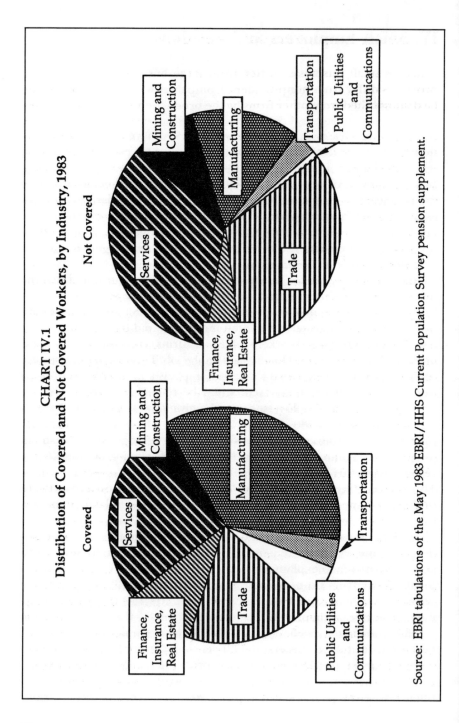

CHART IV.1

Distribution of Covered and Not Covered Workers, by Industry, 1983

Covered

Not Covered

Source: EBRI tabulations of the May 1983 EBRI/HHS Current Population Survey pension supplement.

66

Firms with Pension Plans

Just as small businesses differ from large businesses, pension plan providers differ from nonproviders. Companies with pension plans can be distinguished from other firms by the production requirements of the firm (the work place) and the type of workers meeting those production requirements. Providers and nonproviders exhibit different industrial patterns, different capital and management requirements, and different rates of unionization. The work force of firms with pension plans differs from that of nonproviders in terms of age, job tenure, and earnings.

Characteristics of the Work Place—The production of goods and services translates into specialized work place requirements. Employment skills needed for success in one industry may not be important in another. Broadly speaking, the skills used in manufacturing are different from those of the service sector. Furthermore, jobs vary within an industry and even among companies producing similar products. These differences in the work place may lead to differences in pension coverage.

The industrial composition of covered and uncovered workers is dissimilar; covered workers are more likely to be in manufacturing than in services. In 1983, 36 percent of workers with pension coverage were in manufacturing, 21 percent were in services, and 18 percent were in wholesale and retail trade (chart IV.1).[1] By contrast, only 15 percent of workers without coverage were in manufacturing, 33 percent were in services, and another 33 percent were in trade. Industrial differences between providers and nonproviders hold regardless of firm size.

Nonetheless, industry alone cannot explain why some small firms have pensions while others do not, as differences in coverage rates by firm size are as great as differences in industry-specific coverage rates for firms of the same size. Workers in very large firms in all industries are more likely to have pension coverage than those working for smaller employers. In particular, 92 percent of workers in very large manufacturing firms and 63 percent of workers in very large retail trade firms were covered by a pension plan. In contrast, only 18 percent of workers in very small manufacturing firms and 8 percent of retail workers in very small firms were covered. Direct measures of differences in production requirements, such as the ratio of capital to labor, may provide more information about the factors that influence plan sponsorship.

Capital Intensity—Capital-intensive firms are those that make greater investments in plant and equipment on a per employee basis. Higher capitalization and increased technology have historically boosted manufacturing

---

[1] These data are from the 1983 EBRI/HHS Current Population Survey pension supplement.

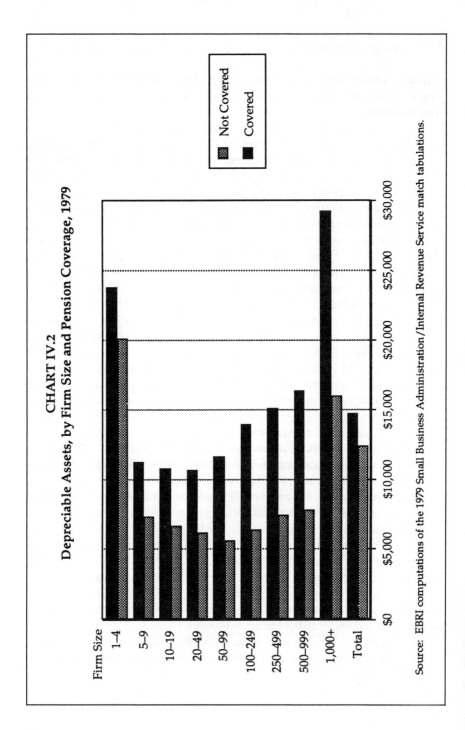

CHART IV.2
Depreciable Assets, by Firm Size and Pension Coverage, 1979

Not Covered
Covered

Firm Size

1–4
5–9
10–19
20–49
50–99
100–249
250–499
500–999
1,000+
Total

$0 $5,000 $10,000 $15,000 $20,000 $25,000 $30,000

Source: EBRI computations of the 1979 Small Business Administration/Internal Revenue Service match tabulations.

productivity and wages. Service firms have traditionally been more labor intensive, using less plant and equipment per worker. Small firms are less capital intensive than large firms. Nevertheless, companies of all sizes offering pensions are more capitalized and less labor intensive than those without pensions.

Depreciable assets per employee in 1979 averaged $14,700 for firms with pension coverage, compared to $12,500 for firms without pension plans (chart IV.2).[2] Firms offering pension plans are more highly capitalized in most industries.[3] Although large employers use more capital-intensive methods of production than small employers, firms contributing to a pension plan tend to be more highly capitalized, suggesting a link between capital investment and the costs and benefits of pension provision.

Management Intensity—Management intensity, like capitalization, is a fundamental attribute of a firm's production process. The simplest theory of supervisory control presented in chapter III suggests that firms with higher management ratios will be less likely to provide a pension than firms providing less supervision. Other arguments can be used, however, to link greater management intensity to higher rates of pension coverage. Employers may sponsor pensions in management-intensive settings because pensions provide managers incentives to improve their supervision (Oi, 1983). Firms with low management-worker ratios may also have simple production requirements that do not require complex supervisory evaluations.

The data show that management-intensive firms are more likely to have a pension plan. Overall, 13 percent of employees with pension coverage were in management, compared to only 9 percent of workers without a pension plan (chart IV.3). Medium-sized firms with pension coverage are the most management intensive, followed closely by firms sponsored by very small employers.[4] Since small management-intensive companies are unlikely to find worker supervision very difficult, these plans could be established to improve the tax-liability status of the owner. This hypothesis is analyzed in chapter V.

---

[2]These figures are based on corporate tax-return data from the SBA/IRS match file and measure the ratio of capital to labor abstracting from land values.
[3]Depreciable assets per employee in real estate firms, holding companies, and other investing companies are not higher, however, in firms that sponsor pensions. These companies often act as central administrators or developers of buildings or enterprises and have a relatively small staff in comparison to those holdings. Depreciable assets per employee in these three sectors combined average $63,170 per worker. Holdings would be even higher on a per worker basis if nondepreciable assets were also included.
[4]Unincorporated small-business owners are not included in the data.

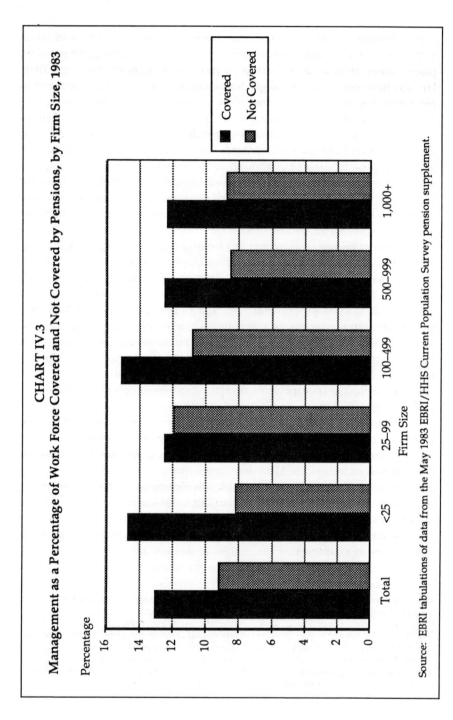

CHART IV.3

Management as a Percentage of Work Force Covered and Not Covered by Pensions, by Firm Size, 1983

Percentage

Covered
Not Covered

Firm Size

Total <25 25–99 100–499 500–999 1,000+

Source: EBRI tabulations of data from the May 1983 EBRI/HHS Current Population Survey pension supplement.

Unionization—As unionization is no longer expanding, the collective bargaining status of a company can be regarded as a characteristic of the work place rather than as a reflection of particular individuals at the firm. Unions have bargained strongly for pension plans, and firms subject to collective bargaining are more likely to have pensions than nonunion shops. Thirty percent of workers with pension coverage are unionized, compared to only 5 percent of workers without pension plans. Large firms are more likely to be unionized than small employers, but pension coverage tends to be proportionately higher in smaller firms under union contract.[5] More than one-third of covered workers in very large firms are unionized, compared to 16 percent of those without coverage. Eighteen percent of covered workers in very small firms are unionized, compared to 2 percent of those without coverage. While unionization contributes to pension coverage, it does not fully explain the coverage propensities of large and small employers.

Characteristics of the Work Force—Companies producing different goods and services hire different types of workers to run their businesses efficiently. A firm's work force reflects the skills needed to operate that business, and compensation is provided accordingly. Employers seeking workers willing to commit to a continued employment relationship will be looking for a more stable work force and will use pensions as a personnel tool to encourage continued employment.

That prediction is confirmed by 1983 data showing that workers with pension coverage spent more years on the job than those without a pension (table IV.1).[6] Job tenure averaged 8.9 years for the covered work force and 4.3 years for those without coverage. Job tenure for covered and uncovered workers differed by industry, but, within industries, workers without pension coverage had considerably fewer years on the job regardless of firm size. Pension plans effectively divide the work force into short-tenured and long-tenured employees. These findings are consistent with the hypothesis of a long-term employment contract.

Prime-age and full-time workers are also more likely to have a pension plan. Prime-age workers (between ages 25 and 64) account for 84 percent of those with pension coverage and 67 percent of uncovered workers. Full-time workers (working 2,000 hours or more) account for 79 percent of all workers with pension coverage and only 59 percent of workers without a pension. Prime-age full-time employees are more likely to be career-minded workers whom employers hire for the long term.

---

[5]For instance, see Andrews, 1985. For an extended discussion of research in this area, see chapter V.

[6]These data are based on the 1983 EBRI/HHS Current Population Survey pension supplement.

71

TABLE IV.1

Average Tenure by Coverage Status and Firm Size, by Industry, 1983

Industry	Total	<25	25–99	100–499	500–999	1,000+
			Firm Size			
Total						
Covered	8.9 yrs.	7.5 yrs.	7.4 yrs.	7.4 yrs.	8.0 yrs.	9.9 yrs.
Not covered	4.3	4.3	4.3	4.4	4.4	4.5
Manufacturing						
Covered	10.9	8.4	9.2	8.8	10.6	11.7
Not covered	5.3	5.1	4.8	5.6	6.7	6.1
Wholesale Trade						
Covered	9.1	9.7	7.0	7.9	8.9	10.7
Not covered	5.8	5.8	5.8	5.5	a	a
Retail Trade						
Covered	6.7	7.7	7.1	5.7	6.2	6.7
Not covered	3.5	3.6	3.4	3.2	3.3	3.1
Finance, Insurance, and Real Estate						
Covered	7.3	7.3	5.9	7.1	a	7.9
Not covered	4.4	4.7	4.1	4.0	3.5	4.4
Services						
Covered	6.3	6.5	5.8	6.2	6.1	6.5
Not covered	4.2	4.2	4.2	3.8	3.3	4.1

Source: EBRI tabulations of data from the May 1983 EBRI/HHS Current Population Survey pension supplement.
[a]Number is too small to be statistically reliable (less than 75,000 in that population).

By contrast, older, younger, and part-time workers are less attached to the labor force. Employers are unlikely to expect them to remain with the firm. Part-time workers may not seek out firms sponsoring pension plans since they are less likely to participate. Older and younger workers are unlikely to qualify for pension benefits and may be less concerned about pension coverage. These workers are often employed by very small companies without pension plans. Sixty percent of uncovered younger workers (under age 25) and 73 percent of uncovered older workers (aged 65 and older) work for very small firms (table IV.2). Very small firms hire 58 percent of all uncovered workers, compared to an overall employment share of 30 percent of the work force. Part-time workers (working fewer

TABLE IV.2
Pension Coverage, by Participant Age and Firm Size, 1983

Firm Size	Age (in years)		
	16–24	25–64	65 +
Covered	100.0%	100.0%	100.0%
1–25	9.8	10.1	21.8
25–99	12.2	9.5	15.6
100–499	16.2	15.0	20.5
500–999	7.4	6.6	8.0
1,000 +	54.4	58.3	34.2
Not Covered	100.0	100.0	100.0
1–25	60.0	56.4	73.3
25–99	15.9	19.6	10.8
100–499	10.0	11.6	7.3
500–999	3.0	3.2	1.0
1,000 +	11.0	9.3	7.5

Source: EBRI tabulations of data from the May 1983 EBRI/HHS Current Population Survey pension supplement.

than 1,000 hours a year) often work for very small firms without pension plans. Seventy-four percent of uncovered workers working less than 1,000 hours a year work for employers with fewer than 25 employees. Such part-time workers need not be included in employer-sponsored pension plans under current pension law.

Higher earnings are related to greater job skills and time on the job. In 1983, the average annual earnings of employees covered by pension plans were $20,000, compared to $11,600 for uncovered workers (chart IV.4). Average earnings of covered workers in large firms are generally higher than average earnings of covered workers in small firms.[7] Earnings of workers in firms without pension coverage are generally similar to one another.

What Small Employers Think about Pension Plans

Firms with pension plans are more capital intensive, hire more higher-paid workers, and employ more managers. These facts provide indirect

[7]This holds for most industries and occupations with few exceptions (the most notable is in retail trade, where small firms tend to pay more).

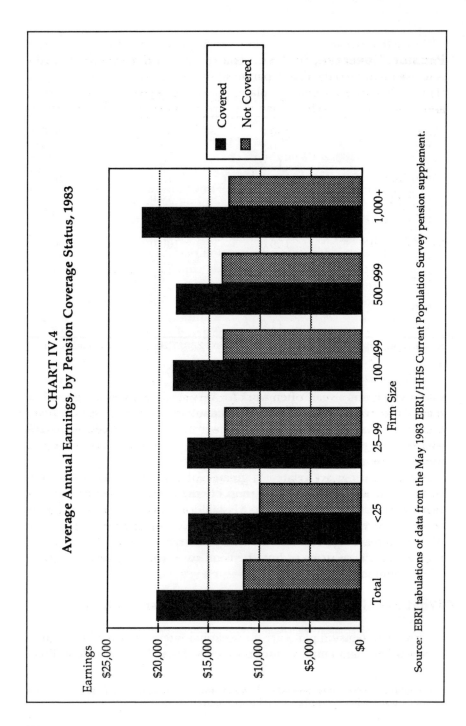

CHART IV.4
Average Annual Earnings, by Pension Coverage Status, 1983

Covered
Not Covered

Earnings

$25,000
$20,000
$15,000
$10,000
$5,000
$0

Total   <25   25-99   100-499   500-999   1,000+

Firm Size

Source: EBRI tabulations of data from the May 1983 EBRI/HHS Current Population Survey pension supplement.

evidence that firms of all sizes offer pensions primarily for business reasons. Another way to discover why some small firms provide pension plans is to ask them directly. Five separate studies have asked small employers (1) why they sponsor pension plans, (2) why they do not sponsor plans, and (3) why they canceled a plan they previously sponsored. This section reviews and compares the responses to these studies. Although the importance of specific findings varies from study to study, several consistent themes are found throughout. These include concerns about profits, the well-being and desires of workers, government regulation,[8] and the tax advantages of pension plans. Small-business owners themselves provide the building blocks for an economic model of pension coverage.

Why Have a Plan?—One study conducted for the Small Business Administration (SBA) questioned small employers and pension actuaries about their reasons for starting a pension plan.[9] The profitability of the firm and the tax deductibility of pension contributions were among the primary reasons for establishing a plan. Union negotiations and general competitive needs were also discussed. Employers mentioned profit sharing as being an incentive for plan formation as well as concerns about their employees' welfare. The study reported that owners were interested in pensions from the standpoint of their own retirement income and as a means to shelter current income from taxation.

A second SBA study (Justin Associates, 1985) also asked small employers why they established a pension plan.[10] Some employers indicated that they wanted to retain good employees (8 out of 13 firms); others said they established a pension plan to accumulate funds for retirement (5 of 13). The employers also mentioned the tax advantages of pension plans and the need for a plan under some union contracts.

A National Rural Electric Cooperative Association (NRECA) study (Korczyk, 1988)[11] indicated that most cooperative members provided a pension plan because their employees needed coverage. They also said they needed to maintain a plan to compete for workers. Only a minority of owners reported wanting plans for themselves.

A National Federation of Independent Business (NFIB) study (Dennis, 1985) found that 29 percent of those surveyed started their pension plan

---

[8]The effect of government regulation is discussed more thoroughly in chapter VI.
[9]Conducted by James Bell and Associates, 1984, in conjunction with ICF Inc., this study interviewed 18 employers about pension and health plans.
[10]Conducted by Justin Research Associates, 1985, for the Small Business Administration, this study questioned a small sample of 31 firms.
[11]That survey, conducted by the Opinion Research Corporation, interviewed 822 members of the National Rural Electric Cooperative Association (Korczyk, 1988).

to keep valued employees.[12] Other responses echoed this theme: employers reported that employee needs were a primary reason to start a plan. Some employers cited competitive pressures and union negotiations (mentioned more frequently by older plans). Other reasons for plan formation were tax advantages and personal motives—each cited by 11 percent of the employers.

In another study, commissioned by the Employee Benefit Research Institute (EBRI) and the American Association of Retired Persons (AARP), small employers were brought together in focus groups to discuss the purposes of pension plans.[13] Both employers who provided plans and those who did not regarded pensions as a potential reward for good employee performance on the job, similar to a bonus. Small employers also believed that pensions ought to reduce turnover (although they were not sure whether they did). These employers indicated that pensions should instill loyalty and show workers that the firm is a good place to work. Providers felt that a pension benefited them and their key employees personally and mentioned that pensions had income tax advantages.

Why Not Provide a Plan?—The reasons employers cited for not having a plan paralleled those given for plan formation. The relative importance assigned to those reasons was somewhat different, however. Financial factors were often a crucial reason for not providing a pension plan.[14] NRECA survey respondents indicated that cost was a prime reason for not providing a plan. Another major reason they mentioned was that they had no need for a plan.

Many respondents to the NFIB study said that they did not provide a pension plan because they could not afford one (39 percent). Another 9 percent listed start-up problems, and 6 percent indicated that their

---

[12]The survey conducted by the National Federation of Independent Business (NFIB) received completed interviews from 1,439 NFIB member firms (Dennis, 1985). Unlike some of the studies cited earlier, this analysis is based on a structured questionnaire. The relatively large sample ensures that the analysis is not based on the response of any one firm that is more likely to be unrepresentative of small employers as a whole. This is one of the primary data bases used in the chapter V and chapter VII analyses. See appendix A for a detailed description of the data.

[13]In focus groups, eight to ten individuals discuss an issue of interest. Participants can express opinions or come to conclusions that would not necessarily be included in a structured survey. EBRI and AARP used the Opinion Research Corporation (1986) to conduct two focus groups in each of three cities—one in New Jersey, one in Texas, and one in California. Two groups were conducted at each site. One group consisted of owners and managers of firms that employed 50 workers or fewer and provided a pension plan. The other group consisted of similar employers who did not offer retirement plans. Professional firms of accountants, physicians, and attorneys were not included.

[14]The financial viability of the firm as a precondition to plan provision was only emphasized by respondents to the Bell study.

employees preferred direct compensation.[15] When asked what incentives would cause nonproviders to start a plan, 38 percent said the single most important incentive would be increased profitability. Another 20 percent indicated that they would be encouraged to start a plan if the tax advantages of the plan increased. Twelve percent said they would be more interested in providing a plan if they could reinvest the funds in their own business. Another 16 percent in essence reported they would consider a plan, depending on the strength of employee demand.

In the focus groups, the financial status of the firm was not mentioned as a significant reason for not having a plan. However, in face-to-face conversations with other business owners, employers may be unwilling to discuss the financial position of their firm. Two influences were mentioned consistently: the cost of plan contributions and the burden of administering a plan.

Employers also spoke about the demand of their employees for retirement benefits. They suggested that employees with lower incomes would prefer higher pay. They noted that, because their industries were characterized by high worker mobility, their workers would not be interested in a pension plan that required vesting. They also felt that retirement income was a remote goal at best for younger workers. Finally, employers suggested they preferred to pay bonuses to reward performance selectively.

The employers in the SBA-Bell study indicated that their firms were not profitable enough to justify a pension plan. But they also indicated that pension plans were complicated to establish, and that young workers preferred cash compensation. Employers in the Bell study stated that profitability was the most important consideration in starting a plan.

The Justin Associates study confirmed the finding that employers perceived that pension plans were not affordable or worthwhile unless the firm made consistent profits. Cost-related factors (including start-up and administrative costs) were cited as deterrents to plan formation by 12 of the 16 firms answering the question. Some responded that a pension would not be worthwhile because they employed part-time employees or had high worker turnover. Other employers felt that their employees could already provide for their retirement and preferred to build up equity in their own firm. Employers also said that complex and changing regulations prevented them from starting a pension plan.

Why Terminate?—The SBA-Justin Associates study noted that the primary reason for plan termination was lack of revenue or insufficient profits. The NFIB study found that 25 percent of employers responding cited reduced profitability or sales, and 8 percent cited increased administrative costs.

---

[15]The nonresponse rate for the question was substantial—about one-third of those surveyed.

But government regulation also played a role in plan termination. Thirty-five percent of firms that terminated plans said they did so because of changing and complex regulations. Other labor force changes influenced 17 percent of the employers who had terminated a plan. Over one-third of the firms that canceled a plan subsequently established another plan.

The Economics of Plan Provision

Small employers have definite opinions about what considerations are important for plan sponsorship. Other evidence also indicates that employers play the decisive role in a decision to provide pension coverage. Employers may use pensions to encourage worker loyalty, longevity, and productivity on the job. Recent studies support the concept that pensions are provided with a continuing employment relationship in mind (see chapter III). Consequently, economic analysis needs to focus on the employer side of the pension equation to see why firms offer plans. In short, in the economic equation of plan provision, the costs of providing a plan must be balanced against the benefits to the firm.

The Costs of Plan Provision—The decision to sponsor a pension plan is similar to other business decisions. Businesses will sponsor a plan if it is cost effective to do so. The plan sponsor must be willing to pay at least as much as the plan will cost. According to the NRECA survey, costs are an important reason why employers with pension coverage select particular plans (Korczyk, 1988). Plan costs include start-up costs, continuing costs of administration, and the costs of plan amendments and revisions (including those stemming from legislative changes). Continuing expenses include investment management fees, audit fees, plan recordkeeping fees, legal fees, internal administration and related staff compensation, and employee communications.

Many plan costs must be paid directly by the sponsoring employer and cannot be paid from the pension fund (Hallenbeck and Hall, 1988). According to a survey of employers sponsoring profit sharing plans, 44 percent said that they paid investment management fees through the plan (Hewitt Associates, 1988). But virtually all legal fees, internal administrative costs, and employee communications were paid by the company. Thus, the bulk of costs represent additional employer expenses.

Studies have shown that per capita administrative costs are greater in smaller pension plans than in larger plans (table IV.3). Mitchell and Andrews (1981) used data from the first ERISA annual report (the 5500 form) to investigate multiemployer plans. Holding other factors, such as asset size, constant, they reported that administrative expenses per participant declined from $138 for plans with only 100 participants to $13 for plans with 20,000 members.

TABLE IV.3

Administrative Costs per Participant

Number of Participants	Multiemployer Plans			State and Local	Small Private
	Mitchell and Andrews[a] 1975	Cooper and Carlsen[b] 1978	Cooper[c] 1983	Pope[d] 1977	Dennis[e] 1985
3–4	—	—	—	—	$186
20–99	—	—	—	—	39
100	$138				
250	92				
375	—	$78	$170	—	—
500		68			
1,000	50	54	103		
2,500		43[f]	85[f]	$50–63	
3,000	31				
12,000		23	56	—	—
20,000	13	—	—	—	—
25,000	—	—	—	26–32	—
100,000				17–21	
300,000	—	—	—	12–16	—

Source: Derived from Robert D. Cooper, *Pension Fund Operating Expenses, the Summary Report and Fact Book* (Brookfield, WI: International Foundation of Employee Benefit Plans, 1984); Robert D. Cooper and Melody A. Carlsen, *Pension Fund Operations and Expenses, the Technical Report* (Brookfield, WI: International Foundation of Employee Benefit Plans, 1980); William J. Dennis, Jr., *Small Business Employee Benefits* (Washington, DC: National Federation of Independent Business Research and Education Foundation, 1985); Olivia S. Mitchell and Emily S. Andrews, "Scale Economies in Private Multiemployer Pension Systems," *Industrial and Labor Relations Review* (July 1981): 522–530; Ralph A. Pope, "Economies of Scale in Large State and Municipal Retirement Systems," *Public Budgeting and Finance* (Autumn 1986): 70–80.
[a]Mitchell and Andrews, 1981.
[b]Cooper and Carlsen, 1980.
[c]Cooper, 1984
[d]Pope, 1986.
[e]Dennis, 1985.
[f]Represents average costs for plans with 2,750 participants.

Two other studies of multiemployer plans conducted for the International Foundation of Employee Benefit Plans (Cooper and Carlsen, 1980; Cooper, 1984), also based on annual ERISA forms, report findings comparable to those of Mitchell and Andrews. For 1978, total operating costs were $23 per participant for plans averaging 12,000 members and $78 per participant for plans averaging 375 participants.[16] Operating costs rose

---

[16]The figures do not hold asset size constant.

considerably in 1983 (in nominal terms) to $56 per participant for plans averaging 12,000 members and $170 per participant for plans averaging 375 participants. Thus, the costs of large plans increased 118 percent on a per participant basis, while those of small plans increased 143 percent, compared to an increase in the overall price level of 52.7 percent. These figures suggest that smaller plans became relatively more expensive to administer.

Looking at state and local government plans, Pope (1986) also identified significant economies of scale with increasing plan size. He studied large pension systems ranging from 1,000 to 650,000 employees and found that average administrative costs in 1980 for a plan with 2,500 participants ranged from $50 to $63 per participant, compared to costs of between $26 and $32 per participant for plans with 25,000 participants and between $12 and $16 for plans with 300,000 participants. These figures are roughly comparable to those of multiemployer plans.

Small-Employer Costs—The administrative costs reported by small-employer plans appear lower than those of multiemployer plans and state and local plans (table IV.3).[17] Direct comparisons, however, may be misleading. For one, multiemployer plans may be more expensive since the plans are administered outside the direct purview of employers. Small employers may have plans with relatively simple provisions and low record-keeping costs. Furthermore, small employers tend to sponsor defined contribution plans; these are generally less costly than defined benefit plans. Defined contribution plans do not require actuarial evaluations to determine contribution amounts and to ensure that the plan is in compliance with the law. Perhaps most important, small employers probably do not report all the internal costs related to plan administration.

The underreporting of administrative costs has also been observed for large single-employer plans.[18] In large firms, recordkeeping duties and investment management are likely to be delegated to particular individuals or departments. In small firms, the situation is more complicated; the same general office staff may take care of recordkeeping and payroll records while the owner/manager may decide on the investments made by the plan. Costing-out these functions would be difficult, and small employers would be unlikely to make the calculation voluntarily without a strong incentive to do so.

---

[17]These costs are reported in the 1985 National Federation of Independent Business survey of small employers.

[18]Based on unpublished analysis of ERISA annual reporting forms (Form 5500).

While many small employers in the NFIB survey—44 percent—reported managing their plans in-house, the survey did not differentiate plan record-keeping procedures from the internal management of plan assets. According to the 1988 Hewitt survey of profit sharing plan sponsors, 17 percent of plans with less than $1 million in assets and 28 percent of plans with $1 million to $6 million in assets managed their funds internally. Internal recordkeeping was even more prevalent, however. Nearly one-half of all the profit sharing plans with assets under $6 million reported internal recordkeeping.

The underreporting of the full costs of plan administration notwithstanding, the reported administrative expenses of small-business pension plans declined with increased sales and employment except for the very smallest firms. Costs peaked at $212 per participant for firms with $200,000 to $499,999 in sales and declined to $20 per participant for firms with sales of over $10 million. Similarly, those with three or four employees paid $186 in administrative costs on a per employee basis while those with 20 through 99 employees paid only $39 per employee.

More extensive research shows that the administrative costs of small firms decrease on a per participant basis with increasing numbers of participants and increasing fund contributions (Andrews, 1989a).[19] As a result, small employers would be less likely to sponsor a pension plan than larger employers, because they face higher per capita administrative expenses and would need a more compelling economic reason for plan sponsorship.

The Benefits of Plan Provision: Willingness to Pay—Costs are not the entire story for an employer trying to decide whether pension plan sponsorship will pay. Factors that influence a business' willingness to pay for a plan include the financial condition of the firm and the impact of the plan on future profits and productivity. These economic motives are closely related to the shape of the small employer's work force and the general level of information the employer has about pensions.

Profits—Small employers consistently indicate that more profitable companies can afford to sponsor pension plans. Certainly, profit sharing plans have been heralded for years as a way for small employers to involve their employees directly in the success of the business while allowing employers the financial flexibility to forgo contributions in bad years. The profitability of the firm would not be a consideration for plan sponsorship, however, if employers could simply reduce the wages of their employees

---

[19]These findings are comparable to those of Mitchell and Andrews, 1981, indicating that there are economies of scale in financial management and in benefits administration in multiemployer plans.

and substitute pensions instead. The nature of the pension commitment is tied to the use of pension plans to facilitate long-term employment relationships, however, and the requirement under law that pensions be established on an ongoing basis. Employers cannot establish and terminate a series of pension plans at will and expect that these plans will be tax qualified by the Internal Revenue Service (IRS).

Since pensions represent a long-term commitment for the employer, the initial impact of plan sponsorship will be on profits. Ongoing profitability is also important for plan sponsorship because of the up-front employer expenditures necessary to start (or terminate) a pension plan. Since these costs must be amortized over the life of the plan, an employer would be unwilling to incur start-up (or shut-down) costs for a business that was operating on the margin, particularly if plans are established to encourage worker longevity with the firm.

The Employment Relationship and Productivity Gains—Pensions have been shown to have two distinct, interrelated effects on employment. First, research has shown that employees covered by pension plans have longer job tenure and lower turnover rates than workers without pension coverage (Schiller and Weiss, 1979; Mitchell, 1982; Viscusi, 1985; Ippolito, 1986). Second, an equally strong body of research has shown that pensions can be used by employers to encourage retirement (Quinn, 1977; Burkhauser, 1979; Gustman and Steinmeier, 1986; Fields and Mitchell, 1984). These findings are consistent with the presumption of a continuing employment relationship between the firm and the employee. If employers expect their workers to stay on the job, pensions can encourage workers to continue with the firm through benefit accruals and vesting schedules that tilt compensation to the future. Pension plans may also be the best way for employers to encourage lifetime careers since benefit eligibility formulas, such as early retirement incentives, provide an inducement for employees to leave the firm at a time when their productivity may be starting to diminish.

Although most evidence implies that employers use pension plans as a part of personnel policy, the rationale for a continued employment relationship has been left largely unspecified. Small employers may find that workers with a continued commitment to the firm increase their productivity by improving their firm-specific job skills (learning on the job) and through greater overall effort on the job. Small businesses that gain from pension sponsorship may be more capital intensive (mechanized and computerized) and need workers with greater sophistication and knowledge. Hammermesh (1980) argues that larger, more capital intensive firms provide examples of that combination of capital and skills. That combination would induce firms both to pay higher wages and to provide a pension plan.

82

Barron, Black, and Loewenstein (1987) suggest that large employers will be more highly capitalized to reduce the number of employees they must hire and supervise. In addition, they will select more highly qualified applicants and provide them greater training. This argument suggests that pension coverage is more likely in firms with higher capital-labor ratios. Smaller firms with greater capital costs may take the same approach. Similarly, firms with higher capital-labor ratios needing more highly skilled workers will, on average, pay their workers more.

Employee Demand—Although theory suggests that pensions can be an effective management tool to improve company productivity, if a group of employees want a pension plan, the willingness of the employer to provide a plan may be reinforced (Dorsey, 1982; Woodbury, 1983). Over a career horizon, pension contributions may be more valuable than equivalent wages for higher-paid workers facing higher marginal tax rates. Because wages are taxed as current income, a worker must earn more than a dollar to save a dollar for retirement.[20] But a dollar put in a pension fund is not taxed until retirement, when many retirees may be facing lower marginal tax rates than they paid while they were working.[21] Furthermore, interest earned in the pension fund accrues on a tax-deferred basis.[22]

Pension funds provide a more favorable environment for retirement-income accumulation for employees with higher marginal tax rates. In addition, higher-paid employees may be more likely to save for retirement (or other purposes) than lower-paid workers. Consequently, companies with higher-paid workers are more likely to offer a pension plan to retain valued employees, and those workers on their own are more likely to demand a plan.

But lower-wage workers may also find pensions a good way to save for retirement. Defined benefit plans provide additional cost savings for all employees because they are insurance arrangements. Since the asset value of the pension plan does not remain within the participant's estate, the assets the plan must accumulate are lower than those that would be needed to accumulate the same savings on an individual basis. Furthermore, pension benefits are less costly than individually purchased annuities because employer-sponsored plans do not face adverse selection. Since retirees with long life expectancies are well represented among purchasers of

---

[20]Individual retirement account contributions confer the same advantages as a pension plan up to the taxable limit (which varies with income and pension plan participation).

[21]Many consider this advantage reduced since tax reform because of anticipated increases in taxes in the future.

[22]Other investments may provide tax-deferred income as well. These range from many state and local bonds, unrealized capital gains on marketable securities, and the capital gains on a primary residence.

individual annuities, adverse selection increases the cost of annuities to insurance carriers; these costs are passed on to the consumer. Finally, even defined contribution plans providing lump-sum distributions at retirement, without the advantages of group insurance, give participants access to professional money managers they might not otherwise be able to afford.

That there is a demand for retirement income saving is suggested from data on voluntary pension plan contributions. For example, one survey of teaching institutions, including primary and secondary schools and colleges and universities (TIAA/CREF, 1987), found that of the eligible employees under age 40, 26 percent of clerical workers, 59 percent of faculty, and 72 percent of administrative officers participated in voluntary pension plans.[23] Participation rates increased for employees aged 40 and over—63 percent of all eligible clerical staff, 83 percent of faculty members, and 91 percent of administrative officers (table IV.4). This pattern of pension saving is similar to that found by income class for 401(k) plans and IRAs.[24]

TABLE IV.4
Pension Plan Participation:
Colleges, Universities, and Independent Schools[a] with a Wholly Voluntary Pension Plan[b] for One or More Classes of Employees: Percentage of Total Participating, 1986

	Faculty	Administrative Officers	Other Professionals	Clerical-Service
All Eligible Employees	74.4%	85.2%	59.9%	47.0%
Eligible Employees under Age 40	59.0	72.3	46.3	25.9
Eligible Employees Aged 40 and above	83.1	91.0	70.0	63.4

Source: Teachers Insurance and Annuity Association-College Retirement Equities Fund and Education Research Unit, *Research Dialogues* (January 1987), table 2, p. 3.
[a]Independent schools are defined as primary or secondary private schools not operated by a governmental unit.
[b]Teachers Insurance and Annuity Association-College Retirement Equities Fund (TIAA-CREF) plans and, at 78 institutions, pension plans with premium allocation options, including TIAA-CREF.

---

[23]Presumably, on average, these occupational breakdowns reflect different salary scales.
[24]See Andrews, 1985. Percentage contribution rates differ, however.

Labor Force Composition—Few employers hire only one type of worker at one rate of pay. Most companies have a mix of employees in different occupations and at different pay scales. The mix of workers within the firm may affect the willingness of employers to establish plans because worker performance is not uniformly improved with more experience on the job. Pensions may differentially affect the productivity of workers in different occupations. And not all workers want pensions. Companies whose production processes require a range of skills must hire workers with different characteristics. The jobs the company has to fill can affect its decision to offer a pension plan.[25]

Several studies consider the drawbacks of having a single pension plan covering different types of jobs within a firm. Investigating the effect of pensions on retirement, Nalebuff and Zeckhauser (1985) show that one single plan may not provide appropriate retirement incentives for different groups of workers. Goldstein and Pauly (1976) suggest that if different types of workers are provided identical benefits within a single work force, some workers might be paid more in terms of total compensation than they would if all workers were the same type.

Within companies with different types of workers, larger firms would have greater incentives to provide a pension plan since they may have more leeway to target plans to specific groups of workers or lines of business. Through collective bargaining, employers may have different plans for salaried and hourly employees. Large corporations, such as the Ford Motor Company, may have hundreds of pension plans. Small employers would have less flexibility under current law to exclude workers from the pension plan they provide, and would be less able to provide more than one plan for different groups of workers. Since small firms cannot segment their workers as effectively, small employers with relatively more high-skilled, high-income workers will be more likely to sponsor pension plans. While this is an economic outcome, based on the costs and benefits of plan sponsorship, it may conflict with public policy concerns about pension equity.

Information—A firm's willingness to sponsor a pension plan may also depend on the accuracy of the information the employer receives about the costs and benefits of a plan for the firm. If employers underestimate the positive effect of pensions on worker productivity, the costs of a pension may seem too high. If employers underestimate worker interest in

---

[25]This discussion does not take into consideration differences in tastes or savings preferences among similar individuals in identical jobs who receive identical rates of pay. Presumably, workers could then take jobs based on their preferences, depending on the type of pension the employer provided.

pension benefits, the costs of providing a plan may also seem too high. Businesses may be misinformed about administrative costs or about the availability of a cost-effective plan to meet their needs. To the extent that it is relatively more costly (in terms of time and money) for owner-managers of small firms to investigate their pension options, small employers will be less likely to provide a plan.

Summary and Conclusions

If pensions play a role in the personnel policy of a firm, the willingness of the firm to sponsor a pension plan can be viewed as a decision based on the costs of doing business. Employers would benefit from a pension plan if worker productivity were improved. Since by law pension plans must be broadly based, employers must balance the benefits of providing pensions to employees whose job performance will improve with a pension against the costs of providing pensions to employees whose job performance will not improve. For that reason, small companies will be less willing than large businesses to have pensions. Small employers would also have less reason to substitute the incentive of a pension plan for more effective employee evaluation on the job. In addition, pensions cost small employers more than large employers on a per employee basis because of the scale economies of running a plan. On these grounds alone, smaller employers have less of an incentive to sponsor pension plans than larger companies.

Pensions may also be less prevalent in small companies for reasons that are not directly related to firm size but are related to the nature of the business the small employer is operating. In particular, the production processes and work forces employed by many small businesses do not call for the type of long-run employment relationships that make pension sponsorship financially worthwhile. Because many small employers are less highly capitalized and their employees less skilled than those of larger employers, the productivity gains accruing from long-term employment relationships and pension sponsorship are reduced. Many small employers pay lower wages than large employers, so their workers gain less of a tax advantage from having a pension plan. Hence, the demand for pension plans on the part of small-business employees is likely to be less.

In economic terms, the combination of cost, productivity, and labor force considerations indicate that pensions will be more costly for small firms and that the benefits of plan sponsorship tend to be less. Consequently, the economic attributes of small businesses sponsoring pension plans should be closer to those of large plan sponsors. Although aggregate statistics roughly support this hypothesis, the relative importance of particular economic factors needs to be assessed more thoroughly before evaluating how changes in policy may influence pension coverage. Chapter V investigates the importance of economic influences on pension coverage as well as the potential use of pensions by small business owners for personal tax-planning purposes.

V. An Economic Analysis of Pension Coverage

Introduction

Effective policies to increase the number of small employers who voluntarily provide plans must be based on knowledge about the relative importance of economic factors related to pension coverage. To determine the effectiveness of pension policy proposals, the following questions need to be answered. First, how much of an influence do firm size, the work force, and earnings have on the likelihood of pension coverage? Second, how effective is unionization in improving coverage? And, third, how would employers react to decreased administrative costs?

As chapter VI considers, current law not only provides employers with incentives to establish plans but also seeks to prevent abuse by ensuring that employers include a broad cross section of employees. In addition, special rules have been enacted requiring faster vesting standards and benefit accruals for some plans to prevent small-business owners from establishing plans that provide few benefits for their employees. To evaluate the effectiveness of such rules, we need to assess whether small employers are more likely than large employers to establish plans for personal tax-planning purposes.

To address the issues outlined above, chapter V presents economic findings that assess the extent to which business considerations, worker demand, and administrative costs influence pension coverage among large and small employers. Chapter V also reviews other factors not necessarily related to the production process, such as the use of advisors by small employers to gain information about pensions. Finally, differences in pension coverage among firms are assessed to determine whether small firms establish pension funds primarily for personal tax-planning purposes.

Management, Productivity, and Pension Plans

Economic theory suggests that employers use pensions to promote a long-term employment relationship with their employees and to take advantage of increased worker knowledge gained on the job. In addition, large employers who cannot consistently evaluate the performance of their work force may sponsor pensions to reward good performance and make losing a job more costly for workers. Large employers may also be able to sponsor a number of plans, each targeted to particular employee groups. The validity of these theses is investigated with the help of economic analysis that simultaneously adjusts for the effect of more than one influence on pension coverage.

Firm Size as a Factor—Even after taking into account differences in the work place such as industry and earnings, workers in smaller firms and workers in smaller plants (or establishments) are less likely to have a pension plan.[1] Employees working for firms with fewer than 500 workers are less likely to have a pension than those at firms with 500 or more workers. Similarly, employees at work sites with fewer than 100 workers are less likely to have a pension plan than those at larger work sites. Some smaller work sites may represent different lines of business for the employer. Self-contained businesses of this type would be easier to manage and might also be subject to different bargaining agreements.

These findings are supported by analysis from a somewhat different perspective. In 1979, the likelihood of a corporation making a pension contribution was 21 percent for corporations with fewer than 100 employees and 51 percent for corporations with 100 or more employees, after accounting for differences in industry and capital intensity.[2] Even among small firms, those with larger employment bases are more likely to sponsor a pension. The likelihood that a small business will sponsor a pension plan increases by 3.2 percentage points for every 10 additional employees on the job (table V.1).[3]

These findings, in conjunction with research on the effect of firm size on earnings (reported below), lend support to the hypothesis that larger firms structure their pensions to improve output on the job when the evaluation of individual performance within a group of workers becomes more difficult. Nonetheless, owners of very small businesses may also be less likely to sponsor a pension plan if they can fund their own retirement in another manner.[4]

Production and the Work Force—Several recent studies support the theory that the nature of the production process influences plan sponsorship. Hutchens (1987) found that employees are less likely to have a pension in jobs in which repetitive tasks are performed. His results support the contention that pensions are provided because worker effort is harder to monitor in complex operations. Allen and Clark (1987) investigated

---

[1]These findings analyze pension coverage based on the May 1983 EBRI/HHS Current Population Survey pension supplement. See appendix B for specific equations.

[2]These findings are based on analysis of the SBA/IRS match file. See appendix B for specific equations.

[3]Nonetheless, a 1 percent increase in employment results in only a 0.14 percent increase in the pension coverage rate. This analysis is based on National Federation of Independent Business (NFIB) data. See appendix B for specific equations.

[4]See below for a more thorough analysis of this hypothesis.

TABLE V.1
Effects of Factors Influencing Pension Coverage Rates

Effect of	On	Leads to Increase of
10 additional employees[a]	Likelihood firm will provide coverage	3.2 percentage points
1 more year on job[b]	Likelihood of being covered by a pension	1.3 percentage points
200 more hours annually[b]	Likelihood of being covered by a pension	1.4 percentage points
$1,000 increase in annual earnings[b]	Likelihood of being covered by a pension	1.2 percentage points
$1,000 increase in payroll per employee[a]	Likelihood firm will provide coverage	1.6 percentage points
$1,000 increase in payroll per employee[c]	Likelihood of corporate contribution to a plan	1.1 percentage points
$10 decrease in administrative costs[a]	Likelihood firm will provide coverage	1.3 percentage points

Source: Employee Benefit Research Institute.

[a]Small-firm pension coverage model based on the National Federation of Independent Business small-employer survey.
[b]Pension coverage model based on the May 1983 EBRI/HHS Current Population Survey pension supplement.
[c]Analysis of the Small Business Administration/Internal Revenue Service match file.
Note: See appendix A for description of estimates.

the effect of pensions on productivity and reported that, on average, pensions should raise labor productivity by increasing job tenure.[5] Work by Dorsey (1987) suggests that the type of plan chosen by a firm is related to productivity. He found that defined benefit plans were provided more frequently in industries needing skilled workers.

Time spent on the job is often correlated with job skills and proficiency. Employees covered by a pension plan have more years on the job and work longer hours than those without pension coverage. The likelihood that a worker is covered by an employer-sponsored pension plan increases by 1.3 percentage points for every additional year on the job (table V.1).[6] For each additional 200 hours worked annually, the likelihood of pension coverage rises by 1.4 percentage points.[7] Those who are on the job less than a year are less likely to work for firms with pension plans. Employers hiring workers for low-skilled jobs may have no business justification for sponsoring a pension plan since these workers are easily replaced and gain few additional job skills by working longer. Short-tenure and part-time workers also may not want pension coverage or expect to qualify for benefits. These findings are consistent with an economic theory of pension provision that suggests that pensions are part of a long-term employment contract to improve productivity in the firm.

Earnings and Pension Plans

According to analysis from three different perspectives—that of the worker, the small employer, and the corporation—higher earnings are consistently related to higher pension coverage rates even after taking into account the effect of other factors. From the worker's perspective, for every additional $1,000 in earnings, workers are 1.2 percentage points more likely to be covered by a private pension plan.[8] From the small employer's perspective, a $1,000 increase in payroll per employee in small firms

---

[5]Nonetheless, their empirical findings were not statistically significant.

[6]A 1 percent increase in job tenure results in a 0.16 percent increase in the pension coverage rate. Equations are estimated based on the 1983 May EBRI/HHS Current Population Survey pension supplement. The NFIB data do not show that firms with more part-time workers are less likely to have a pension plan. The survey has little demographic detail, however, and responses about the age distribution of the full-time and part-time work force may be inaccurate. For more information about the NFIB data, see appendix A.

[7]A 1 percent increase in hours worked results in a 0.26 percent increase in the pension coverage rate. This analysis is also based on EBRI/HHS Current Population Survey pension supplement data for 1983.

[8]In this case, a 1 percent increase in earnings (holding hours constant) leads to a 0.34 percent increase in the pension coverage rate. These estimates are based on analysis of the May 1983 EBRI/HHS Current Population Survey pension supplement. Greater detail is found in appendix B.

results in a 1.6 percentage point increase in the likelihood of pension sponsorship.[9] From the corporation's point of view, after controlling for firm size and the ratio of capital to labor, a similar increase in payroll per employee leads to an increase of 1.1 percentage points in the likelihood of a corporate contribution to a pension plan (table V.1).[10]

These combined findings support the hypothesis that earnings are an important influence on pension coverage. This relationship may prevail for more than one reason. On the one hand, higher wage earners may have a greater demand for pensions.[11] On the other hand, higher wage earners may have the skills that employers want to maintain within the firm, which causes the employers to structure their compensation packages to encourage continued employment.

While most workers know whether or not they have a plan and may want a pension in retirement, many have very little knowledge about the precise role their pension plan plays in their total compensation (Mitchell, 1988). This suggests that the linkage between pension coverage and earnings at least in part measures the relationship between pension provision and the business considerations of the firm.

Employer Finances and Plan Costs

Economic arguments suggest that unprofitable firms will not institute pension plans because start-up costs (and potential termination costs in the event of financial distress) would create financial hardship. Thus, a financially marginal firm would need a compelling reason to establish a pension plan. As noted in chapter IV, even financially sound small employers need greater inducements for plan formation than large companies as per participant administrative costs are greater.

The relationship between profits and plan sponsorship can be measured directly and indirectly. Direct measurement indicates that companies

---

[9] A 1 percent increase in average payroll per employee leads to a 0.78 percent increase in the likelihood of plan sponsorship. These results are based on an analysis of the NFIB data. Appendix B provides greater detail.

[10] These findings, based on an analysis of the SBA/IRS match file, are very similar to those from the NFIB data. A 1 percent increase in average payroll per employee leads to a 0.7 percent increase in the likelihood of a corporate contribution to a pension fund. The results are found in appendix B.

[11] A number of studies find that differences in marginal tax rates influence pension contributions and coverage growth (Long and Scott, 1982; Woodbury, 1983; Barth, Cordes, and Friedland, 1984). Since marginal tax rates are closely related to earnings, the greater propensity for those with higher earnings to have pension coverage may be related to tax incentives to defer income.

making pension contributions are more profitable than other firms.[12] The role of profits can be analyzed indirectly for small employers using gross sales as a substitute for profitability. Profits are identically equal to sales less the costs of production. Holding labor costs constant, small firms with lower sales generally are less likely to have a pension plan.[13] In particular, firms with sales under $500,000 are less likely to provide a pension than firms with sales of $500,000 or over, even if other company characteristics are the same. These findings suggest that more profitable firms are more likely to have a pension plan. But sales volume is also related to the capital intensity of production. Thus, firms with higher sales may be more capital intensive and use a more skilled work force.[14]

A key factor from the point of view of public policy is the role administrative costs play in plan formation among small employers. Theoretically, policies designed to reduce administrative costs would lead more small employers to sponsor plans on a voluntary basis. Based on estimates of administrative costs that small employers would incur if they decided to sponsor a plan, a $10 decrease in administrative costs per employee would raise the chances that a small firm will provide pension coverage by 1.3 percentage points, after accounting for other economic factors such as sales, industry, and payroll per employee (table V.1).[15] In other words, a 10 percent decline in administrative costs per worker for small employers would increase pension coverage, on average, by 2.7 percent. While pension coverage is cost sensitive, large cost reductions are needed to significantly improve pension provision.

---

[12]This finding is based on statistical analysis of the SBA/IRS match file. EBRI's SBA/IRS match data are grouped by industry and firm size, making more extensive analysis of the role of profits technically infeasible. Individual observations are not available for public use. See appendix A for more information.

[13]This analysis of small firms is based on the NFIB survey. See appendix B for specific equations.

[14]Analysis presented in appendix B using the SBA/IRS match file statistically confirms the findings presented in chapter III that corporations providing pension plan contributions are more capital intensive than other companies. Substituting capital-labor ratios from the SBA/IRS match file for sales and industry in the NFIB analysis indicates that higher capital-labor ratios raise the likelihood of plan sponsorship (see appendix B). The evidence suggests that the relationship between sales and pension coverage may result from the relationship between capital intensity, profits, and plan sponsorship.

[15]Since actual cost data are available only for NFIB firms that have a pension plan, the costs that firms would have to pay if they wanted to become plan sponsors must be estimated. Administrative costs were estimated for both providers and nonproviders for statistical reasons. Plan sponsors were estimated to pay administrative costs of $59 per employee compared to estimated administrative costs of $68 per employee that would have to be paid by nonsponsors if they decided to start a pension plan. See Andrews, 1989a, for a detailed description of the methodology behind these projections.

Additional Influences on Plan Formation

Factors that are secondarily related to the production process, worker demand, or plan costs may also influence pension coverage. These include the extent of unionization, the type of industry, and the amount of information that employers have about pensions.

Unionization—Union workers are more likely to have pension coverage than nonunion workers, and unionization raises the pension coverage rate of workers in small firms more than that of workers in large firms. Andrews (1985) reports that 73 percent of workers in small firms covered by a union contract have pension coverage, compared to only 28 percent of workers in small firms not under union contract. Furthermore, union workers in firms with fewer than 25 employees are 51 percentage points more likely than nonunion workers in very small firms to be covered by a pension plan. Union workers in firms with 25 through 99 workers are 34 percentage points more likely to have a pension than nonunion workers in similar firms.

Other research confirms these findings. Gustman (1986) reports that union members in large firms have slightly higher pension coverage rates than union members in small firms, but nonunion workers in large firms have much higher coverage rates than their nonunion small employer counterparts.[16] Freeman (1985) states that unions raise the probability of pension coverage for workers in small firms by 46 percentage points, compared to an 8 percentage point gain for workers in very large firms.[17]

Several explanations have been proposed for the effect of unionization on pension coverage. One explanation suggests that the demand for pensions is greater in a unionized environment because union decisions are based on member votes, and are weighted more heavily toward the desires of older, long-tenure workers (Freeman, 1985). Another argument counters that in some unions, younger members are in favor of pensions to encourage older workers to retire more quickly and open promotion paths.[18] Pensions may also provide a premium to higher-paid union

---

[16]This research uses the 1983 Survey of Consumer Finances sponsored by the Board of Governors of the Federal Reserve System.

[17]The results are found using the May 1979 Current Population Survey pension supplement. Using another data set, the Bureau of Labor Statistics Expenditures for Employee Compensation survey, Freeman finds a 60 percent increase in coverage due to unionization for workers in firms with fewer than 500 employees, compared to a 6 percent coverage-rate increase for workers in firms with 500 or more employees.

[18]Telephone conversation with Paul Jackson, Wyatt Company (12 December 1988).

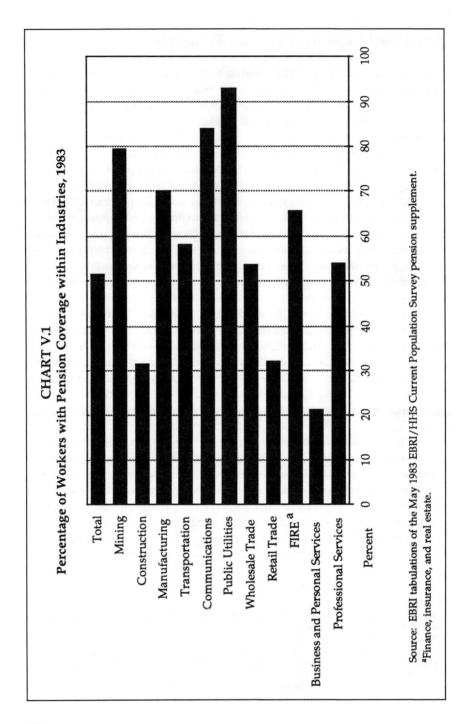

CHART V.1
Percentage of Workers with Pension Coverage within Industries, 1983

Source: EBRI tabulations of the May 1983 EBRI/HHS Current Population Survey pension supplement.
[a]Finance, insurance, and real estate.

96

workers that makes job loss very costly, or they may be related to the train-ing and retention of unionized workers (Gustman, 1986).[19]

Despite the potential for unions to wield economic power over many small employers, the vast majority of employees in small firms are not unionized. Gains in unionization seem unlikely because it is difficult to organize a relatively unskilled, decentralized work force.[20] As a conse-quence, gains in pension coverage are unlikely to stem from increased unionization among small employers.

Industry—The industry in which a business operates traditionally has been considered an important determinant of pension coverage since strong differences in pension coverage rates have been observed. In 1983, coverage rates ranged from 93 percent in public utilities, 84 percent in communications, and 70 percent in manufacturing to 32 percent in re-tail trade and 22 percent in business and personal services (chart V.1).

Many factors that influence pension coverage, such as earnings and firm size, vary by industry and may be the true explanation for differ-ences in industry coverage rates. Coverage rates can be "adjusted" to take account of these factors. For instance, on an unadjusted basis, workers in durable goods manufacturing have higher pension coverage rates than workers in finance, insurance, and real estate or than workers in whole-sale trade and professional services. Yet after accounting for the influence of other factors, workers in these three service-providing industries have relatively higher pension coverage rates than workers in durable goods manufacturing.[21]

While the impact of industry on pension coverage reflects the influence of other factors, different data sets do not provide consistent findings on industrial rankings after accounting for the effect of these influences.[22] The lack of uniformity in industrial rankings suggests that pension

---

[19]Ippolito, 1985, theorizes that collectively bargained pension funds are purposely under-funded to ensure that union workers have a greater stake in the continuation of the firm and share in the risks of the business.

[20]See chapter II discussion of trends in unionization.

[21]Based on analysis using the May 1983 EBRI/HHS Current Population Survey pension sup-plement. Allen and Clark, 1987, also report that after adjustment, workers in wholesale trade have a relatively greater likelihood of pension coverage than the raw numbers in-dicate and that workers in durables manufacturing have less of an advantage.

[22]The NFIB data for small firms show that pension coverage is highest in wholesale trade and manufacturing firms. After adjusting for the effect of other factors, the NFIB data show that employers in finance, insurance, real estate, banking, and nonprofessional services are more likely to have a pension plan than small employers in other industries. The 1984 Survey of Income and Program Participation (for prime-age male workers in small firms) shows that workers in communications, wholesale trade, and manufacturing have the high-est likelihood of being covered by a pension plan before adjustment for other influences. After accounting for differences in wages, firm size, job tenure, and unionization, workers in professional services have relatively higher coverage rates than workers in other industries.

coverage rates by industry reflect the influence of other factors related to pension coverage. Because any one data set provides information on a limited subset of the factors that affect pension coverage, the degree to which industry is an independent factor cannot be determined. In other words, differences in pension coverage by industry may simply reflect a correlation with related factors not explicitly included in the analysis. We must be wary of policy prescriptions based on perceived differences in industry coverage rates.

Information—Many observers have suggested that employers and employees do not recognize the need for a pension plan and that pensions must be sold to the business owner. Economists might argue that if employers are uninformed about plan costs and benefits, better information could affect pension coverage rates.

The National Federation of Independent Business (NFIB) asked its members about their most important source of information on pensions and retirement income. After adjusting for differences in payroll, firm size, and costs, companies whose primary source of information was an accountant, insurance agent, magazine, or other publication had pension coverage rates that were 15–25 percentage points less than for firms getting information from trade associations, financial planners, and investment advisory firms, business consultants, lawyers, and bankers.[23]

Firms obtaining pension information from accountants and insurance agents may be less likely to have a plan for several reasons. Insurance agents who advise small businesses may not be familiar with pension plans or may find that pension plans are not their most profitable product. Firms actively considering a pension plan may seek multiple sources of information other than accountants and insurance agents. Financially sophisticated entrepreneurs may actively search for the best advice on all financial matters. Improvements in financial planning may include attractive pension or capital accumulation plans. And some advisors may provide better pension packages to small employers or be more persuasive in explaining the benefits of pension sponsorship.

Personal Motives for Pension Plans

The economic arguments presented in chapter IV, bolstered by the empirical findings of this chapter, have provided a consistent explanation for pension plan sponsorship by firms of all sizes. But another factor is the attitude of workers. Workers also favor pension coverage as a means to save for retirement. The demand for pensions is not restricted to

---

[23]See appendix B.

rank-and-file employees; business owners and highly compensated executives find tax deferral attractive as well. In fact, support for high contribution levels for highly compensated employees has been based on the premise that the employer-sponsored pension system will be weakened if top management has no active interest in rank-and-file plans.

Personal financial considerations affect all business decisions, of course, as long as profits motivate economic performance. Thus, self-interest among owners and managers in firms of all sizes is not an issue. However, some observers have speculated that small employers establish pension plans primarily in their own personal interest without providing commensurate benefits for their employees. These doubts led to provisions of the Tax Equity and Fiscal Responsibility Act of 1982 (TEFRA) requiring special standards—top-heavy rules—for plans in which more than 60 percent of accumulated benefits were earmarked for key employees. The definition of key employees, in part, hinged on ownership in the firm, and, hence, the top-heavy rules were most likely to apply to small employers.[24] Some feel these rules prevent abuse; others think they add to plan costs without serving a comparable public policy purpose. To evaluate the need for such rules requires an assessment of the extent to which small firms establish plans solely for the personal benefit of the owner.

Why Do Small Employers Sponsor Fewer Plans?—Personal considerations may influence the behavior of employers in several ways. To build up equity for their own retirement, small employers may invest in their businesses instead of sponsoring pension plans. This hypothesis predicts that only small-business owners who cannot reinvest in their business will establish a pension plan for personal reasons.[25] Evidence on managerial salaries presented in chapter III suggests that owner-managers of small firms have greater discretion in setting their own wages than managers of larger corporations. Small-business owners may take little in salary and invest in their companies instead.

Unfortunately, the predictions based on this hypothesis are uncertain. If small employers are more likely than large employers to establish plans primarily to shelter their personal income, pension coverage rates would be higher in small firms after taking into account the influence of other factors. If large employers are more likely than small employers to use

---

[24]These rules require faster vesting standards and more favorable benefit accruals for rank-and-file members of top-heavy plans. The top-heavy rules are discussed in greater detail in chapters VI and VII.

[25]Although recent arguments suggest that the Omnibus Budget Reconciliation Act of 1987 (OBRA '87) will stop the formation of new defined benefit plans (see chapter VI), for the most part small firms have traditionally favored defined contribution plans. Thus the arguments related to plan formation in a defined contribution framework remain valid.

pensions to shelter the income of top executives, the pension coverage rates of large employers will be higher.

Earlier analysis has shown that smaller firms are less likely to sponsor pensions than larger firms even after accounting for the effect of other influences on coverage. This could support the argument that small employers have less need to shelter income for retirement through a pension plan than large employers. But economic considerations also lead to the prediction that large firms are more likely to sponsor pension plans than small employers. The evidence is indeed inconclusive.

If personal financial considerations influence the establishment of pension plans by small-business owners, they ought to respond to economic factors in a less consistent manner than larger enterprises. Statistical analysis suggests, however, that pension coverage based on economic factors can be predicted more accurately for extremely small employers than for larger small employers.[26] Nonetheless, firms with exceptionally high payrolls per employee ($50,000 or more) that were excluded from the analysis as outliers[27] may be more likely to establish plans for nonbusiness reasons. Firms with very low sales are no less likely to have a pension plan than larger businesses, suggesting that they may establish their plans for personal reasons.

Small employers may signal their personal interest in a pension through the advisors they use for information about pension plans. Firms that use accountants and insurance agents for pension advice may be more willing to reinvest in their business or shelter income using other insurance products instead of sponsoring a pension plan. But business owners who learn about pensions from accountants and insurance agents may not have evaluated all their options before deciding on plan sponsorship.

Do Small Businesses Discriminate?—The purpose of the top-heavy rules is to ensure that employees receive their fair share of benefits in plans that have a strong owner interest. Small employers could presumably establish plans that are favorable to themselves, exclude their employees from the plan, fail to vest those who participate, or provide their employees fewer benefits.[28]

---

[26]These findings are based on the NFIB survey. The Spearman correlation coefficient of the residuals of the pension coverage forecasting equation with the total number of employees was 0.28, suggesting less accurate prediction (heteroscedasticity of residuals) with increasing firm size and not with decreasing firm size.

[27]These firms were omitted because it was not clear whether the monthly payroll figures reported by certain employers represented valid observations or whether some employers reported annual figures instead of monthly estimates.

[28]Following current usage, pension coverage refers to the provision of any plan by a particular employer. Participation in a plan means that the employer has a plan and the employee is included in it. Not all employees are always included in an employer's plan. Vesting means that the pension participant has met the years of service required under the plan to be entitled to a benefit at retirement.

Statistical evidence does not indicate, however, that small employers discriminate in participation and vesting requirements. In 1983, among all covered workers, the percentage of employees who participated in private-sector employer-sponsored plans was not influenced by firm size (Andrews, 1985). Furthermore, plan participants working for small companies were more likely to be vested than participants in large companies even before 1982, the year the top-heavy rules were enacted (Rogers, 1981). These findings do not support the contention that most small employers exclude their employees from future benefit entitlement.

Another way owner-managers may look out for themselves is by providing more generous plans. Owners are included in over 85 percent of small-employer pension plans. Small employers might be willing to pay for a "Cadillac" plan that provides them extra service. This hypothesis can be tested by comparing the estimated administrative costs of plan sponsors with estimated administrative costs that firms without plans would have to pay for a plan. Statistical evidence suggests that all employers will be charged equally for plan administration and that cost differences stem from economies of scale (Andrews, 1989b).

Small-business owners who are included in their plans may establish better plans for themselves. The compensation costs of small businesses sponsoring plans that include the owner are more sharply skewed toward pension contributions.[29] On average, contributions amount to 6.5 percent of compensation for small businesses. For firms in which the pension plan covers the owner, contributions amount to an average of 8.3 percent of compensation, after adjusting for differences in other factors such as plan costs, average pay, and the size of the firm. This suggests that owners may establish better pension plans when they are included.

For defined contribution plans, the principal type of small-employer plan, increased contributions would be passed on to all employees.[30] Although some small employers may discriminate against their employees, statistical evidence indicates that, on average, employees of small firms benefit from their plan if one is provided and benefit even more if their employer is in the plan.

Professional Practices and Pension Plans—Small professional corporations are most frequently cited as examples of employers who establish plans strictly as tax shelters (doctors, lawyers, accountants, actuaries, and

---

[29]Compensation includes wages and salaries, health insurance premiums, and pension contributions.

[30]The relationship between owner participation and plan generosity is further complicated since higher pay per employee tends to reduce the share of compensation spent on pensions if other factors are taken into account. Top-heavy rules may require firms with more low-paid workers to contribute a larger share of compensation for those workers.

architects). Discriminatory behavior by professional-service providers would mean that their employees would be more likely to work in an office with a pension plan but less likely to participate in the plan and less likely to be vested.

Concerns about the behavior of professional corporations may be warranted. Professional-service workers account for 34 percent of employees with coverage in very small firms compared to 14 percent of workers without coverage.[31] The distribution of covered and uncovered workers is not as skewed in other industries and other firm size categories. Once differences in economic factors and firm size are accounted for, employees in professional services are still more likely to be covered by a pension plan and less likely to be plan participants than other workers (Andrews, 1985). Consequently, professionals may establish plans primarily to meet their own needs and those of their higher-paid employees. But these findings are not uniformly supported by data from other sources[32] and may reflect data omissions which influence industrial patterns of coverage and participation rather than discriminatory practices by professional corporations. Nonetheless, the possibility of discrimination by those in professional practices cannot be overlooked.

Summary and Conclusions

Research indicates that an economic analysis of pension coverage provides a realistic way of appraising the pattern of coverage in large and small firms. Economies of scale in plan administration have been well documented. Direct evidence of the influence of administrative costs on pension coverage has now been provided. If administrative costs are $10 less per employee, the result is an increase in the likelihood of plan sponsorship of 1.3 percentage points for small employers.

Gains in employment, job tenure, or average payroll increase pension coverage rates, but increases have to be relatively substantial in percentage terms to make much of a difference. Firms with higher profit rates

---

[31]Based on analysis of the May 1983 EBRI/HHS Current Population Survey pension supplement.

[32]According to the SBA/IRS match file, coverage is also higher in professional-service corporations after accounting for differences in firm size. Analysis of 1984 Survey of Income and Program Participation data for prime-age male workers in small firms confirms that men in professional services are more likely to be covered by a pension plan than workers in other industries, but they are no less likely to be plan participants. By contrast, taking into account the effect of other economic factors, the NFIB data on small employers do not show that smaller firms supplying professional services have different coverage patterns than other firms. The proportion of participants in firms having a pension plan is no lower for professional-service firms than for other companies.

and more capital intensive production are more likely to sponsor pension plans. Higher sales, a proxy for profitability and capitalization for firms with similar employment, lead to increased pension coverage among smaller employers. While pension coverage also varies by industry, the effect of industry on coverage is clouded. Since each data set contains different information, industry differences may simply represent influences on pension coverage that are not included in the analysis.

Other influences on pension coverage fit an economic theory of pension provision less neatly. In particular, firms that get information about pensions from advisors other than accountants and insurance agents appear more likely to offer a plan. Employers using these sources may be more sophisticated or the marketing strategies employed by some advisors may be more persuasive. At the least, information about pension plans does not appear to be uniformly provided to small firms.

The fact that small-business owners are less likely to offer a pension plan than large employers may reflect the ability of small employers to shelter income within their businesses, an ability not as easily implemented by corporate management. But the plans formed by large employers could be motivated by the desires of key executives as well. Evidence suggests that in large and small firms alike, pensions are primarily established according to cost-effective business criteria as a means to motivate employees. Statistical analysis does not indicate that plans are provided by either large or small employers solely to satisfy the personal financial considerations of owners and managers. Employees of small firms tend to benefit when their employer is included in the plan.

Policy concerns have also focused on small professional corporations. The top-heavy rules established under TEFRA were intended, in part, to ensure that such plans are not discriminatory. Analysis shows higher than normal coverage among professional-service employees but lower than average participation rates. These findings may indicate that small professional offices establish plans for their own personal financial objectives and then restrict participation to relatively few of their employees. But the variability in industry coverage rates after accounting for other factors cautions us against taking these findings too literally.

Issues of fairness and equity are the concerns of public policy and not those of the market. While pension coverage depends on the economic conditions of the firm, subsequent chapters will show that pensions do not operate in a free-market environment. All firms are influenced by government regulation and react to regulatory changes. The next chapter studies the impact of legislation on the growth of the retirement income system.

VI. Pension Policy and Small Employers

Introduction

The federal government has been actively involved in pension law for almost seven decades. For many years, federal pension law was praised for facilitating and encouraging plan formation. More recent changes have been criticized, however, as discouraging growth, although the intent of these changes was to ensure that plans were financially sound and equitable.

Chapter VI discusses the history of pension legislation and indicates which provisions are particularly important to small employers. Legislation before 1974 is reviewed, as is the Employee Retirement Income Security Act of 1974 (ERISA), the foundation of current law. Throughout the 1970s and 1980s, Congress has enacted many amendments to ERISA. In 1986, significant amendments were passed in conjunction with the Tax Reform Act. In 1987, new requirements for defined benefit plans were passed as provisions of the Omnibus Budget Reconciliation Act. These laws have combined to define the pension system in which small businesses operate.

Legislative intent and market outcomes are not always synonymous, however. Not surprisingly, small-business owners have their own opinions about the pros and cons of pension legislation. Chapter VI also investigates what small-business owners say about government regulation, and uses their responses as a framework to develop an economic theory of pension regulation. Finally, the chapter provides empirical evidence about the effect of government activity on plan formation during the late 1970s and early 1980s.

The Background: through ERISA

With few exceptions, small-business pension plans are subject to the same federal legislation as large company plans, although small companies may be affected by the legislation in different ways. While ERISA is the foundation of modern pension law, earlier legislation promoted the expansion of the private employer-sponsored pension system. Some of those early laws were particularly important to small businesses (table VI.1).

Pensions were first provided tax-deferred status when the Revenue Act of 1921 exempted the interest income of stock bonus and profit sharing plans from current taxation. The Revenue Act of 1926 extended this tax

TABLE VI.1
A Review of Selected Pension Legislation Affecting Small Business, 1921–1974

Year Enacted	Legislation	Provisions
1921	Revenue Act	• exempted net interest income from taxes of stock-bonus and profit sharing plans
1926	Revenue Act	• extended tax exemption to pension trusts
1938	Revenue Act	• gave participants some rights to plan assets
1942	Revenue Act	• coverage rules enacted • limited allowable employer contributions • permitted integration of pension plans with Social Security
1962	Self-Employed Individuals Tax Retirement Act	• provided for Keogh plans (lower contribution limits than those of corporate plans)
1974	Employee Retirement Income Security Act (ERISA)	• vesting standards, stronger reporting and disclosure requirements, and participation standards • stricter fiduciary requirements • established the Pension Benefit Guaranty Corportion (PBGC) • raised Keogh contribution limits • established individual retirement accounts (IRAs) for those not participating in an employer-sponsored plan

Source: Employee Benefit Research Institute.

exemption to pension trusts. The preferred tax treatment enjoyed by pension plans since that time has helped both large and small employers and their employees.

Small employers are more likely than large employers to use profit sharing plans to provide primary retirement benefits. These plans enable employers to make contributions to a pension fund based on the profitability of the firm. Thus, contributions need not be made for years in which the company has low profits. This contribution flexibility is particularly important to small firms with limited cash reserves. Many employers also feel that linking retirement income to profits gives employees a greater stake in the company's performance. Consequently, legislation providing tax-deferred status to profit sharing plans was particularly important to the many small employers who established plans.

The Revenue Act of 1938 made pension trusts irrevocable, that is, participants were provided rights to plan assets for the first time. The Revenue Act of 1942 established employee eligibility rules for coverage,[1] contributions, and benefits to prevent plans from discriminating in favor of officers, shareholders, and highly compensated employees. Taken together, these requirements are generally termed nondiscrimination provisions. To ensure that plans did not discriminate against lower-paid employees, the law required that 70 percent of the employees—or a "fair cross section"—either were participants or were potentially eligible to participate in the plan. Although plans could not provide proportionately greater benefits to higher-income employees, they could integrate plan benefits with Social Security. Using integration, the plan could look at the combined Social Security and pension benefits a participant would receive at retirement to provide a target benefit equal to a similar percentage of preretirement earnings for all employees.[2]

The theme of nondiscrimination through equitable coverage and fair integration provisions reappears in subsequent pension legislation. Recent congressional efforts to insure that plans do not discriminate have been directed, in part, toward small employers.

---

[1] The term "coverage" as used in the tax code differs from the use of coverage in statistical studies. The legal reference is to the proportion of employees who are potentially eligible to become plan participants. By contrast, statistical analysis usually considers that all employees who work for an employer sponsoring a pension plan are "covered" while those actually included in the plan are "participants." In statistical terminology, those who are not participants may be excluded by the employer because they are not in the group of employees who were "covered" (in tax code terms) or because they do not meet the plan participation standards based on age and hours worked.

[2] Thus, integration allows pension benefits to be relatively higher for those earning above the maximum amount subject to Social Security taxes than for those earning below the Social Security tax base.

107

The Self-Employed Individuals Tax Retirement Act of 1962 constituted another milestone for small-employer plans. This legislation enabled unincorporated businesses, farmers, and those in professional practices to establish Keogh plans (named for Congressman Eugene J. Keogh (D-NY)) for their retirement. For the first time, small unincorporated business owners could start a pension plan for themselves and their employees. These plans originally had less generous contribution limits than those of corporate plans. Contribution and benefit limits were extended in the 1970s and 1980s, however, so that Keogh limits are now identical to those of corporate pension plans.

The next major legislative event was the 1974 enactment of ERISA. ERISA is considered the most sweeping pension legislation ever undertaken. While the basic tax structure remained essentially the same under ERISA, participation and vesting standards were provided for the first time. Participation standards generally specified that legally covered employees could be excluded from the plan only if they worked fewer than 1,000 hours annually or if they were under 25 years of age.[3] Several different vesting standards were allowed. The most predominant was 10-year cliff vesting in which a plan participant was entitled to benefits only after 10 years of participation under the plan. Workers had to be vested in their plan at least as quickly as these standards specified. ERISA's vesting standards may have accelerated the trend toward shorter vesting among large employers (Employee Benefit Research Institute, 1986). Pre-ERISA vesting provisions among small employers are not known, although small plans had somewhat shorter vesting schedules than large plans immediately following ERISA.

ERISA included fiduciary and funding requirements as well. Funding standards for defined benefit plans under ERISA were intended to promote fiscal responsibility among ongoing plans. In addition, most retirement benefits from defined benefit plans were guaranteed by the newly created Pension Benefit Guaranty Corporation (PBGC) in the event a plan terminated. If a plan terminated with insufficient funds to cover benefit liabilities, the PBGC would have a claim on 30 percent of the company's net worth—a provision that was of initial concern to small firms. The PBGC was to be funded through premiums paid on a per participant basis. As premiums have increased over the years, small employers with defined benefit plans may be finding these costs more of a financial burden.

ERISA specifically excluded several groups of plans from PBGC coverage, including plans established and maintained by a professional service

---

[3]The provisions are somewhat more complicated.

employer that do not have more than 25 active participants.[4] More generally, since small firms are less likely than large firms to sponsor defined benefit plans, the establishment of the PBGC was relatively less important for small employers.

ERISA strengthened reporting and disclosure requirements to provide better plan information to the federal government and plan participants. While all firms must provide information to plan participants on an ongoing basis, the costs of providing summary plan descriptions and annual reports and of responding to other participant requests may be higher for small employers on a per participant basis. Internal Revenue Service (IRS) regulations enable annual reporting requirements to be somewhat less lengthy for small plans (those with fewer than 100 participants), and require full reporting only every three years. Nevertheless, the regulatory relief provided may not be enough to make up for higher per participant reporting costs.

ERISA also permitted workers who were not included in an employer-sponsored plan to establish individual retirement accounts (IRAs). This legislation was intended to enable those without coverage to have the benefits of a pension plan. Workers in small firms were to be potential beneficiaries of this change since employer-sponsored pension coverage is lower in small firms. Less than 5 percent of eligible workers contributed to an IRA in 1978, however, before IRA eligibility was expanded to plan participants as well.[5]

Post-ERISA, Prior to Tax Reform

Since ERISA, changes in pension legislation have been enacted almost every year (table VI.2). Many of these changes may have had a greater impact on small employers than on large firms. Seven major bills were enacted into legislation between 1978 and 1986. The Revenue Act of 1978 was followed by the Multiemployer Pension Plan Amendments Act of 1980 (MEPPAA). The Economic Recovery Tax Act of 1981 (ERTA) and the Tax Equity and Fiscal Responsibility Act of 1982 (TEFRA) came close behind. In 1984, the Deficit Reduction Act (DEFRA) was added and the Retirement Equity Act (REA) was enacted later that year. Finally, in 1986, the same year as tax reform, the Single-Employer Pension Plan Amendments Act (SEPPAA) was passed. These new laws all affected small employers.

---

[4]Several other exceptions are specified under ERISA as well.

[5]Based on findings from the May 1979 Current Population Survey pension supplement. While eligibility was expanded in 1982, the 1979 survey provides the most recent data available on the use of IRAs when eligibility was restricted.

TABLE VI.2
A Review of Selected Pension Legislation Affecting Small Business, 1978–1987

Year Enacted	Legislation	Provisions
1978	Revenue Act	• established simplified employee pensions (SEPs) with tax-exempt contributions • established cash or deferred arrangements (401(k) plans)
1980	Multiemployer Pension Plan Amendments Act (MEPPAA)	• increased multiemployer plan premiums • required faster funding • imposed liability on employers leaving the plan
1981	Economic Recovery Tax Act (ERTA)	• established universal IRAs for all workers • increased Keogh contribution limits and increased SEP compensation limits • placed a 10 percent tax on early withdrawals
1982	Tax Equity and Fiscal Responsibility Act (TEFRA)	• made compensation and benefit limits the same among all pension plans (increased self-employed limits to equal those of corporations) • tightened ability to integrate defined contribution plans with Social Security • placed a penalty on early distributions to key employees • introduced top-heavy rules
1984	Deficit Reduction Act (DEFRA)	• reduced limits on maximum plan contributions and benefits in real dollar terms • placed a penalty on early distributions to 5 percent owners • changed 401(k) rules and top-heavy rules

1984	Retirement Equity Act (REA)	• reduced age of plan participation and vesting and extended definition of break-in-service • required written spousal consent to choose to stop pension benefits upon death of participant • provided benefits to surviving spouses of worker who dies before retirement age • provided that private pensions could be divided in divorce
1986	Single Employer Pension Plan Amendments Act (SEPPAA)	• limited terminations to those who could cover commitments and those in distress • raised PBGC single-employer premium
1986	Tax Reform Act (TRA)	• reduced vesting requirements, established minimum coverage and participation rules • imposed 10 percent penalty on all preretirement distributions and 15 percent excise tax on pension distributions above a certain level • reduced averaging period for calculating taxes on lump-sum distributions • capped 401(k) pretax contributions and compensation used in contribution or benefit calculations, and changed contribution limits for profit sharing plans • 415 limits maximum benefits **(continued)**

TABLE VI.2 (continued)

Year Enacted	Legislation	Provisions
1986	Tax Reform Act (continued)	• restricted IRA eligibility • changed rules on Social Security integration • new definition for highly compensated employees for non-discrimination rules • permitted some SEPs to act like 401(k) plans with elective pretax contributions
1986	Omnibus Budget Reconciliation Act (OBRA '86)	• contributions and accruals continue regardless of age
1987	Omnibus Budget Reconciliation Act (OBRA '87)	• increased single-employer premiums and added a variable portion dependent on plan's funded status • required defined benefit plans to make quarterly contributions • required faster funding of past service liabilities • made plan contributions over 150 percent of termination liability no longer tax deductible

Source: Employee Benefit Research Institute.

Revenue Act of 1978—The Revenue Act of 1978 established simplified employee pensions (SEPs). SEPs are individual accounts similar to IRAs, with higher contribution limits. Unlike IRAs, contributions are generally provided by the employer. Employers originally could make contributions for each employee for up to 15 percent of salary, with a $7,500 limit. Dollar limits on contributions were raised by subsequent legislation to the $30,000 defined contribution plan level.[6] Employer contributions are not subject to Social Security, unemployment insurance, or income tax withholding. While any employer can establish a SEP, they were intended to be a low-cost way for small employers to start a plan.

Many small employers are eligible to establish so-called "model" SEP plans. Model SEPs are standardized plans that are started by simply filling out IRS Form 5305. Employers with other pension plans cannot establish model SEPs, however. Employers who have terminated a defined benefit pension plan are also ineligible. Model SEP benefits cannot be integrated with Social Security, although other SEP plans can have integrated benefits. Reporting requirements are simplified for model SEP plans; filing for other SEPs is subject to the normal ERISA procedures.

SEPs have stricter requirements than other pension plans to ensure that officers, highly compensated employees, and those with more than a 10 percent equity interest in the firm are not favored. Employer contributions originally were required for each employee who reached age 25 (now age 21) and who worked for the employer three out of five calendar years.[7] To ensure that all eligible employees are included, SEP contributions have to be made for eligible workers who left the firm during the plan year.[8] In addition, all eligible employees must agree to participate in the plan or the plan cannot be provided.[9] Two participation exceptions are provided: one for employees in collective bargaining units who have negotiated for retirement benefits and another for employees who are nonresident foreigners. Contributions could not be made on cash compensation[10] in excess of $100,000 (now $200,000).

---

[6]These limits are for combined employer and employee contributions.

[7]Now, such employees must have earned $300 a year or more.

[8]This includes former workers whose whereabouts are unknown and those who died during the year.

[9]Although most employees would be unlikely to refuse a noncontributory plan, this provision has caused concern among would-be providers.

[10]In pension law, the term used is "compensation," which is roughly defined as wage and salary payments, tips, bonuses, and other cash payments. Employee benefits are not included. The economic definition of compensation is the total cost to the employer of both wages and benefits. To avoid confusion, the term "cash compensation" is used to indicate payments referred to as "compensation" in pension law.

Employers can wait until April 15 of the next year (the income tax filing date) to start a SEP and, just as annual contributions are not required in profit sharing plans, employers do not have to make annual contributions to their SEPs. Immediate vesting is required, however. Originally, employees could contribute to SEPs only if their employer's contributions were less than the IRA limit. After ERTA, all employees could contribute up to an additional $2,000.

Distributions from SEPs, like IRA distributions, originally were not eligible for the 10-year forward averaging formula that could be used to calculate taxes due on lump-sum benefit distributions from pension and profit sharing plans. They are now eligible for 5-year forward averaging, however. Distributions are taxed less heavily under forward averaging than they would be under normal income taxation. SEPs also cannot include loan provisions that enable participants to borrow money from the plan.[11]

The Revenue Act of 1978 also sanctioned cash or deferred arrangements through the addition of section 401(k) to the Internal Revenue Code. Plans established under this section are frequently called 401(k) plans. Under 401(k) plans, employees can make contributions using pretax dollars. Contributions and interest are not subject to federal income taxes until the funds leave the pension system, when a participant changes jobs or retires. This is an exception to the principal of taxation known as "constructive receipt," which specifies that income should be taxed when the individual has control and discretion over its use. As a consequence, employers were reluctant to sponsor 401(k) plans until the IRS issued preliminary regulations in 1981. Employers were assured they could rely on these guidelines.

Since 1981, 401(k) plans have become extremely popular, particularly in larger companies. Between 1985 and 1988, participation among full-time workers rose from 26 percent to 36 percent.[12] In 1985, 5 percent of small employer plans were in 401(k) plans.[13] These plans can be advantageous for small employers because they share plan costs with their employees. Nonetheless, the relatively high administrative costs of 401(k) plans (Justin Associates, 1985) and special nondiscrimination rules[14] may have discouraged their use among small employers.

---

[11]Additional changes in SEPs under the Tax Reform Act of 1986 are discussed later in this chapter.

[12]These findings are based on Bureau of Labor Statistics surveys of medium and large employers (U.S. Department of Labor, 1986–1987).

[13]These findings are based on EBRI tabulations of the NFIB survey.

[14]Before tax reform, the minimum coverage rules for qualified plans required plans to include either a specified percentage of employees or a fair cross section of employees. Those tests became more complicated after tax reform. Before tax reform, the percentage of pay contributed by the higher-paid group could be no more than a specified percentage higher than that of the lower-paid group (depending on two tests). Again, tax reform complicated those procedures. See EBRI, 1987, for a more complete description.

Multiemployer Pension Plan Amendments Act of 1980—In 1980, MEPPAA substantially altered the relationship between multiemployer plans and the PBGC. While only 5 percent of small-employer plans were multiemployer plans in 1985,[15] their businesses were affected by the regulatory changes. MEPPAA increased per participant premiums used to finance PBGC guaranties and also required faster funding of unfunded liabilities. Depending on the collective bargaining situation, these requirements could have affected small-employer compensation costs adversely. MEPPAA also required employers who withdrew from multiemployer plans to continue funding the benefits of workers they had hired in the past. This was a liability that many employers never realized they had and one that could be financially disruptive to small employers.

Economic Recovery Tax Act of 1981—Universal IRAs were instituted for workers under ERTA—and then restricted in 1986 under tax reform. Under ERTA, IRA limits were raised from $1,500 to $2,000 per employee (or 100 percent of cash compensation), with top limits for one-earner couples of $2,250. After ERTA, IRA contribution rates rose from less than 5 percent for nonfarm workers who were not plan participants to over 12 percent. Universal availability and better marketing may have encouraged more uncovered workers to save for retirement. Nevertheless, the increase in IRA participation represented a limited increase in total retirement income coverage.

ERTA had other consequences for small employers. Keogh contribution and benefit limits were increased, and the dollar limit on contributions to SEPs was raised from $7,500 to $15,000 per participant. The maximum cash compensation that SEP contributions could be based on was raised from $100,000 to $200,000. These changes were intended to encourage small employers to establish pension plans regardless of the legal structure of their business.

Tax Equity and Fiscal Responsibility Act of 1982—TEFRA finally placed self-employed businesses on an equal footing with corporations by making contribution and benefit limits the same for all pension plans. This eliminated incentives for professional practices to incorporate their businesses solely to maximize pension contributions.

TEFRA also contained a number of changes which were met with less enthusiasm by the business community. These changes were, in part, precursors to the Tax Reform Act and were primarily intended to limit the benefits of highly compensated owners and managers. The legislation sought to ensure that pension plans were not used just to shelter the income of the highly compensated.

---

[15]Based on EBRI analysis of the NFIB survey.

TEFRA enacted maximum benefit and contribution limits that were lower than those provided under ERISA. Specifically, contribution limits for defined contribution plans were reduced from the lesser of 25 percent of compensation or $45,475, to the lesser of 25 percent of compensation or $30,000. Maximum annual pensions from tax-qualified defined benefit plans were lowered from the lesser of 100 percent of cash compensation[16] or $136,425 a year, to the lesser of 100 percent of cash compensation or $90,000 a year. These limits would affect the highly compensated in large establishments and the pensions of successful owner/operators of small firms.

In addition, the ability to integrate defined contribution plan benefits with Social Security was tightened. Before TEFRA, the difference between the percentage contribution applied to earnings too high to be taxed under Social Security (earnings greater than $32,400 in 1982), and the percentage contribution applied to earnings below the Social Security maximum could be up to 7 percentage points under a defined contribution plan. After TEFRA, the maximum contribution differential was initially 5.4 percentage points.[17]

Perhaps most important for small employers, TEFRA introduced "top-heavy" rules. Under these rules, plans have to apply special standards if more than 60 percent of accumulated benefits are earmarked for key employees. For defined benefit plans, the calculation is made according to accrued benefits; for defined contribution plans, the calculation is based on account balances.

Under the top-heavy rules, key employees are defined for the current year and over a four-year look-back period as: officers (revised in 1984 to exclude those earning less than 1.5 times the dollar limit on contributions in a defined contribution plan—currently $30,000); the 10 employees with the largest ownership share in the company (having at least a one-half of 1 percent ownership interest and earning more than $30,000 a year); those with more than a 5 percent interest in the company; or those with more than a 1 percent ownership interest in the firm who receive cash compensation in excess of $150,000.

Small-employer plans are more likely to be top-heavy than large-employer plans because the ratio of shareholders to employees in the plan is likely to be higher. Five percent shareholders in major corporations are probably institutional investors such as pension funds; 5 percent owners in small corporations may be just members of the management

---

[16]This applies to compensation for the highest three consecutive calendar years during which the employee was a participant in the plan.

[17]It rose to 5.7 percent after 1983.

team. Management can easily have a 1 percent ownership interest. Furthermore, small firms may also fail the 60 percent top-heavy test if their employees have shorter average job tenure and lower average wages than those of large employers.[18]

Top-heavy plans must provide minimum benefits (or contributions) that are not integrated with Social Security to plan participants who are not key employees. In top-heavy plans, only the first $200,000 of an employee's cash compensation may be taken into account. The minimum benefit for those who are not key employees in defined benefit plans is 2 percent of average annual cash compensation for the five years of consecutive service with the highest compensation, not to exceed 20 percent of average annual cash compensation. The minimum contribution for those who are not key employees in defined contribution plans is the lesser of 3 percent of cash compensation or the highest contribution rate for a key employee.

Top-heavy plans also have stricter limits on allowable benefits for key employees when the employer sponsors both a defined benefit and a defined contribution plan. Plans in which key employees have 90 percent of accrued benefits are never allowed to increase the overall combined plan limits beyond the single plan limits.

One of two vesting standards must be satisfied by top-heavy plans. The first standard requires employees to be 100 percent vested after three years of service under the plan. The second option is six-year graded vesting, which requires employees to be at least 20 percent vested after two years of plan participation, with a graded increase in this percentage over the next four years of service and 100 percent vesting after six years of service.

Many small employers adopt the top-heavy rules without making the calculation to determine if their plans fall in the top-heavy category. Other sponsors whose plans may not be top heavy at all times make a calculation each year, so they can take advantage of normal ERISA standards for years in which the plan is not top heavy. The intent of the top-heavy rules is to ensure that rank-and-file employees of small companies benefit from their employers' pension plans and that the plans are not just tax shelters for owners and managers.

Deficit Reduction Act of 1984—DEFRA further reduced the limits on maximum plan contributions and benefits in real dollar terms (adjusted for inflation) by postponing inflation adjustments until 1988. DEFRA also made changes in the rules applicable to 401(k) plans and made some

---

[18]Although nationally representative data are not available, as Calimafde, 1987, noted, "It would be interesting to analyze the multiple plans of large companies to determine the level of benefits going to highly paid and lower-paid employees."

technical changes to the top-heavy rules. Small employers would have to be aware of these changes to keep their 401(k) plans and other retirement plans in compliance with the law. Keeping up with and understanding even relatively small changes are, in general, more expensive for small employers on a per employee basis.

Retirement Equity Act of 1984—Under REA, ERISA was amended to reduce the age of plan participation from 25 years to 21 years and the usual age at which vesting standards begin to apply from 22 years to 18 years. In addition, REA extended the definition of a break in service from one to five years. That is, all years with the plan must be counted toward vesting for former workers who are reemployed within five years (defined as five consecutive one-year breaks in service at most or a period of time equal to earned service).

REA also requires that spouses of employees consent in writing if a couple chooses to waive the normal joint-and-survivor form of benefits, the effect of which is to stop pension benefits at the death of the plan participant. REA also provided pension benefits to surviving spouses of workers who die before retirement age. Unless both spouses waive the preretirement survivor option, benefits will be provided to a vested worker's surviving spouse whether or not the participant was retired or was eligible for retirement at the time of death. REA also specified that in the case of certain domestic relations orders (including divorce settlements and legal separations), private pensions could be divided upon divorce. In general, REA required additional recordkeeping that may be more costly for small employers.

Single-Employer Pension Plan Amendments Act of 1986 [19]—After Allis-Chalmers and Wheeling-Pittsburgh Steel Corporation terminated plans in 1985 with unfunded liabilities of over $400 million, the PBGC faced a potential doubling of its deficit. Threats to the financial stability of the PBGC single-employer insurance system from these and other potential terminations led to a significant restructuring of the program for single-employer plans.

Before SEPPAA, employers could terminate their plans at will, regardless of the financial position of the firm or the plan. After SEPPAA, two types of voluntary terminations were recognized. Plans could terminate voluntarily through a standard termination if their assets could meet their benefit commitments. Other voluntary terminations would be permitted only as distress terminations contingent upon a determination from the PBGC. Distress terminations required the plan administrator to show,

---

[19]For a more thorough discussion of SEPPAA see EBRI, May 1986.

using specific criteria, that the firm was financially unable to continue the plan.

The law also changed the conditions of employer liability to enable the employer to continue payments to the PBGC even after plan termination. Finally, SEPPAA raised the single employer premium from $2.60 per participant to $8.50. Needless to say, these costs and requirements would weigh more heavily on small employers who sponsor defined benefit plans.

The Tax Reform Act of 1986 and Beyond

In addition to lowering income tax rates and broadening the base of taxation, the Tax Reform Act of 1986 (TRA) included many employee benefit provisions. Among those provisions was a change in vesting rules expected to increase future retirement income. Vesting rules were changed to one of two standards—either five-year cliff vesting or a graded schedule in which participants must be 20 percent vested after three years of service with an additional 20 percent each subsequent year and full vesting after seven years of participation. More liberal vesting schedules are always allowed.

TRA imposed a 10 percent penalty on lump-sum preretirement distributions from employer-sponsored pension plans in addition to the usual income tax liability on the distribution. Distributions rolled over into an IRA escape current taxation including the penalty, however, and add to future retirement income.

Earlier legislation levied penalty taxes on distributions in special circumstances. Under TEFRA, early distributions for key employees were subject to a penalty, and under DEFRA, distributions to 5 percent owners were penalized. Before TEFRA, a penalty was applied to amounts distributed to participants who were at least 5 percent owners of the business. These earlier provisions affected small employers more than others, and were instituted to prevent pension plans from being established as tax avoidance schemes. By contrast, under TRA, the 10 percent penalty tax was intended to preserve pension benefits for retirement.

Other TRA provisions affected upper-income employees and owner/managers of small firms. Plan participants with higher earnings were no longer eligible to make contributions to an IRA on a pretax basis. Contributions to 401(k) plans were capped at $7,000 (indexed for inflation). The amount of cash compensation that could be included in pension benefit or contribution calculations was limited to $200,000—the same as top-heavy plans and SEPs. Maximum early retirement benefits were actuarially reduced, in line with maximum benefit amounts for normal retirement. An excise tax was placed on all pension distributions above a certain level. In addition, maximum defined contribution plan contributions were capped at $30,000, with no further adjustment for inflation until the maximum allowable defined benefit plan pension reaches $120,000 through inflation indexing.

Other TRA provisions changed the taxation of retirement distributions. The 10-year period over which lump-sum distributions could be allocated for tax calculation purposes was reduced to five years for most participants. Lump-sum distributions had received particularly favorable tax treatment under 10-year forward averaging. Many felt that these low rates could no longer be justified since they chiefly benefited higher-income retirees.

Some TRA provisions will affect small employers more than larger firms. For instance, tax reform changed the way in which employers could integrate their pensions with Social Security benefits. Very small plans are more likely to have integrated benefits. Minimum coverage rules were also enacted to ensure that employees were not summarily excluded from plans. Businesses with few employees have less leeway to get around the coverage rules by carving out more than one plan or forming subsidiaries. Changes in employee leasing standards (for temporary employees leased from firms that pay their salary and benefits) are also more likely to affect small employers since rules that affect any workers hired by small firms will affect the way the business operates.

TRA also applied the definition for highly compensated employees to all employee benefit plans, but not in exactly the same way as the top-heavy rules. Under TRA, highly compensated employees are defined as (1) 5 percent owners; (2) those earning more than $75,000; (3) those earning $50,000 or more and among the 20 percent highest paid; and (4) officers of the company earning $45,000 or more. Because of the TRA rules, small employers now must test their plans for nondiscrimination according to two different definitions—one under TRA and one under the top-heavy rules. This added test is likely to be administratively difficult for small plans.

Rules for profit sharing were changed under TRA. Profit sharing plans are extremely popular among small employers, accounting for about one-third of all plans. Profit sharing plan contributions are limited to 15 percent of the aggregate cash compensation of the plan participants. Under TRA, these plans can no longer apply the unused part of their prior-year contribution limits to exceed their contribution limit in another year. In other words, if very low contributions had been made in unprofitable years, they cannot be balanced against very large contributions in profitable years once the annual contribution limit has been reached. Under TRA, however, plan contributions can be greater than the employer's current or accumulated profits. Thus, contribution flexibility in one area has been replaced by another, perhaps less desirable, alternative.

TRA permits some SEPs to act like 401(k) plans, with elective pretax employee contributions up to a $7,000 contribution cap. Only employers with 25 or fewer employees in the preceding year may establish a salary-reduction SEP. Salary-deferral SEPs are allowed only if 50 percent or more of all eligible employees elect to make employee contributions. These plans may be established based on employee contributions only.

Omnibus Budget Reconciliation Act of 1986—By the end of 1986, a movement to provide pension equity to older workers coalesced in Title IX, Subtitle C of OBRA '86, which stipulated that benefit contributions or accruals were to continue regardless of age for workers participating in defined contribution or defined benefit plans. Regulations issued by the IRS make the law retroactive for current workers in defined benefit plans who passed their plan's normal retirement age before 1988, the year in which the legislation became effective. By contrast, retroactive allocations were not required for defined contribution plans.

While small employers hire more workers over normal retirement age (which many pension plans define as age 65), as chapter IV shows, these older workers tend to work disproportionately for firms without a pension. Since the new benefit provisions impact more heavily on firms with a greater proportion of older workers, they may tend further to discourage plan formation by small employers.

Omnibus Budget Reconciliation Act of 1987—In 1987, further significant regulatory changes for defined benefit pension plans were made. The impetus for new legislation was the financial status of the PBGC. The PBGC's insurance program would have been in deficit if the premium had not been increased from $8.50 to $16 per participant.

However, this legislation did more than simply raise funds to cover the immediate deficit. Employers were required to make contributions to defined benefit plans on a quarterly basis rather than annually. Further, the basic premium ranged from $16 for well-funded plans to a maximum of $50 for those with large unfunded liabilities. For years, sponsors of well-funded plans have objected to subsidizing underfunded plans that ultimately dumped their liabilities on the PBGC. To some extent, variable-rate funding now penalizes plans that do not meet funding standards.

The 1987 legislation also requires faster funding of past service liabilities. Existing liabilities must be amortized over 18 years rather than 30 years.[20]

---

[20]Unfunded new liabilities are amortized based on the funded ratio (FR)—adjusted value of assets over the current liability—according to the following formula: $0.30 - ((FR - 0.35)*0.25)$. The last term is set to zero if the term is negative.

These amortization periods as well as some other provisions of OBRA '87 do not apply to plans with fewer than 100 participants, however, and are phased in for plans with between 100 and 150 participants.

While requiring better funding, OBRA '87 also stipulates that plan contributions in excess of 150 percent of the termination funding ratio are no longer a tax-deductible expense and are subject to a penalty tax. Employers now face a much narrower funding range. In particular, the necessity for multiple actuarial evaluations to ensure that a multiplicity of rules are met will increase administrative costs for those plans. Many consider that this legislation will significantly impede the formation of new defined benefit plans by small and medium-sized firms.

What Small Employers Say about Pension Legislation

Small employers have formed definite opinions about the effects of government regulation on pension plan sponsorship. Four of the surveys discussed in chapter IV also asked employers about their attitudes toward government regulation.[21]

Pension Legislation and Plan Formation—The Bell study provided mixed findings about how government regulation (or the paperwork involved in setting up a plan) affected decisions by small employers to offer pension plans. Four out of seven employers indicted that legal complexities and paperwork deterred them from sponsoring a plan. Justin Associates reported:

> Many of the small businesses in our survey (apparently correctly) believe that the regulations are so complex that the time and money required to comply are greater than the benefits available from a pension plan. These firms also mentioned regulatory uncertainty and burdensome paperwork.

The National Federation of Independent Business (NFIB) survey asked employers to indicate their single most important reason for not providing a retirement plan. Three reasons were provided in the survey that directly or indirectly reflected the impact of the regulatory environment: "changing and complex regulations"; "too much cost, red tape, and hassle to start one"; and "administrative costs to keep one are prohibitive."

---

[21]These studies include the one by James Bell and Associates, 1984, for the Small Business Administration (SBA); the Justin Associates study, 1985, also for the SBA; the National Federation of Independent Business (NFIB) survey (Dennis, 1985); and the EBRI/AARP cosponsored focus groups (Opinion Research Corporation, 1986).

Based on survey findings, government regulation was not the most important deterrent to plan formation.[22] Only 1 percent of NFIB employers cited "changing and complex regulations" as the most important reason for not providing a plan while another 9 percent cited start-up costs and red tape.

The Employee Benefit Research Institute/American Association of Retired Persons (EBRI/AARP) focus group study provided additional insights into the impact of federal regulation on plan formation. Nonproviders believed that retirement plans involved a great deal of paperwork and knowledge of complex regulation but, when pressed for specifics, were generally poorly informed about pension law. By contrast, many providers said that plan administration was not burdensome (except for those who sponsored defined benefit plans).

Plan Administration and Plan Termination—Constant change in government regulation was cited by 37 percent of NFIB employers as the most important problem in maintaining a retirement plan.[23] Other government regulations were also regarded as a problem. Seven percent of plan sponsors expressed dissatisfaction with the top-heavy rules, and another 2 percent were upset about multiemployer withdrawal liability. Two percent of sponsors reported that ERISA restrictions on the use of plan assets were a problem. Overall, 48 percent of plan sponsors said that government regulation was difficult to handle, while another 15 percent had problems with administrative costs.[24]

Changes in government laws and regulations were also a source of dissatisfaction for the 65 percent of the NFIB employers who were generally satisfied with their plan. These responses are consistent with the finding that government regulation was the most important reason for plan termination among NFIB employers; complex and changing regulations were reported as the cause of 35 percent of plan terminations.

What Do These Studies Mean?—While government regulation of pension plans is a problem for small employers, the four studies surveyed do not provide a consistent assessment of how government regulation affects plan sponsorship in small firms. The Justin Associates report shows that regulation discourages plan formation. The EBRI/AARP focus groups confirm those findings. The Bell study findings are mixed, however, and the NFIB data indicate that government requirements are a relatively unimportant factor in the decision to provide a plan.

---

[22]Many firms did not respond to the question, however, and others could have considered that government regulation was a secondary reason for not having a plan.

[23]Nonresponse was high, however, with 32 percent not answering the question.

[24]Thirty-two percent of those asked did not reply to the question.

The assessment of government regulation among plan providers in each of the four studies differs as well. In the EBRI/AARP focus groups, plan providers considered regulatory complexity less of a problem than non-providers who knew less about the regulatory environment. In contrast, NFIB employers were concerned about government requirements, whether or not they were satisfied with their plan. Government regulation was also the most important reason given for plan termination.

The study findings are influenced, in part, by the selection of the study group. In the EBRI/AARP focus group discussions, the presence of other business owners and managers in the room could affect what the group members said. While the Bell and the Justin studies conducted unstructured in-depth confidential interviews, they interviewed a very small number of respondents. Further, the Bell study interviewed pension experts who would not necessarily reflect the attitudes and knowledge of the small employers who actually make the decision on whether or not to provide a plan. The NFIB survey represents a large sample of small employers, but the structured questionnaire could have constrained the types of answers provided in some areas.

While all these studies have merit, the direct responses of small-business owners provide only partial information about the economic effects of government regulation on employer-sponsored pension plans. What individuals say does not always indicate how they do or will act. Consequently, economic analysis provides an alternative method to assess how government regulation affects plan sponsorship among small employers.

The Economics of Regulation

In a market economy, employers will balance the costs of instituting a pension plan against the benefits they receive. Chapter V shows that employers will institute a plan if it encourages their employees to be more productive or if it ensures the firm access to better workers. In addition, employers will establish a plan if the firm is profitable enough to absorb administrative and start-up costs over the long run. If the tax advantages of pensions are valuable to employees and long-run compensation costs can be reduced, a pension plan will be attractive to employers. Within this economic framework, government regulations also increase or reduce the costs of plan formation. Because regulation can affect the benefits and costs of establishing a pension plan, legislative change will determine whether the economics of plan sponsorship still work for the employer.

Past pension legislation can be analyzed within this framework. The favorable tax treatment provided pension plans reduces the costs of plan sponsorship. Since pension contributions are treated as current business expenses, funded plans are a good business decision. Pension plans are also regarded favorably by employees because they can defer individual income taxes on pension contributions until retirement. By making benefits more secure, ERISA may have increased the demand for pensions among employees.[25] The provisions that may have made pension coverage more attractive include funding standards, PBGC insurance, vesting and participation standards, and better information about plans through summary plan descriptions.

Since pension law encourages different types of plans, employers can match pension sponsorship to their business situation. In particular, developments such as Keogh plans, 401(k) plans, and SEPs may have made tax-favored pensions more attractive to certain small employers. By 1982, Keogh plans offered unincorporated businesses and their employees the same tax advantages as corporations. Salary-reduction plans (or 401(k) plans) allow the employer to share the costs of plan sponsorship with employees and let workers target their own contributions for retirement. SEPs provide an inexpensive alternative for some employers, and salary-reduction SEPs may give very small employers the benefits of a more expensive 401(k) plan.

Other provisions may impose additional costs on employers, however. Funding and fiduciary standards reduce the employer's flexibility to finance corporate expansion through retained earnings. PBGC premiums are a direct cost imposed on a per participant basis for defined benefit plans. Plan descriptions and other reporting requirements also directly increase the administrative costs of the plan.

Another public policy objective has been to discourage small business owners from primarily sponsoring pension plans to limit their own personal income tax liability without providing retirement income to rank-and-file workers. Ideally, public policy should distinguish plans that are primarily designed to reduce the owner's personal income taxes from plans that are an integral feature of the firm's personnel policy. Since these motives may be highly interrelated, the task is complex.

The top-heavy rules are a case in point. To ensure that the tax treatment of pensions does not solely benefit higher-paid owner-managers, Congress set more stringent vesting and integration standards for top-heavy plans to ensure that benefits accrue to lower-paid employees. Yet, the top-heavy rules impose additional costs on smaller companies whose

---

[25]Other researchers disagree with this assessment (Ippolito, 1988). Based on his empirical analysis, Ippolito concludes that ERISA "was not, and is not, a public-interest piece of legislation." In effect, he shows that ERISA did not have an impact on plan provisions. His analysis, however, is integrally tied to the questions he asks, which may not be the right ones in terms of the intent of the legislation.

per worker administrative costs are already higher than those of larger firms. Pension benefits may accrue disproportionately to high-paid, high-tenure owner-managers simply because of the nature of their business. Thus, small top-heavy plans could terminate if the economics of plan provision are no longer favorable to the business while larger companies with a similar benefit accrual structure would not be affected.

Restrictions that cap contributions and benefit payments could also make pension plans less appealing to some businesses. Very high benefit limits affect relatively few managers, but as limits are reduced, more managers will receive lower pension contributions. If pensions become a less effective way to manage the work force, firms might consider plan termination and provide nonqualified plans to key management employees.

REA also may have raised the costs of plan provision for some employers. The required five-year break-in-service provision increases record-keeping costs, particularly in firms with high employee turnover. This provision could discourage small businesses from setting up a plan, particularly since many of the small employers that do not currently sponsor plans face high worker turnover. Similarly, potential benefit distributions for former spouses upon divorce add to administrative costs. And the extension of future benefit payments to the spouses of workers who die before retirement age could be administratively costly.[26]

A constant theme reiterated by small employers is their concern about regulatory complexity and frequency of legislative change. Complex regulations require costly expert advice in establishing and maintaining a pension plan. Frequent legislative change, at a minimum, requires the costly revision of plan documents. Such changes in the law also can lead to significant plan redesign. Thus, no matter what the nature of the change, if it is frequent or complex, it will be costly.

Empirical Findings—If pension legislation has curbed plan growth, its effects have been gradual. The pension coverage rate for private-sector employees declined from 56 percent to 52 percent between 1979 and 1983 (Andrews, 1985). Nonetheless, the number of pension plans has continued to increase (EBRI, 1989). Growth was robust between 1977 and 1982, with plan expansion averaging 10.5 percent annually. Net plan formation slowed in 1983 and 1984, with slight losses in the absolute number of defined benefit plans in 1984; plan growth rebounded from 1985 through 1987. This pattern does not provide a clear signal that pension legislation has constrained pension plan growth. Nor do the plan count estimates provide sufficient information to analyze statistically the effects of pension

---

[26]See Fini (1988) for interviews of benefit consultants and benefit managers.

legislation enacted between 1974 and 1986. In any event, given different enactment dates and possible anticipatory behavior on the part of plan sponsors, the effect of specific pieces of legislation on plan formation in general probably would be impossible to evaluate.

Based on an economic theory of pensions in which employers balance the costs and benefits of plan formation, the overall impact of recent legislation could be estimated if the effect of changes in other factors in the economy influencing pension coverage are measured adequately. After taking into account changes in factors such as the industrial distribution of the work force, firm size and enterprise size, and other worker characteristics, statistical analysis based on this premise shows that coverage rates in 1983 were lower than those posted in 1979.[27] In other words, the pension coverage rate declined in ways that cannot be explained by any of the measures included in the analysis that are known to affect pension coverage.

As a consequence, the reason for the decline may well have been the ever-expanding number of changes in legislation that necessitate plan revisions and increase costs. While this is a reasonable hypothesis, other factors not included in the analysis may have reduced pension coverage as well. For instance, data on profitability and the ratio of capital to labor were not included. Neither was information on other changes in the tax code or other costs of production. These factors may have had as strong an impact on coverage as changing pension legislation.

Other research, demonstrating that recent legislative change has affected the type of plans provided, strengthens the hypothesis that at least some of the coverage decline is related to revisions in ERISA. Based on analysis similar to that presented above, Clark (1989) suggests that changing federal pension regulation has increased the relative cost of defined benefit plans and provided new options for defined contribution plans, thus shifting the form of primary pension coverage for many employees. Ippolito (1988) also indicates that large firms were more likely to create defined contribution plans between 1974 and 1981. He did not find a comparable change for small businesses. Thus, while recent pension regulation may have contributed to a reduction in the coverage rate and altered the distribution of plan types among large and medium-sized firms, its impact on small employers relative to larger firms remains unclear.

---

[27]This analysis is based on private-sector employees (excluding railroad workers) and uses pooled data from the May 1979 and 1983 Current Population Survey pension supplements. See appendix B for the equation that was estimated.

Summary and Conclusions

The thrust of pension legislation over the past 50 years has been an ongoing effort to combine incentives for plan formation with safeguards for pension participants. The growth in plan formation provides indirect evidence that the tax incentives were successful. The impact of legislation over the past 10 to 15 years is less clear. ERISA focused on participant safeguards, which may have lowered the benefits of plan provision for some employers and led to lower coverage rates.

Statistical evidence indicates that the pension coverage rate has declined since 1979, even after adjusting for shifts in the age distribution of employment and the industrial composition of the labor force. Nevertheless, given the complex nature of the economy, this decline could be as much a result of poor business conditions as of legislative change. The pension plan market may be saturated under current economic conditions.

Legislation intended to encourage plan formation among small employers and their employees has been noticeably unsuccessful. A small percentage of the self-employed—just 5 percent in 1979—have instituted Keogh plans. That percentage has declined—even though ERTA and TEFRA enabled Keogh plans to mirror those of corporate employers. Furthermore, few employees without pension plans contribute to an IRA—only 12 percent in 1982. Finally, SEP plans have not gained much support. In 1985, only 6 percent of small employers sponsored SEPs. Consequently, many in Congress are searching for alternative ways to make pension plans more attractive. In lieu of voluntary solutions, some have recommended mandating coverage of all employees. It appears appropriate to evaluate the possibilities for voluntary change, however, before considering that solution.

VII. Policies to Encourage Growth in Pension Coverage

Introduction

New proposals to improve pension policy have met with a mixed reception. On the one hand, policymakers still seek to improve coverage, particularly among small employers, so that more workers will receive benefits from both Social Security and employer-sponsored pensions upon retirement. On the other hand, further legislative change is beginning to be viewed with intense suspicion, certainly by those outside of the policy community, since the host of new pension laws enacted in recent years are suspected of threatening the system's stability. Statistical analysis suggests that these suspicions may not be entirely unwarranted. Small employers themselves are particularly wary of any further changes, although they still would welcome legislation that would make plan formation more feasible and lift regulatory burdens (Arthur Andersen & Co., 1986).

Chapter VII discusses key legislative proposals aimed at encouraging plan formation. These proposals include the expansion of SEPs, the easing of regulatory requirements, and the granting of additional tax preferences to small-employer plans. In addition, this chapter reviews measures to ensure that preretirement cashouts are maintained until retirement.

First, the policy rationale for proposals in each of these areas is investigated with particular emphasis on its relationship to small employers. Then, specific bills are outlined that have been proposed by Congress in recent years. Finally, the potential impact of these legislative proposals on plan growth is examined from the perspective of the economic theory of pension provision and regulation developed in chapters IV and VI. The impact of a cost-reducing tax credit for small plans is simulated based on the analysis developed in chapter V of how costs influence pension coverage. These findings are compared to other simulations of plan sponsorship that assume long-run changes in the economy and in the market for pension plans.

Proposed Areas of Legislative Change

Recent interest in improving coverage and benefit entitlement for employees working in small firms has focused on four areas: (1) encouraging coverage by simplifying plans that would be available to small employers and their employees, (2) streamlining the regulatory process, (3) directly reducing the costs of plan provision, and (4) preserving benefit distribu-tions for retirement. Proposals in each of these areas are in response to perceived gaps or inconsistencies in the system.

Simplified Pensions for Small Employers—Congress is cognizant of the fact that small employers cannot afford the same type of pension plans that large firms can afford. Consequently, under the Revenue Act of 1978, sim-plified employee pensions (SEPs) were introduced to provide a low-cost plan for small employers. The experiment has not led to substantial in-creases in pension coverage, however, as relatively few employers have taken advantage of SEPs. Under the Tax Reform Act of 1986 (TRA), salary-reduction SEPs were authorized for employers sponsoring very small plans on the theory that this feature would encourage coverage without adding to employer costs because contributions could be made on a voluntary basis.

Although lawmakers understand that SEPs have not achieved much suc-cess to date, the idea of a low-cost pension plan that would be easy for small employers to sponsor continues to gain support. Some observers believe small employers may not have adopted SEPs because the employ-ers have had only limited information about these plans. Others suggest that more flexibility may be needed. In sum, there is continued congres-sional interest in encouraging simplified pension plans that would pro-vide equitable pension benefits for small-firm employees.

Improving the Regulatory Environment—Economic theory suggests that efficient regulation (through regulatory tiering) would permit small firms to follow more lenient regulatory requirements to compensate for the fact that large employers benefit from regulatory economies of scale. An ex-ample of regulatory tiering is the Employee Retirement Income Security Act (ERISA) reporting and disclosure requirements, which allow firms with fewer than 100 participants to file full reports (Form 5500-C) every three years rather than annually. Another example is the exemption from Pen-sion Benefit Guaranty Corporation (PBGC) insurance for professional-service providers with fewer than 25 employees.

Policymakers have noted, however, that in most cases small pension plans are not allowed much relaxation from the ERISA regulatory stan-dards and, in some cases, are burdened by stricter regulation than large firms. In particular, the top-heavy rules described in chapter VI put heav-ier compliance burdens on small employers. Firms either must determine that their plans are not top heavy before they can follow the ERISA stan-dards used by other plans, or assume top-heavy status and follow more restrictive standards than those used by other employers. Proponents of regulatory relief would argue that the extra costs faced by small firms resulting from faster vesting schedules will reduce plan formation or cause the termination of worthwhile plans.

But by imposing less stringent standards and easing compliance for small firms, regulatory tiering may also preserve small plans that do not operate in the public interest (Brock and Evans, 1986). That is, more plans may be established primarily for tax planning purposes. The top-heavy rules were initially imposed to ensure that benefits were provided fairly in plans that appeared to benefit owner-managers disproportionately.

Broader regulatory issues would also include questions about differences in regulatory costs and access to information faced by firms of different sizes. Small firms do not have the same access to pension professionals, and it is generally more costly for them to protect the pension benefits of their workers to the same extent as large employers do. Greater federal assistance could ease the way.

Reducing the Costs of Pension Plans—Plan simplification and regulatory burdens are public policy concerns because small firms find the establishment of a pension plan, its continuation, and its termination more costly than larger employers do. Chapter V presented information indicating that per capita costs are higher for smaller firms. Small employers themselves consistently indicate that these costs can only be met by profitable firms. Chapter IV showed how profitability can affect an employer's willingness to make the initial investment in plan formation. Start-up costs are related to regulatory requirements as well.

The Internal Revenue Service (IRS) recently increased user fee schedules for pension plans. Employers must pay the IRS $400 to start a pension plan with fewer than 100 participants.[1] IRS approval for plan amendments can be expensive for small employers, ranging from $50 to $1,000 for rulings on plan provisions, funding methods, new plan years, and numerous other changes (U.S. Department of the Treasury, 1988). In addition, financially troubled employers might shrink from making a commitment to a pension plan, since plan terminations are also costly. If plans with fewer than 100 participants terminate, the IRS charges $200. Consequently, legislative interest has also focused on finding direct ways to reduce the costs of plan provision for small employers.

Preservation—The preservation of pension benefits is one aspect of pension portability.[2] The idea behind pension preservation is that retirement

---

[1]Some small employers have reportedly stopped applying for IRS approval since it is not mandatory.

[2]In the broadest sense, pension portability refers to the transfer of pension entitlement from one retirement plan to another. Incomplete pension portability may lead to benefit losses from (1) a lack of pension entitlement upon job change and/or (2) the loss of future income through the current consumption of preretirement distributions. Discussions about pension portability center on (1) vesting, (2) portability of credited service, and (3) portability of cash distributions (preservation). The Tax Reform Act of 1986 improved vesting by reducing the original ERISA vesting standards. It has often been noted that without

income benefits, once accumulated in a pension plan, should be used to provide income in retirement. Preretirement distributions at job change are most frequently cashed out to the employee leaving the sponsoring company, although they may also be transferred directly to another retirement plan. Most defined contribution plans and some defined benefit plans distribute vested benefits in the form of a lump-sum cash distribution when a plan participant changes jobs. If preretirement cashouts are invested in another pension plan, an IRA, or directly by the employee, these funds will continue to earn an investment return until retirement. Future retirement benefits are lost, however, when lump-sum distributions are used for current consumption instead of for retirement saving. Recent evidence suggests that most distributions are spent rather than saved (Andrews, 1985; Atkins, 1986).[3]

Interest in preservation also stems from the fact that more employees now participate in defined contribution plans for both primary and secondary benefit entitlement. The fear is that these benefits will be lost to the system when employees change jobs. The perception is that people now change jobs more frequently, although statistics indicate relatively little difference in job tenure by age and sex (table VII.1). Nevertheless, the job tenure of women is lower than that of men, and more women are now in the labor market. While benefit preservation is not an issue that policymakers have directly targeted to small employers, the issue is more important to small-firm plan participants who are more likely to be vested and who are more likely to participate in defined contribution plans than it is to participants in larger companies. Furthermore, because employees in small firms without plans tend to have shorter job tenure, measures to expand coverage could also incorporate preservation provisions to ensure that increased coverage would result in greater income at retirement.

Legislative Proposals to Expand Coverage and Improve Benefits

Five bills were introduced in Congress in 1987, 1988, and 1989 that, in part, were intended to encourage plan formation among small employers

---

portability of credited service, retirees who have only one job will have higher retirement benefits from a defined benefit plan based on a final-pay formula than retirees who have similar careers and the same type of pension plan but have worked for more than one company (Munnell, 1982). There have been no legislative proposals for across-the-board portability of credited service because it would be difficult to achieve and could have undesirable economic consequences. Nonetheless, the Retiree Health Benefits and Pension Preservation Act would also authorize the U.S. Treasury to study portability issues. For a more complete discussion of portability issues, see EBRI, 1986 and 1987.

[3]Larger preretirement distributions are more likely to be saved; however, most distributions are for amounts less than $5,000.

TABLE VII.1
Median Years with Current Employer, by Age, Sex, and Race, Selected Years, 1951–1987

Worker Characteristics	1951	1963	1966	1968	1973	1978	1981	1983	1987
				years with employer					
Aged 16 Years and over[a]									
Men	3.9	5.7	5.2	4.8	4.6	4.5	4.0	5.1	5.0
Women	2.2	3.0	2.8	2.4	2.8	2.6	2.5	3.7	3.6
Difference	1.7	2.7	2.4	2.4	1.8	1.9	1.5	1.4	1.4
25–34 Years									
Men	2.8	3.5	3.2	2.8	3.2	2.7	2.9	3.8	3.7
Women	1.8	2.0	1.9	1.6	2.2	1.6	2.0	3.2	3.1
Difference	1.0	1.5	1.3	1.2	1.0	1.1	0.9	0.6	0.6
35–44 Years									
Men	4.5	7.6	7.8	6.9	6.7	6.9	6.6	7.7	7.6
Women	3.1	3.6	3.5	2.9	3.6	3.6	3.5	4.6	4.9
Difference	1.4	4.0	4.3	4.0	3.1	3.3	3.1	3.1	2.7
45–54 Years									
Men	7.6	11.4	11.5	11.3	11.5	11.0	11.0	13.2	12.3
Women	4.0	6.1	5.7	5.1	5.9	5.9	5.9	6.9	7.3
Difference	3.6	5.3	5.8	6.2	5.6	5.1	5.1	6.3	5.0

(continued)

TABLE VII.1 (continued)

Worker Characteristics	1951	1963	1966	1968	1973	1978	1981	1983	1987
				years with employer					
White, 16 Years and over[a]									
Men	4.0	5.9	5.5	5.0	4.7	4.6	4.0	5.3	5.2
Women	2.3	3.0	2.8	2.4	2.8	2.6	2.4	3.6	3.5
Difference	1.7	2.9	2.7	2.6	1.9	2.0	1.6	1.7	1.7
Black, 16 Years and over[a,b]									
Men	3.1	4.1	3.4	3.3	4.0	3.7	4.0	4.7	4.4
Women	1.7	2.9	2.8	2.0	3.3	3.6	3.3	4.4	4.3
Difference	1.4	1.2	0.6	1.3	0.7	0.1	0.7	0.3	0.1

Source: U.S. Department of Commerce, Bureau of the Census, Current Population Reports, Labor Force Series P-50, no. 36 (5 December 1951); Special Labor Force Reports, Bureau of Labor Statistics series on job tenure, nos. 36, 77, 112, 172, and 235; and Bulletin 2162 as quoted for years 1951–1981 by June O'Neill, *Journal of Labor Economics* (January 1985); 1983 data from Ellen Sehgal, "Occupational Mobility and Job Tenure in 1983," *Monthly Labor Review* (October 1984): 18P23; 1987 data from unpublished U.S. Department of Labor, Bureau of Labor Statistics data as previously published in the series on job tenure.

[a]Aged 14 years and over in 1951, 1963, and 1966.
[b]Includes other nonwhite races through 1968.

(table VII.2). The first, the Pension Portability Act (H.R. 1961, H.R. 1962, and S. 944), was introduced in 1987.[4] These bills represent an expansion of an earlier bill, the Retirement Universal Security Arrangements Act of 1985 (H.R. 3098). The Pension Portability Act would increase coverage and preserve benefits through a number of measures, including changes in SEPs. As its title implies, the bill seeks to use pension rollovers to enhance system portability and ensure benefit preservation through a new type of retirement plan.

The second bill, the Portable Pension Plan Act of 1987 (H.R. 1992) seeks to preserve benefits, improve SEPs, and help small employers. The third bill, the Pension Portability Improvement Act of 1987 (S. 1349 and H.R. 2693) is also aimed at improving pension preservation and encouraging SEPs. In each of these bills, the preservation provisions are intended to ensure that preretirement distributions are saved until retirement and the SEP provisions are aimed at encouraging new small-employer plans. The most recent bill, the Retiree Health Benefits and Pension Preservation Act of 1989 (H.R. 1866), would also improve preservation and extend SEPs.

The Small Business Retirement and Benefit Extension Act of 1987 (SBRBEA) (S. 1426 and H.R. 2793) is entirely devoted to making plan sponsorship easier for small employers. SBRBEA would ease the current legislative burden faced by small firms and provide a tax credit toward their plan administration expenses.

Simplified Employee Pensions—All four portability bills have provisions to facilitate SEPs. Under the Pension Portability Act, SEP reporting and disclosure would be simplified. Both the Portable Pension Plan Act and the Pension Portability Improvement Act would allow firms of any size to have salary reduction SEPs. Such SEPs are now limited to businesses with fewer than 25 employers. Both of these bills and the Retiree Health Benefits and Pension Preservation Act also require employers to provide a SEP salary reduction plan if requested by an employee. These salary reduction plans would allow greater pretax contributions than an individual retirement account (IRA).

The Regulatory Environment for Small Employers—The focus of regulatory change has continued to be on the top-heavy rules. SBRBEA would phase out these rules on the grounds that they are costly and unnecessary due to tax reform. In particular, TRA provided a new definition of highly compensated employees, limited integration with Social Security, capped countable cash compensation, and shortened vesting standards. Proponents of a phaseout of the top-heavy rules believe that the TRA

---

[4]H.R. 1962 amends ERISA while H.R. 1961 amends ERISA and the tax code.

TABLE VII.2
Proposed Pension Legislation Affecting Small Businesses

Name of Bill	Bill Number(s)	Main Provisions
Pension Portability Act of 1987, 1988	S. 944, H.R. 1962 (1987) and H.R. 1961 (1988)	• provides for a new type of retirement plan, the portable pension plan, run by financial institutions • extends simplified employee pensions (SEPs) to all employers without a plan with a salary reduction provision and simplified requirements • increases portability, especially for cashouts which could be placed in a portable pension plan
Portable Pension Plan Act of 1987	H.R. 1992	• establishes SEPs for all businesses that have not provided pensions within last five years and at the request of any employee • increases portability by offering exiting employees a lump-sum transfer to a new plan, individual retirement account (IRA), or SEP • calls for simplification and clarification of regulations • increases tax on preretirement cashouts from SEPs and IRAs
Pension Portability Improvement Act of 1987	S. 1349, H.R. 2693	• provides for rollovers to IRAs and defined contribution plans and distributions in the form of a lifetime annuity or similar payout • establishes SEPs for all businesses without a currently qualified plan
Retiree Health Benefits and Pension Preservation Act of 1989	H.R. 1866	• provides for rollovers to IRAs and defined contribution plans and distributions in the form of a lifetime annuity or similar payout • establishes SEPs for all businesses that have not provided pensions, at the request of any employee • authorizes U.S. Treasury to study portability issues
Small Business Retirement and Benefit Extension Act of 1987	S. 1426, H.R. 2793	• phase-out of top-heavy restrictions for small employers • allows tax credit of 14 percent of contributions to nonhighly compensated employees for small firms • delays effective date for nondiscrimination rules

Source: Employee Benefit Research Institute.

changes make the top-heavy rules duplicative, and therefore costly, to small employers.[5] Proponents also argue that, rather than imposing top-heavy rules, Congress should decide which provisions best meet legislative objectives for all plans.

The Portable Pension Plan Act contains another provision that is specifically intended to improve the overall regulatory environment for small employers. Instead of adding new rules and regulations, the act specifies that the Department of Labor should provide outreach to small employers so that they may become better informed about pension plan options. Many feel that SEPs have not gained more popularity because they have not been widely publicized. The Employee Benefit Research Institute/ American Association of Retired Persons (EBRI/AARP) focus group findings support this perception and indicate, more generally, that many small employers have limited knowledge about pensions.

Lower Costs for Small Employers—SBRBEA would directly reduce the pension costs of small employers. The bill provides a tax credit equal to 14 percent of employer contributions for nonhighly compensated employees. The tax credit reaches a maximum of $3,000 for defined contribution plans and $4,500 for defined benefit plans. This differential reflects the presumption that defined benefit plans cost small employers more per worker. The tax credit is phased out for businesses with 50 to 100 employees.[6]

Preservation Provisions—The Pension Portability Act, the Portable Pension Plan Act, the Pension Portability Improvement Act, and the Retiree Health Benefits and Pension Preservation Act all seek to maintain preretirement distributions in a retirement income plan. The first, the Pension Portability Act, introduces a new pension instrument called a portable pension plan that would be established by financial institutions rather than by employers. Firms wishing to provide pension coverage for their employees without the fiduciary responsibilities or administrative obligations of plan sponsorship could make contributions to a portable pension plan. As such, these plans are intended to provide another low-cost option to small employers to encourage plan formation. Portable pension plans could also be used by employees and employers to roll over preretirement distributions.

Under the Portable Pension Plan Act, employers would have to make direct transfers to portability maintenance accounts—such as a defined contribution plan, an IRA, or a SEP—when a vested plan participant left

---

[5]See Calimafde, 1987.
[6]This phaseout is parallel in concept to the treatment of tax-deductible IRA contributions at higher earnings levels.

the company. They could not directly transfer preretirement distributions to the departing employee. Defined contribution plans would have to offer transfers upon job termination but defined benefit plans would not. Defined benefit funds could maintain benefit accruals and provide a vested worker with a pension at retirement age. Defined contribution plans would not have to accept distributions from other plans, however.

The bill would make it more difficult for employees to receive preretirement distributions (and presumably more difficult to spend them). Only SEPs and IRAs would be allowed to make distributions directly to the employee. This leaves open the possibility that former plan participants could cash out their IRAs after transfers were made from their pension plans. But, the penalty tax on preretirement cashouts would be increased from 10 percent to 20 percent of the distribution—also as a means of preserving early pension distributions until retirement.

The Pension Portability Improvement Act and the Retiree Health Benefits and Pension Preservation Act include the most stringent of the preservation requirements. Distributions could not go directly to employees before they reached age 59 ½ and, at that time, would be tied to postretirement life expectancy. Preretirement transfers could be made to a new employer's retirement plan or to a rollover IRA. Such funds could also remain in the plan of the original employer. The bill would require defined contribution plans to accept rollovers from other plans. By contrast, the Portable Pension Plan Act would require the General Accounting Office to study ways for defined contribution plans to accept rollovers.

Proposed Legislation and Pension Coverage

The effect of recent legislative proposals on plan formation can be analyzed according to the economic criteria developed in chapters IV and VI. If plans can be better tailored to fit the business situation of the employer, boosting productivity and profits, more employers will be willing to provide a plan. If the costs of plan administration are lowered, more employers will be able to sponsor a plan. Finally, if pension plans become more attractive to employees, more workers will want to work for firms with pension plans. The proposals introduced in Congress in 1987, 1988, and 1989 can be analyzed from these perspectives.

Changes in Simplified Employee Pensions—According to the EBRI/AARP focus group sessions, many small employers did not favor the stringent SEP participation and vesting requirements (EBRI, 1986). The lower administrative cost of a SEP did not appear to be sufficient, in and of itself, to turn plan sponsorship into a profitable business decision for many employers. Because participation must be virtually universal and vesting must

138

be immediate, small businesses might have to include employees who do not want a pension. Furthermore, because of immediate vesting, SEPs cannot be used to encourage the continued employment of those workers whom the firm expects to become more productive over time. Assuming these are the primary disincentives to SEP sponsorship, simplified disclosure and reporting procedures are unlikely to increase coverage unless participation and vesting standards are eased as well.

Expanding the use of salary reduction SEPs to employers of all sizes is unlikely to revolutionize the small-plan market. SEP nondiscrimination rules may limit their popularity among small employers who are reluctant to shoulder the administrative costs of plan provision for temporary employees. Moreover, although salary reduction plans are the fastest growing segment of the pension universe, and salary reduction SEPs have low-cost 401(k) features, lower-paid small-firm workers are less likely to take full advantage of these salary reduction possibilities.

In 1982, however, only 12 percent of all workers who were not plan participants made an IRA contribution. This 12 percent probably represents those uncovered workers who are willing to save for retirement and suggests that few workers without coverage are apt to ask their employers for a salary reduction SEP. With the average earnings of production workers at $16,250 in 1987, relatively few could afford an IRA contribution of more than $2,000. Furthermore, workers who are not already plan participants earn, on average, less than participants. Higher SEP limits would not make salary reduction SEPs more attractive than IRAs for most employees. In fact, the average wage earner in 1987 would have had a savings rate of over 12 percent with a $2,000 IRA contribution. By contrast, the national savings rate was only 3.7 percent of personal disposable income in 1987. Nondiscrimination requirements cannot be met if only higher-income workers opt for a salary reduction SEP. If employers provide matching contributions, more employees will participate, but matching contributions impose additional costs on the small employer. Consequently, unless current savings behavior changes radically, employers who currently sponsor SEPs will be the primary ones to adopt salary reduction features.

The EBRI/AARP focus groups also indicated that relatively few small employers knew about SEPs. More aggressive marketing strategies by financial institutions might increase SEP formation. A stronger sales approach could go a long way toward expanding employer demand for the product. Financial institutions successfully stepped up their marketing of IRAs after all workers became eligible to make contributions in 1982. But financial institutions must be convinced that SEP marketing will be profitable before they are likely to launch a sales campaign.

The Regulatory Environment for Small Employers—SBRBEA would repeal the top-heavy rules for small employers on the grounds that provisions in TRA make the top-heavy rules redundant. These rules are difficult to analyze in economic terms since little can be gleaned about social welfare gains or losses stemming from the top-heavy legislation. Chapter V demonstrates that small employers generally do not sponsor plans only to manage their personal income taxes. Statistical analysis does not clearly indicate that the top-heavy rules have improved benefit entitlement in small firms. Furthermore, small-employer plans could be top-heavy because of salary and tenure factors and not because the plan was intentionally trying to favor highly compensated employees. Unless evidence can be provided that small firms generally exclude their employees from plan participation and benefits for other than business reasons, the fate of the top-heavy rules must be decided based solely upon judgmental criteria—that is, upon the opinions of policymakers about what is fair and equitable.

One important question in terms of pension equity is whether each and every plan should ensure that the highly compensated receive no more than their "fair" share of benefits from a pension plan, or whether individuals with similar earnings and job tenure should be able to receive similar retirement benefits, regardless of the size of the firm. In the first case, vesting should be faster for low-wage workers in small firms, and the benefits of highly compensated small-firm managers should be capped. In the second case, vesting should be the same in all firms, and highly compensated workers in small firms should have the same contribution limits as executives of major corporations.

Another equity issue arises if the more favorable tax treatment of pensions given to top management in major corporations is considered a subsidy. The argument is as follows. Small employers can shelter income by reinvesting it in their own businesses. Many corporate executives do not have that option. Consequently, pension plans may act as a government-sanctioned subsidy to highly compensated executives that both promotes retirement income and (implicitly) levels the tax-shelter playing field between top management and small-business owners.

Another regulatory issue touched on in recent legislation is the provision to enable a regulatory agency—the Department of Labor—to supply small employers with better information about pension plans than they might otherwise have. As chapter V shows, employers receiving pension information from accountants and insurance agents are less likely to establish plans than employers learning about pensions from other sources. Simulations based on the analysis of the factors affecting pension coverage presented in chapter V[7] suggest that if firms receiving pension information from accountants and insurance agents behaved like firms that dealt with financial planners, the small-firm pension coverage rate could increase from 22 percent to 31 percent. Yet the real question is how to turn this potential for increased coverage into reality. The Department of Labor would have to be willing to support its outreach program with extensive research before its efforts could be rewarded.

Will Lower Costs Increase Coverage?—Proposals to expand SEPs and those to ease regulatory burdens seek to encourage coverage by reducing the costs of plan provision for small employers. SBRBEA directly addresses the issue of costs by providing a tax credit for small employers of up to 14 percent of the employer's pension fund contribution. The tax credit approach implicitly recognizes that one reason small employers are less willing to offer a pension plan is that they face higher administrative costs per plan participant than large employers.

A 14 percent tax credit leads to a sizeable projected increase in the percentage of small employers providing pension plans. Simulations indicate that such a tax credit could increase the number of workers in small firms covered by a pension plan by as much as 55 percent.[8] According to this projection, some 3.9 million more workers would have been covered by a pension plan if the tax credit had been in effect in 1987 (table VII.3). That gain would have raised the pension coverage rate among private-sector workers in small firms from an estimated 22 percent to 34 percent of all employees and would have raised the total pension coverage rate for private-sector workers from an estimated 51 percent to 55 percent. The small-employer credit, of course, would only expand coverage among small employers.

But not everyone who works for an employer sponsoring a pension plan is actually a plan participant. Some employees are excluded from the plan because of the type of job they hold, while others fail to meet age and tenure requirements. Consequently, a 14 percent tax credit would add fewer actual plan participants. The simulations indicate that 2.9 million more workers would have become participants in employer-sponsored plans in 1987, which would have raised the small-firm participation rate

---

[7]See appendix B for greater detail.

[8]The simulation is based on the equation used in chapter V to evaluate the effect of administrative costs on the probability of pension coverage. The increase in the likelihood of coverage among small firms was applied to groups of employees from the 1983 Current Population Survey pension supplement. The figures developed were updated to 1987. The simulation assumed that all small-employer plans were eligible for a maximum credit of $3,000. Since two-thirds of all small firms sponsor defined contribution plans and new plans are more likely to be defined contribution plans, the assumption appears reasonable and conservative. See appendix B and Andrews, 1989a, for more information.

TABLE VII.3

Estimated Effect of a 14 Percent Tax Credit on Contributions on Small-Firm Pension Coverage, 1987

Firm Size	Increased Number of Covered Workers (thousands)	Estimated Tax Credit (millions)
Total Workers	3,885	$1,101
1–24	2,733	948
25–99	1,152	153

Note: Employee Benefit Research Institute projections based on small-employer simulation model using National Federation of Independent Business data and May 1983 EBRI/HHS Current Population Survey pension supplement updated to 1987 labor force and price levels.

from an estimated 17 percent to 26 percent. For the private sector as a whole, the participation rate would have grown from an estimated 41 percent to 44 percent of employees. The projected cost to the U.S. Treasury of a 14 percent tax credit would have been about $1.1 billion in 1987. Up to $3.1 billion in additional taxes also could have been deferred as a result of contributions to new small-employer plans.

Under SBRBEA, the 14 percent tax credit is simply a credit for plan sponsorship that can be deducted from corporate, sole proprietor, or partnership tax liability. A broader-based proposal would be to subsidize all small-plan sponsors whether or not they owed taxes. This would be the equivalent of a small-employer pension-based "negative income tax."[9] A pure tax credit that did not include a "negative income tax" component, as proposed under SBRBEA, would encourage only those small businesses that pay taxes to sponsor pension plans. Companies without taxable income would not respond to the tax credit. An estimated one-third of all small businesses pay no income tax.[10]

A 14 percent small-business "negative income tax" (including the phase-out and maximums) leads to an even larger simulated increase in the

---

[9]This term is usually used in the context of welfare reform measures that would provide a minimum income to all Americans through the income tax system—taxing some and providing cash transfers to others.

[10]IRS data indicate that many companies of all firm sizes have no tax liability. Somewhat more than 30 percent of all corporations with assets of $250,000 or more did not report net income in 1984 and paid no taxes. The percentage of sole proprietorships without reported net income was more than 25 percent lower. Since average assets per firm were over $250,000 for all small employers in the SBA/IRS match file, one-third of all small businesses are estimated to pay no income tax.

percentage of small-firm workers covered by a pension plan. A small-employer "negative income tax" could have ensured that 5.8 million additional workers had pension coverage in 1987—1.9 million more than under the 14 percent tax credit (table VII.4). The pension coverage rate for those working for small employers would have been 40 percent in 1987 under a 14 percent subsidy, compared to a coverage rate of 34 percent under the SBRBEA tax credit. The total projected coverage rate for all employees would have been raised to 58 percent.

A "negative income tax" would have added 4.4 million plan participants to employer-sponsored plans, raising the participation rate among those working for small employers in 1987 to 28 percent. The projected participation for all workers would have been 46 percent in 1987. The U.S. Treasury would have to spend more under a "negative income tax" than under a tax credit—an estimated $1.7 billion in 1987. Up to $4.6 billion in additional taxes would have been deferred for new pension contributions, which would have reduced federal revenues by an estimated $6.3 billion in 1987.

The efficacy of the "negative income tax" in stimulating pension coverage stems from a substantial reduction in the real administrative costs faced by employers. On average, projected administrative costs faced by small employers taking advantage of the "negative income tax" would have been around $860 per firm in 1987 before receiving the subsidy. The average projected government subsidy or tax credit (assuming taxes were owed) enjoyed by employers sponsoring pension plans would have been around $1,850 per firm in 1987. In other words, the tax credit or subsidy provided to small employers is projected to be higher than estimated ongoing

TABLE VII.4
Estimated Effect of a 14 Percent Subsidy on Contributions on Small-Firm Pension Coverage, 1987

Firm Size	Increased Number of Covered Workers (thousands)	Estimated Tax Credit (millions)
Total Workers	5,827	$1,652
1–24	4,099	1,422
25–99	1,728	230

Note: Employee Benefit Research Institute projections based on small-employer simulation model using National Federation of Independent Business data and May 1983 EBRI/HHS Current Population Survey pension supplement updated to 1987 labor force and price levels.

administrative costs. However, since 44 percent of plans are managed internally, according to the 1985 NFIB survey, some small employers have greater administrative costs in terms of staff time than actually reported. Thus, the credit or subsidy would also pay for the costs of internal staff time.

Nonetheless, not all employers could afford to sponsor a pension plan, even with subsidized administrative costs. That subsidy would not cover start-up costs—such as search time, consultant costs, and government user fees—that can be expensive for plan sponsors.

Employee preferences would also continue to influence plan formation in a voluntary system even if administrative costs are subsidized by the government. Unless long-run productivity gains offset the firm's expenditures on plan contributions, the costs of pension sponsorship will outweigh the benefits, particularly if few employees are interested in costly pension coverage. If a company tries to offset pension costs by lowering wages (or restricting raises), employees will look for other jobs. The company will be unable to hire comparable workers at lower than market wages. Even after a subsidy is provided, if pension sponsorship is not a financially viable business decision, plans will not be established.

Preservation Proposals—All four proposals seeking to preserve preretirement distributions for retirement would control participant access to pension fund assets. Since Congress has shown increased reluctance to grant special tax treatment for any purpose, restricting pension fund distributions to retirement income purposes would help justify the continued tax deferral of pension contributions and earnings.

Tightening participant access to funds, however, can affect the attractiveness of pensions to employees. If participants value higher income in retirement, restricting access to pension income will not change the demand for pensions. But if participants count on access to preretirement cashouts, new restrictions will make pensions less attractive. Employee responses will depend on the nature of the restriction and how retirement income saving is perceived.

EBRI simulations show that manufacturing workers holding four jobs between ages 25 and 64 could lose 43 percent of their pension benefits at retirement by spending all preretirement cashouts (EBRI, 1987). By contrast, workers who invest cashouts of exactly $3,500 from each of three jobs would, by retirement, have saved an amount equivalent to over 80 percent of a typical clerical worker's full-career pension. Preservation would be most important to employees of small firms who are covered by defined contribution plans. These employees may also receive relatively small distributions. The effect of plan preservation would be greatest in conjunction with other policy measures that effectively increase pension plan sponsorship in small companies.

Other Sources of Growth

Of all the proposals recently under consideration, the 14 percent tax credit offers the greatest promise of quickly increasing pension coverage in small firms. But is this the only avenue for coverage growth? Under certain conditions, increased plan sponsorship also can take place if productivity gains are forthcoming and economic growth is more robust.

Real Wage Growth—As noted in chapter V, studies consistently show that earnings influence pension coverage. This finding is consistent with a theory of plan provision in which employers use pensions to encourage a continuing employment relationship with their employees. Workers with higher wages in firms of all sizes are more likely to have a pension. Pension coverage is thought to increase productivity, and hence earnings, by encouraging more experience on the job. Further, those in high-wage occupations may be harder to replace, and firms will have a greater reason to retain those workers. Finally, higher-wage workers are more likely to want a pension plan. Consequently, if real wages rise, plan sponsorship should increase.

Real average hourly earnings grew at a 1.98 percent annual rate between 1952 and 1972 and declined by 0.24 percent between 1972 and 1985. Many believe that real wage growth will resume in the future and that the most recent period represents an aberration. Nevertheless, real wage growth is expected to be weaker than it has been historically. The pessimistic assumptions of the board of trustees of the Social Security Trust Fund (1988) assume a 0.9 percent annual long-run real-wage growth rate. The board's two intermediate assumptions show more optimistic long-run growth in real wages of 1.4 percent and 1.9 percent per year. Many observers feel that the intermediate assumptions are too optimistic and prefer to use the pessimistic alternative.[11]

Real wage growth of approximately 0.9 percent per year would increase the average payroll per employee for small employers from around $15,000 to $20,000 in 1985 dollars by 2020 when many of the baby boom generation will be retiring.[12] Moderate growth at a long-run 1.4 percent rate would raise payroll per employee in small firms to about $23,500 (in constant dollars) while more expansive growth at 1.9 percent would raise payroll per employee in small firms to about $27,500 (in constant dollars).

---

[11]The board's pessimistic assumption for real wage growth in the 1989 report was reduced to 0.8 percent.

[12]For more information, see appendix B.

According to simulations based on the chapter V analysis of the effect of earnings on coverage, real wage growth of 0.9 percent per annum could increase the pension coverage rate among workers in small firms from 22 percent to 27 percent. Faster real wage growth would produce greater gains in pension coverage. Real wage growth at a 1.4 percent rate would increase the coverage rate to 31 percent of small-firm workers. Growth of 1.9 percent could bring the coverage rate to 36 percent by 2020.

A Combination of Factors—Nonetheless, real wage gains do not provide as much of an incentive for coverage growth among small employers as a 14 percent "negative income tax" would provide. The combined effects of real wage growth and improved information, however, are virtually equivalent to a 14 percent federal subsidy—that is, raising the pension coverage rate to 37 percent of all workers in small firms. Alternatively, a "negative income tax" for small-employer pension plans, combined with a real $5,000 gain in payroll per worker could raise the pension coverage rate for workers in small firms from 22 percent to 46 percent. At a 0.9 percent growth rate, this would take place by the year 2020. At a 1.4 percent annual growth rate, the same pension coverage rate would be achieved before the year 2010. If real wages grew at 1.9 percent annually, the pension coverage rate among small-firm employees would reach 41 percent by the year 2003, even before the retirement of the baby boom generation.

The greatest spur to pension coverage growth among workers in small firms could occur if all potential simulated sources of increased coverage worked together (a "negative income tax," real wage growth, and improved access to information about pensions). In that case, the coverage rate among workers in small firms could increase by 35 percentage points, from 22 percent to 57 percent of small-firm private-sector workers. This rate is higher than the 51 percent total coverage rate posted for all private-sector employees in 1983. The challenge is finding out how to make this happen.

Further research is needed to determine why advice offered by accountants and insurance agents is less likely to lead to pension plan formation than advice received from other sources. Greater knowledge about the options suggested by various sources could provide a basis for achieving greater pension coverage. Do the insurance agents consulted by small employers specialize in liability or life insurance, and have a limited interest in pension plans? Do accountants warn their clients about the complexities of plan formation and neglect to highlight the benefits? Do banks offer low-cost asset management options? Are small firms that use financial planners more interested in providing benefits? The answers to these questions are crucial to the development of the small-employer market.

In addition, the possibility for advanced technologies to improve the small-plan market must be assessed. Computer technology is beginning to make both personnel and benefit management administratively easier. Similarly, families of mutual funds now serving individuals may be able to expand their business to small firms. If many of the costs of plan provision stem from regulatory and administrative tasks that are amenable to computer management, plans can be designed that are tailored to the work force, less expensive for the firm, and more profitable for the provider marketing the product.

Summary and Conclusions

Without significant changes in the small-plan market, increasing pension coverage will not be easy within a voluntary system. Preservation proposals are related to coverage but are not primarily directed toward that end. While SEPs continue to be proposed as a solution to small-employer coverage, if the IRA experience is any guide, most employees will not demand coverage. Reduced SEP reporting requirements are not likely to encourage SEPs unless the required plan provisions are also desirable to firms. More small employers might establish SEPs if ERISA participation and vesting standards could be used since small firms may find it cumbersome to cover all of their short-term employees.

After an evaluation of current legislative proposals in this area, the 14 percent tax credit for small-employer plans has the greatest potential in the short run for raising small-firm pension coverage within a voluntary system. Under such a policy, a simulated 2.9 million more workers would have participated in employer-sponsored plans in 1987. Nonetheless, the pension participation rate among small firms would have only been boosted from 17 percent to 26 percent, and the total pension participation rate would only have been increased by 3 percentage points, from 41 percent to 44 percent.

The public policy issue is whether an estimated annual tax expenditure of $1.1 billion (based on 1987 projections) for a 14 percent tax credit, or roughly $380 per new plan participant (in 1987 dollars), is worth the gain in coverage. In 1978, 1.5 million IRA contributors created an estimated tax expenditure of $745 million (in 1987 dollars), or $500 per participant (in 1987 dollars). Thus, tax expenditures for IRAs soon after the passage of ERISA were greater on a per person basis than those that would result from the proposed 14 percent tax credit. The costs of the tax credit would be higher in future years, however, as plan contributions would increase for a growing labor force and the newly formed small-employer pension funds would start accruing earnings on their investments. Furthermore, coverage gains that result from a tax credit lead to another immediate loss in tax revenues for the government because the taxation of pension contributions is also deferred. The unique feature of the 14 percent tax credit, however, is that those tax revenues are not recovered.

A tax credit for small plans might be politically more attractive if preservation could be ensured. Since most small employers provide defined contribution plans, many small-employer plan participants can expect to receive more than one lump-sum distribution before retirement age as they change jobs. If legislators were confident that pension distributions were used exclusively for retirement income, the cost of a tax credit (or subsidy) might be more palatable.

If a small-employer tax subsidy worked in conjunction with an improvement in the economy, its long-run impact would be greater. Unfortunately, the prognosis for economic growth is uncertain. Wage growth over the past decade has been slow, and compensation gains could be diverted to health insurance premiums if health care cost inflation is not controlled. In addition, businesses interested in developing new pension products for small firms must be willing to accept the risks inherent in entering a new market. The main question that has an influence on the expansion of the employer-sponsored pension system, however, will continue to be whether plan provision is a good business decision for the small employer. Even in an expanding economy, plan formation will not be appropriate for every firm.

VIII. The Economic Implications of Pension Policy

Introduction

Two separate concerns dominate the debate about small-employer coverage. First, are small-employer plans burdened by excessive regulation that discourages further plan formation? And, second, is public welfare reduced if pension accruals favor small-business owners? These small-plan issues represent one aspect of a broader public policy debate. More generally, the interest in small-employer coverage is a direct result of policy interest in the equitable provision of pensions to all wage and salary workers.

Three primary parties are concerned with pension policy—firms, workers, and the federal government.[1] Chapter VIII defines the interests of each and discusses how different policies serve each of their needs. The strengths and weaknesses of proposals to improve the voluntary system are compared to other broader-based policy alternatives, including the mandating of employer-sponsored pensions and the expansion of social insurance.

The ultimate goal of pension policy is the provision of adequate and equitable income to retirees and their families. This standard, which depends on individual perceptions, is investigated in terms of the policy alternatives discussed. Pension policy also involves an ongoing debate about the budget deficit, macroeconomic policy, and savings and investment. This chapter explores the relationship between these broad economic issues and the narrower retirement income policy goals.

Why Have a Plan?

The retirement income needs of employees are met by direct government provision of benefits through Social Security and Supplemental Security Income (SSI) and through a federally regulated voluntary pension system stimulated by tax incentives. This public-private partnership has developed over time without detailed and systematic coordination. Thus, persistent calls have come for a national retirement income policy to address pension issues on a unified basis rather than piecemeal. In view of

---

[1]Other interested parties, of course, range from the families of employees to businesses providing pension services.

the perception that the pension system is fragmented and contradictory, it is useful to step back and outline how business, labor, and government are affected by pension policy. This appraisal provides a framework to evaluate policies directed at increasing pension coverage and providing better benefits for retirees.

The Perspective of the Firm—Employers provide pensions for business purposes. The research presented in chapter IV supports that proposition. Pensions are an integral part of personnel policy to encourage continued employment among workers who are valuable to the firm. A vested benefit ensures that the cost of being dismissed or changing jobs is greater than it would be if only wage and salary payments were involved. Pension plans may foster loyalty and encourage workers to perform to their full capacity. As a consequence, large firms will be more likely to provide pensions than small firms if their corporate managers find it difficult to evaluate the contribution of individual workers.

Pensions are also used to regulate the labor force, easing workers out of their jobs at retirement age. Employers who wish to scale down or shift resources from one operation to another can also use pensions as a management tool that encourages their employees to leave on terms favorable to themselves and to the company. Those workers can afford to retire or redirect their careers without the stigma of unemployment. More generally, by offering retirement benefits, employers can maintain the profitability of their operations. Consequently, pension plans both encourage longer job tenure and induce workers to leave the firm.

The use of pension plans to manage the work force has been encouraged by federal tax policy. Since employers are allowed to fund their plans on an ongoing basis, they can afford to expense pension contributions over time on a reasonable schedule without compromising the financial integrity of the firm. Thus, deductible pension contributions meet the needs of employers to improve worker productivity by encouraging continued employment, hard work, and commitment to the firm.

Large employers who can segment their work force through union contracts or different lines of business may be more likely to offer pensions than small firms. Work force segmentation allows large employers to offer a variety of pension plans tailored to the employment relationship desired by the firm. Small employers have little flexibility to segment their work force because of federally mandated coverage requirements. Furthermore, because a pension by design and by government mandate is a long-term commitment, smaller and less stable businesses will be less likely to offer a plan.

The Perspective of the Worker—The advantages of tax deferral are a prime attraction for employees, making pensions more valuable than individual savings. Some consider this the most important reason for the growth of the pension system (Ippolito, 1985). Tax advantages are likely to be more important to relatively higher-income workers who face higher marginal tax rates: i.e., top management and owner-managers with higher incomes. Nonetheless, the analysis provided in chapter V indicates that even in a small business, plan formation is related to the economic situation of the firm. Little support can be provided for the contention that the establishment of small-business plans is primarily determined by the personal retirement income strategy of the business owner.

Beyond tax deferral, employer-sponsored pensions offer a number of other advantages to all members of the labor force. For instance, they have the advantage of pooled mortality experience (insurance)—even when the plan is not explicitly provided through an insurance company. Pension plans are not individual savings accounts that can be bequeathed to survivors; instead, they spread the "risks" of lengthy retirement across all workers. As such, pensions providing an annuity at retirement are cheaper than individual savings at a given level of retirement income. Defined benefit plans are also less costly than individual annuities purchased on the open market at sex-distinct mortality rates, because the employer's work force consists of a broad group. Covering a broad group avoids the costs of adverse selection inherent in individual annuity purchases (the tendency of persons in poor health not to buy annuities). Finally, employer-sponsored plans provide professional investment management that employees might not be able to afford for the investment of their own savings.

The Perspective of Government—The current tax treatment of pension plans was developed to promote retirement income security and adequacy. Government intervention can be justified in several ways. Rank-and-file employees may be shortsighted in their evaluation of their future retirement needs. Public finance theory demonstrates that market rates of return are generally less than the social rate of return. In other words, to meet the retirement income goals of society, saving might have to be higher than the level desired by individuals on their own. If workers are unwilling or unable to save enough for retirement, the public may call on the government to fill the gap.[2] The public may also call on the government to provide retirement income that is subject to less investment risk and uncertainty than individual saving. In particular, Social Security and defined benefit pension plans have that advantage.

Many of the Employee Retirement Income Security Act's (ERISA's) regulatory provisions offer some degree of consumer protection. Consumer

---

[2]This justification of an income-security policy can be made for Social Security payments and employer-sponsored pensions.

protection measures encompass such diverse provisions as fiduciary requirements, funding standards, and participation and vesting requirements. While most pension funds can be expected to meet high standards of participant protection in any case, these safeguards help justify the tax preferences granted.

While some favor the federal government mandating greater uniformity in the provision of employer-sponsored pensions, many social policy goals of the United States are met by means other than broad-based national programs. The voluntary pension system may be likened to the U.S. system of higher education. College degrees are provided through a mixed system of public and private colleges and universities. Like pension funds, private educational institutions are not taxed. Although federally sponsored colleges and universities would be another way to provide higher education, few argue for a nationalized system, since Americans have a tradition of educational diversity.

Why Defer Taxes?

After the Tax Reform Act of 1986, our system of taxation was expected to follow the model of the comprehensive income tax. All corporate and personal income under a comprehensive income tax is subject to taxation, without exception. Pension contributions and asset income theoretically should be subject to individual income taxes too, in the absence of overriding social policy goals.[3] Contributions to pension trusts would remain a justifiable current business expense.

The comprehensive income tax is only one tax system alternative, however. *Blueprints for Basic Tax Reform*, published by the U.S. Department of the Treasury in 1977 as a guide for tax reform, discusses two "model" tax schemes: one for a comprehensive income tax and the other for a consumption tax (Bradford, 1984). With a consumption tax, consumer spending would be taxed and savings would be exempted from taxation. Prior to tax reform, our tax system acted as a modified consumption tax that exempted or modified taxation of many types of savings, including capital gains, state and local bonds, individual retirement accounts (IRAs), home ownership, and pension funds (Bradford, 1984).

---

[3]Administrative complexities may hinder current taxation, however. These complexities arise in several ways. First, in defined benefit plans it is usually difficult, if not impossible, to allocate the firm's contribution to particular employees. Second, even in defined contribution plans with allocated accounts, the mechanics of assessing taxes on an employee-by-employee basis would be complex. Would the fund pay the taxes or would each employee be taxed individually on funds not yet received? The Congressional Budget Office, 1987, provides a number of suggestions on alternative ways to tax pension fund accruals.

According to economic theory, efficient taxes should not distort economic choices without a clear reason for doing so. In other words, taxation should be neutral. One frequently cited example of a market-distorting tax policy is the implicit tax placed on Social Security benefits when retirees earn above a certain level. In 1989 benefits are reduced by one dollar for every two dollars of earnings above $8,880 earned by Social Security beneficiaries aged 65 to 70.[4] This implicit tax distorts the choices older Americans make between work and retirement.

Taxpayers also choose how much to spend on goods and services and how much to put into savings. The comprehensive income tax distorts investment decisions by taxing both income spent and income saved. By reducing the return on investment, individuals receive less than they would otherwise, and saving may be discouraged.[5] In other words, individuals save less because they receive less than the pretax market rate of return. By contrast, the deferred tax treatment of pensions mirrors a consumption tax and reduces distortions in saving behavior.[6]

Theoretically, a lump-sum tax on all individuals is the only tax that does not distort economic choices. But observers easily agree that such a tax would place a completely inequitable burden on lower-income families. In all probability, no one tax can meet all the equity and efficiency considerations society demands. Many argue that the consumption tax is less equitable than the comprehensive income tax because it disproportionately exempts the rich from taxation. A consumption tax funneled through pension funds, however, is *a priori* less regressive since pensions lead to savings that are relatively broadly based over most of the earnings spectrum (Andrews, 1985). Furthermore, according to *Blueprints*, "The relative burdens of rich and poor are determined by the degree of progressivity of the tax. Either tax is amenable to any degree of progressivity of rates."

All too often proponents of the taxation of pension plan investment returns are opposed to tax expenditures *per se* and do not recognize the merits of any system of taxation other than a comprehensive income tax.[7] As a consequence, their arguments fail to note the benefits of the consumption tax.[8] A balanced appraisal of the tax treatment of employer-

---

[4]For those between age 62 and 65, the earnings over $6,480 are taxed. There is no limit on earnings for those aged 70 and over. The work disincentives faced by younger retirees are scheduled to be reduced in the future, however.

[5]This argument gives rise to the phrase "the double taxation of savings."

[6]Others would argue that these distortions are minimal, in part, because of the relative value of income and substitution effects in terms of savings behavior. For a review of some of the empirical studies in this area see Aaron, Bosworth, and Burtless, 1989.

[7]It can be shown that current taxation can be achieved through the taxation of the investment returns on a current basis and the taxation of contributions at retirement.

[8]For instance, see Congressional Budget Office, 1987.

sponsored pension plans must admit that pension plans add an element of consumption taxation to the tax system, thus reducing some of the economic distortions inherent in the comprehensive income tax. Some observers who would contest the use of tax expenditures for employee benefits on grounds of efficiency would look favorably on the consumption tax element introduced through the tax deferral of pension contributions.

What Voluntary Expansion Means

How would voluntary expansion of the private employer-sponsored pension system meet the social or economic goals of employers, employees, and government? Three generic policies have been proposed: (1) increase the types of plans small employers can sponsor, (2) ease regulatory requirements, and (3) reduce the costs of plan provision for small employers. Under the options currently discussed, greater plan choice would be provided by the expansion of simplified employee pensions (SEPs). Regulatory relaxation would be provided through the elimination of the top-heavy rules, and cost reduction would take place through the 14 percent small employer tax credit.

SEPs and Other Plans—Increasing plan provision options for small employers is laudable in theory if there is a pent-up demand for new types of pension plans. Since their administrative costs are higher, small employers are less likely than large employers to institute a pension plan. Thus, cost reducing options may encourage more small employers to provide pension coverage for their employees. This could improve retirement income without an expansion of federal programs. Greater coverage would add to the consumption tax aspects of our income tax system. But greater coverage will not occur unless small employers adopt these new types of plans. As chapter VII outlines, the incentives for employers to establish new SEPs do not appear to be particularly strong under current proposals.

Top-Heavy Rules—The elimination of the top-heavy rules would offer regulatory relief to small employers. Yet the ultimate impact of these rules on employees and employers is unclear. On the one hand, the top-heavy requirements may have caused some plans to terminate and may have discouraged the formation of new plans. On the other hand, the top-heavy rules may have expanded benefit entitlement within plans.[9] More generally, the evidence does not suggest that regulatory change has had a substantially greater impact on pension coverage in small firms than among large employers.

---

[9]See Andrews, 1989b.

The social and economic consequences of the top-heavy rules are unclear. The top-heavy rules have the effect of allowing top management in large firms to be entitled to higher pensions than owner-managers of small firms with equal salaries. Such discrimination in favor of corporate executives is justified on the premise that more employees are plan participants when large firms sponsor pension plans. (By contrast, the top-heavy rules provide more favorable treatment to lower-paid plan participants in small firms.) But manager-worker ratios result primarily from the employment structure of the business and not from discriminatory hiring practices. The top-heavy rules are inconsistent with principles of horizontal equity (in this case, treating individuals with the same income in the same way).

If the top-heavy rules were repealed, horizontal equity would be restored for individuals with similar earnings in different-sized firms. Costs would be lowered but plan sponsorship would still be more costly for small employers. Some owners probably would establish plans that did not benefit their employees. Others might cover more of their employees if top-heavy compliance were not necessary since the coverage of low-income, short-tenured workers would not compromise their own benefits. In any event, unless very small firms have the same employment structure as large firms, small plans will naturally tend to benefit owners and managers more.

Policymakers might consider taking a broader look at regulatory requirements. Pension law has become more burdensome both because of the many legislative changes requiring plan amendments and because of the growing complexity of plan administration. Simplified common rules and a stable regulatory environment could contribute to the establishment of more plans.

A Tax Credit for Small Plans—A tax credit or a "negative income tax" for small employers would reduce administrative costs and encourage pension coverage. Pension-induced productivity gains would be within the reach of more small employers if pensions were less costly. With greater coverage, more employees would become entitled to future pension benefits. Thus, the social goal of encouraging plan sponsorship would be met. In addition, a tax credit would increase pension coverage while letting employers and employees choose the amount of pension coverage they wanted.

Administrative costs are higher for small businesses because of economies of scale in running a plan and possible economies of scale in compliance. If small plans must pay more per employee to comply with ERISA, then compliance costs should be reduced for small firms. The tax credit, in effect, does just that.

An alternative route to increasing pension coverage among small employers could be to encourage or establish state risk pools, perhaps as part of state employee pension funds, to provide administrative and financial services on a cost-effective basis. But scale economies could only reduce administrative costs to the rates faced by larger plans. A tax credit or subsidy that exceeds plan management costs could encourage plan sponsorship among employers who have little other economic motive to provide a pension.

What a Mandatory System Means

Over the years, proposals have been made to mandate employer-sponsored pensions to supplement Social Security. The most recent proposal, that of President Carter's 1981 Commission on Pension Policy, would have provided pension coverage to a core labor force. The commission recommended that a "minimum universal pension system" (MUPS) be established for all employees over age 25 with one year of service and 1,000 hours of employment with their employer. The minimum contribution would have been 3 percent of payroll, and vesting would have been immediate.[10]

MUPS was based on the ERISA participation standards in effect in 1981. Since that time, the Retirement Equity Act (REA) has reduced the minimum plan participation age to 21. Based on that age, a MUPS would have raised the estimated pension participation rate for very small employers from 12 percent to 54 percent in 1987 (table VIII.1). Estimated participation rates for very large employers would have increased as well, from 70 percent to 86 percent of employees. On average, the estimated total participation rate for private-sector workers in firms of all sizes would have been raised from 41 percent to 71 percent in 1987. Only workers not meeting the MUPS standards would have been excluded from plan participation.

Under the proposed MUPS, a portability clearinghouse (and clearinghouse fund) would also have been established within the Social Security Administration and would have been administered by independent trustees appointed by the president. The clearinghouse would have directly invested and managed pension funds for employers not wishing to administer their own plan. The clearinghouse was supposed to enable small employers to take advantage of the scale economies available to large

---

[10]Perhaps contradictorily, the Commission also recommended that the ERISA vesting standards then in force not be changed. See President's Commission on Pension Policy, 1981.

TABLE VIII.1
Pension Participation Rates: Actual and under MUPS[a]

Firm Size	Percent Participation	
	Actual	Under MUPS
Total	40.5%	70.8%
Under 25	11.7	53.5
25–99	27.3	69.9
100–499	44.0	76.7
500–999	52.0	81.0
1,000 or more	69.5	85.8
Do Not Know	37.5	63.9
Adjusted Total[b]	41.0	71.9

Source: Employee Benefit Research Institute tabulations of data from the May 1983 EBRI/HHS Current Population Survey pension supplement.
[a]Minimum universal pension system.
[b]Calculation omits those who do not know their firm size.

funds.[11] A defined contribution plan approach was adopted to reduce the degree of complexity imposed upon plan sponsors.

In conjunction with the MUPS, the commission recommended a special alternative tax credit for small businesses of up to 46 percent of their qualified plan contributions (up to 3 percent of payroll). Employers could either deduct their contributions or take the credit, whichever was larger. The availability of an alternative tax credit would have benefited businesses taxed at relatively lower corporate tax rates.

No reallocation of resources can be done without cost. At the time, commission estimates indicated that the MUPS would have cost the federal government $10.5 billion in 1984.[12] By 1987, that cost could easily have risen to $12.7 billion with the growth in the labor force and the rise in earnings—more than 10 times the direct cost of a 14 percent tax credit for small employers.

Unlike tax expenditures, mandating does not work in conjunction with market forces. Consequently, firms have to offer pension coverage even if the costs of providing a plan outweigh the benefits. Employers unable

---

[11]In a sense, this is the thrust of the new type of pension plan proposed on a voluntary basis under the Pension Portability Act.
[12]These costs were described as "business tax savings."

to raise their prices or pass on their pension expense to their employees would be forced to reduce other expenditures, change their method of production, lower their profits, or go out of business. The commission estimated an employment loss of about 160,000 workers due to increased pension costs, assuming that companies could not pass on their costs.[13] Because a MUPS would fall disproportionately on small employers, who are less able to weather unanticipated cost increases, the Pension Commission disemployment figure probably represents a lower-bound estimate.

In the long run, the pension commission anticipated that the cost of the MUPS pension contribution would be passed on to workers in the form of lower wages, as many believe Social Security taxes are passed on.[14] In that case, the MUPS would have had no long-run disemployment effects except for minimum-wage workers. However, some workers would be forced to accept pension coverage rather than higher wages. In effect, the MUPS would have reduced the ability of employers and employees to allocate compensation between wages and benefits (and hence would have affected consumption and saving).

A reduction in choice may be an acceptable public policy option if warranted by the benefits of the proposal. The benefits from a mandatory system are twofold. First, mandating ensures that all workers included in the legislation are covered by a pension plan—in the case of the commission proposal everyone aged 25 and over with one year of service, working 1,000 hours a year. In other words, every member of the target group would immediately become a plan participant. Mandating could include a broader spectrum of the work force (for instance, reflecting REA participation changes) or be structured more narrowly (for instance, providing five-year vesting in keeping with the Tax Reform Act of 1986).

Second, mandating ensures that pension coverage is provided more equitably. One of the chief criticisms of the voluntary system has been that workers covered by a plan unfairly benefit from the tax expenditures provided. Furthermore, the critique continues, workers with pension plans have higher than average earnings. A mandatory system would mitigate some of those concerns. Under the commission's MUPS, however, short-tenure, part-time workers would not be participants. Social Security provides higher replacement rates to lower-income workers, and lower-paid workers get a better rate of return on their contributions to Social Security. On the whole, those workers who would not be MUPS participants may have as high replacement rates as workers who participate in employer-sponsored plans.

---

[13]For a discussion of the model, see ICF Incorporated, 1981.
[14]See chapter III for additional discussion of this point.

At What Price Coverage?

Proposals to expand the pension system have been justified on the grounds that employer-sponsored pension coverage reaches just one-half of the work force. But the presence or absence of an employer-sponsored plan does not directly translate into the presence or absence of adequate resources in retirement. The analysis in chapter VII on the effects of different policy proposals to increase pension coverage does not address the more fundamental issue of whether or not such policies are needed. Normative issues, which depend on individual perceptions, are the hardest to address. Nonetheless, the goal of pension policy should be retirement income and not pension coverage *per se*. Policy considerations lie in three areas: income adequacy, pension equity, and macroeconomic policy.

Income Adequacy—Under current policies, retirement income will increase and pensions will become more important. Forecasts show that 83 percent of retired couples born during the baby boom and 60 percent of single individuals will receive income from employer-sponsored pensions (Andrews and Chollet, 1988). Future retirees are expected to be better off in real dollar value terms but have a somewhat lower standard of living relative to the working population. Appropriate income replacement rates in retirement have been pegged at roughly 60 to 80 percent of preretirement earnings, with lower replacement rates needed by upper-income retirees (President's Commission on Pension Policy, 1981).[15] Analysis has suggested that replacement rates in the late 1970s were approaching the lower end of that range (Fox, 1982). The average wage replacement from pensions and Social Security (excluding income from assets) for married men is projected to decline from 49 percent of preretirement income for current retirees to 45 percent of preretirement income for the baby boom (Andrews and Chollet, 1988). Other sex and marital status groupings are projected to have lower replacement rates as well. Average projected replacement rates are below those needed to maintain preretirement living standards and would have to be supplemented by savings.

Some baby boom retirees will have income at the poverty or near-poverty level (within 125 percent of the poverty line) according to projections. Unmarried women (single, widowed, or divorced) will continue to have the greatest needs: 43 percent of single women born in the early decade of the baby boom are projected to be in poverty or near poverty

---

[15]Replacement rates may be measured in many ways. Replacement rates have traditionally been measured against final career earnings. Retirement earnings may be compared to those of the working population, however, or to the career average earnings of the retiree, indexed for inflation.

at age 67. By comparison, only 5.4 percent of single men and 1.6 percent of married couples are projected to have income that low. As a middle-income benefit, employer-sponsored pensions may not be the best means to address this issue. Unmarried women with low lifetime earnings and sporadic labor force histories would not necessarily benefit from additional pension coverage.

Social Security benefits could be retargeted so that low-wage part-time workers receive higher benefits. Increasing Social Security benefits across-the-board has not had widespread support in recent years, however. Furthermore, the perceived regressivity of the payroll tax has discouraged serious consideration of program expansion. Of course, the payroll tax is only regressive when considered on an annual basis. (It is a proportional tax for income up to $45,000.) And when Social Security taxes are measured against benefit payments over a lifetime, Social Security redistributes funds toward those retirees with lower lifetime earnings.[16]

Another way to improve the economic situation of unmarried women in retirement would be to strengthen SSI. For instance, federal guarantees could be raised to the poverty level. In 1987, maximum federal benefits for elderly individuals were only 68 percent of the poverty line. And not all states supplemented SSI benefits. Alternatively, the SSI income and asset tests could be redefined, increasing eligibility. SSI could also provide outreach to insure that all eligible elderly Americans received benefits. Congressional testimony indicates that only 50 percent to 60 percent of the eligible elderly receive SSI (*New York Times*, 1988). According to a study funded by AARP (1988), 22 percent of the elderly poor who were surveyed said they had not heard about the program.

Government spending has become less politically popular, however, and continuing budget deficits have diminished public enthusiasm for expanded federal financing, even on a balanced-budget basis. Thus, the unmet income needs of the poor and near-poor elderly are likely to persist. For most of the population, however, the retirement income system enjoys considerable success by providing retirees with income that mirrors that of younger workers. In view of this success, broad changes in employment-related benefits may not be necessary to ensure income adequacy in retirement.

Pension Equity—Others believe that the distribution of pension benefits is inequitable even if benefits are adequate. Two inequities are cited. The first has to do with the distribution of pension income among retirees

---

[16]In other words, the rate of return to Social Security contributions (payroll taxes) is higher for those with lower lifetime earnings.

and the second with the use of pension plans by owners for personal tax planning purposes.

Those who consider the distribution of pension income inequitable indicate that not all retirees receive income from employer-sponsored plans. In addition, benefits received by retirees with pension income vary. In 1986, the median income from private pensions received by family units headed by a retiree aged 65 or older was $3,190 (Grad, 1988). Sixteen percent of recipients received less than $1,000 annually, and 10 percent received $10,000 or more. This distribution of benefit payments reflects lifetime patterns of pension coverage, lifetime work histories, and differences in lifetime earnings.

A variety of options are available to equalize benefit payments. For instance, Social Security could be augmented by allowing sponsors of pension plans the choice of contracting out of the system if they provide comparable benefits privately. Contracting out is currently permitted in Great Britain. Alternatively, all employees earning more than $5.00 an hour who are not plan participants could be subject to an additional payroll deduction as an IRA contribution. If wages and benefits are traded off in the long run, mandatory IRAs could be administratively simpler than mandatory pension plans and have the same result.

Others would argue for more modest measures, such as several of the recent legislative proposals to increase pension coverage among small employers. An argument can be made that the tax credit proposed under the Small Business Retirement and Benefit Extension Act of 1987 (SBRBEA) would be the best way to target long-term middle-income workers because the credit works in concert with the employer's own business considerations, encouraging plan sponsorship where it is most productive. Nevertheless, pensions are a less important management tool for small businesses for the reasons suggested in chapter III. As a consequence, the percentage of small-firm employees covered by pension plans will always be less than that of large firms. Pension policy that maintains market incentives cannot guarantee benefit uniformity.

There is no consensus about the extent to which public policy ought to affect the distribution of retirement income pension benefits. Thus, there is no consensus on the meaning of pension equity. Public policy could produce an income distribution at retirement that is more equal than that of the active work force. But the overall distribution of retirement income need not be a policy consideration. Retirement income could simply reflect income and savings patterns. Our current retirement income system lies somewhere in between.

Another pension equity issue affects small businesses directly. Congress enacted the top-heavy rules to prevent owners of small businesses from establishing plans solely for their own advantage without benefiting the majority of their employees. Unquestionably, Congress felt that discriminatory plans had been sponsored, and these plans were not then illegal. The top-heavy rules may also have been intended to raise revenue. If plans that benefited few lower-income workers were terminated, tax revenue would be raised at the expense of small-business owner-managers. Since many small-business owners could reinvest their profits, the top-heavy rules were directed at doctors, lawyers, and other professionals whose plans offered anecdotal evidence of abuse.

In providing special rules for small employers, other inequities were introduced into the pension system. Under the top-heavy rules, owners of small businesses cannot accrue pension benefits equal to those received by top managers of large corporations. In contrast, lower-income employees of small firms can vest faster than workers in large companies. If plan coverage rules were simplified and broadened (even adding a 100 percent coverage requirement) and the top-heavy rules lifted, small-business employees would face the same requirements as those working for large firms (aside from the fact that they would be working for companies in which the economic incentives to sponsor a pension plan are weaker).

Macroeconomic Considerations—Greater pension coverage has been praised as a way to increase savings and investment in a nation of heavy consumers. The mandatory pension proposal of the President's Commission on Pension Policy was supposed to limit reliance on Social Security on the assumption that a funded pension system would provide a greater stimulus to the economy. Recent research suggests, however, that the macroeconomic consequences of public and private funding are not necessarily different. Thompson (1988) argues that the economic costs of retirement are independent of the funding mechanism and must be borne by society no matter whether the system is public or private. He states:

> so long as the financing mechanism does not affect the aggregate size of retirement benefits, international trade flows, or the size of the capital stock, it has no bearing on the total social costs of the program.

In other words, benefits paid under either system will cost the same if macroeconomic policy has been used to support similar rates of saving and investment.[17]

National savings can be increased under either a public or a private retirement income system. For instance, if the current projected Social

---

[17]This point is also made by Van de Water and Cullinan, 1988, about health insurance.

Security Trust Fund surplus were maintained and the rest of the federal budget were balanced, the overall budgetary surplus created would serve to reduce consumption and increase savings. Conversely, if funded pensions were expanded and the unified budget were not balanced, additional pension contributions would finance the federal deficit without increasing capital formation.

In sum, savings and investment issues are analytically separable from retirement income issues. Nonetheless, without strong economic growth, more resources will not be available to meet social needs. And strong economic growth is needed to encourage pension plan formation. The challenge is how to stimulate the economy and provide higher real incomes for all Americans.[18]

Conclusions—The time may be ripe for a moratorium on new legislation, since many feel that the pace of change has harmed the pension system and that further legislation could halt plan formation. The defined benefit plan base may have started to erode. Retirement income could be diluted if defined contribution plans are widely substituted for defined benefit plans, because most workers do not save their preretirement distributions until retirement. From the perspective of the small employer, continuing legislative change and scrutiny will make pension sponsorship financially impossible. Legislative stability, incentives for plan sponsorship, and equitable rules should lead to a stronger pension system within a strong economy.

Employment-related retirement benefits may be increased through a continuum of policies. Choices range from expanded Social Security to a mandatory employer-provided pension system and from additional tax incentives to regulatory relief. Which alternative will best meet the needs of the nation? Some proposals are limited in scope while others substantially change the retirement income system. Broad-based changes tend to have the highest social cost. Consequently, the question remains: at what price coverage?

---

[18]For an in-depth recent analysis of many of these issues see Aaron, Bosworth, and Burtless, 1989.

Appendix A. Statistical Appendix

Introduction

Four data sets were used throughout this study to analyze the determinants of pension coverage among small employers.[1] Simulations of economic and policy changes are also based on these data.[2] Three of the data sets are produced by government agencies; the fourth is a survey conducted by a private-sector organization. This appendix describes the general survey and sampling methods used for each data base and its particular use in this study.

The first data set, the Current Population Survey (CPS) pension supplement (for 1979 and 1983), is based on a nationally representative sample of personal interviews of employed persons conducted by the U.S. Bureau of the Census. The second, the Small Business Administration/Internal Revenue Service (SBA/IRS) match file, is a matched sample of two different tax returns filed by businesses in 1979 and compiled by the IRS for the SBA. The third, conducted by the private-sector National Federation of Independent Business (NFIB), is a mail survey based on a sample of the NFIB's small employer membership base. The last data base, the 1984 Survey of Income and Program Participation (SIPP), is based on interviews of a national sample of the population conducted by the Census Bureau.

The CPS Pension Supplements

The May 1979 and 1983 CPS pension supplements were conducted as additions to the U.S. Bureau of the Census' ongoing Current Population Survey. The 1983 survey was designed by the Employee Benefit Research Institute (EBRI) and funded by EBRI and the U.S. Department of Health and Human Resources. The May 1979 survey was funded by the Department of Labor and the Social Security Administration. Tabulations of both surveys are found in chapters I through IV; analysis is presented in chapters V and VI.

The Current Population Survey—The CPS is a monthly survey providing information on the economic status and labor force activity of the U.S.

---

[1] This appendix was prepared by Jennifer Davis based on written documentation and on conversations with the key staff members who compiled each of the data files discussed.
[2] Appendix B describes the simulation methodology and other statistical procedures.

population. The CPS has been conducted for over 35 years for the civilian noninstitutional population of the United States. Monthly estimates are made for total employment, including agricultural workers, self-employed persons, domestic workers and unpaid workers, and wage and salary employees. Estimates are made of total unemployment as well. The CPS also provides information on the number of hours employees work and their occupation and industry.

Individuals in about 71,000 households are selected monthly. From this sample, approximately 60,500 households are eligible for the interview. About 2,500 households are not interviewed, because the occupants cannot be reached. Each household is interviewed over four consecutive months (called a rotation) and again during the corresponding time period a year later, to allow for month-to-month and year-to-year comparisons. Households are selected according to area of residence to produce estimates that are representative of the nation, of individual states, and of other selected areas.

National estimates using the CPS are made by weighting the data for each sample person. The basic weight is a rough measure of the actual number of people that the sample person represents in the U.S. population. The basic weights are then adjusted for noninterviews.

The Pension Supplements—In May 1983, 28,789 interviews were obtained from the 32,535 persons eligible to be surveyed. This interview rate (88.5 percent) was slightly higher than the May 1979 rate. Questions were asked of all those employed for pay. Both surveys have information on pension and retirement plan coverage through employer or union-sponsored retirement plans. The survey data include information on pension participation and vesting as well. Because the pension supplement interviews half of the full CPS sample, the Census Bureau adjusts the original CPS person weights to account for the smaller supplement sample and for persons who could not be interviewed (nonresponses) providing new weights for the survey.

The Data Used in This Study—Tables used in chapters I through IV are generally limited to private sector employees. Tables presented in appendix B used only observations for private wage and salary workers. Workers in the railroad industry were also excluded.[3]

SBA/IRS Match File

The SBA/IRS match file combines data from 1979 business tax forms (Form 1120) with data from two 1979 employment tax forms (Form 941

---

[3]Those covered by Railroad Retirement were not supposed to answer the question. Tabulations indicate, however, that a large percentage of railroad workers responded anyway.

for most employers and Form 943 for agricultural employers). The match was undertaken to provide accurate economic information on assets, receipts, and other financial variables for large and small employers. (Employment and payroll data found on the business tax forms were known to be flawed.) The IRS conducted the match under contract to the SBA and the two files were linked using the employer identification number (EIN) common to both files.[4] Tabulations from the SBA/IRS match file are used in chapters II, IV, and V.

Employment Tax Forms—Most employers must file employment tax Form 941 or Form 943 (for nonagricultural and agricultural employers, respectively).[5] These forms may be filed by subsidiaries or by the parent company. Form 941 is filed quarterly by nonagricultural employers who withhold income taxes, Social Security taxes, or both.[6] Form 943 is similar to Form 941 but is filed annually by agricultural employers.[7]

Employment is reported for the pay period including March 12. If the business is sold or transferred (including changing the legal form of the business) during the quarter, both businesses file a form.[8] If the firm merges or is consolidated with another, the original firm must file for that quarter and show all wages paid for that quarter. The Census Bureau receives a tape of 941/943 forms from the IRS, validates the information, and imputes employment and payroll when necessary.

Business Tax Forms—Business tax Form 1120 is filed by all domestic corporations, real estate, investment trusts, regulated investment companies, insurance companies, and foreign corporations doing business in the United States. This form reports income, gains, losses, deductions, and credits of U.S. corporations. For the 1979 sample, returns with accounting periods that ended from July 1979 through June 1980 were included.[9]

The Sample—A stratified probability sample of 80,000 firms was selected by the IRS out of a total of 2.6 million firms. The sample included all firms

---

[4]Three files were actually assembled—one for sole proprietorship, one for partnerships, and one for corporations.

[5]Those employing only household employees file Form 942 and are not included in the match file.

[6]"Wages" are defined as the total of all wages paid, tips reported, taxable fringe benefits provided, and other compensation paid to employees, even if income or Social Security taxes are not withheld. This does not include pension distributions, annuities, third-party sick pay, supplemental unemployment compensation benefits, or gambling winnings, even if income taxes were withheld on them.

[7]In this case, "wages" are taxable cash wages paid.

[8]The change and the date of the change must be noted on the form as well as the name of the new owner or new business name.

[9]The IRS has recently completed a 1982 match that was not available for this study. In that match file, returns with accounting periods ending January 1981 to December 1983 are included.

with $10 million or more in total assets except for corporations in the financial industries, where a minimum of $25 million in total assets was required for selection. Sampling was proportional to the higher of total assets or net income for broad industrial classifications.

The Matching Process—Each parent company has a unique EIN that appears on the business tax Form 1120. The same EIN appears on the 941 or 943 forms the company files.[10] Since subsidiaries can file employment tax forms, several 941 forms and/or several 943 forms could share the same EIN. Therefore, any number of 941 forms and 943 forms could be linked to each Form 1120, allowing for the entire employment and payroll of a company to be grouped with the parent company's business tax form.

The IRS performed an initial match between the business tax Form 1120 and the 941/943 employment tax files. If a business tax form was not matched to a 941 or a 943 form, the IRS tried to correct the EIN on the 1120 forms using other tax form information. If the EIN number was correct, the IRS checked to see whether the company was required to file Form 941 or Form 943. If the business was not required to file, the record was deleted from the file. Nonmatched business tax forms without employment were also deleted.

Matching Problems—A perfect match could not be achieved for several reasons. First, EINs were not always reported accurately.[11] Second, forms could be filed for different time periods. Third, reporting units differed— subsidiaries could file forms 941 and 943 but only the entire company could file the business tax form. Finally, certain business tax forms had the same EIN.[12] Many problem matches were resolved by the IRS by reweighting or imputation. After imputation, the match file represented 64.1 million employees, or 88 percent of the BLS Establishment Survey benchmark of 72.6 million private-sector nonagricultural employees.

The Data Used in This Study—This study uses data from the corporate match file in chapter II and chapter IV. Appendix B provides information about the equations used in the chapter V analysis. The data were provided to EBRI in tabular form by industry and firm size for all employers—for those making a pension contribution and for those not making a contribution to a pension plan. To preserve confidentiality, the IRS did not make

---

[10]Corporation Form 851, on which a company lists all the EINs used by its subsidiaries, is also used to match all possible 941/943 forms to the correct parent company.

[11]Since the EIN on the 941/943 files were verified by the IRS (and the Census Bureau made no changes to this number), the EINs on these forms are considered correct.

[12]While no two business tax forms (Forms 1120) should have the same EIN, matching EINs could occur legitimately in several ways: multiple year filings, in which the company would use its own EIN or cases in which partners in a partnerships use the same EIN (this is the case particularly for oil and gas exploration and underwriting syndicates).

observations on individual corporations available to EBRI. Information was provided on the dollar value of firm assets, on profit rates, on the dollar value of pension contributions, and the dollar value of health insurance contributions. The tabulations provided average dollar values per company for firms in particular employment size and industry groups and average per employee dollar values per firm for firms in each cell.

National Federation of Independent Business Employee Benefits Survey

The NFIB survey of employee benefits was conducted in September 1985 to investigate why small businesses provide employee benefits (Dennis, 1985). The sample was drawn from the NFIB membership file of approximately 570,000 small employers (excluding businesses without full-time employees) by selecting every seventy-third employer from a list drawn up alphabetically within ZIP codes. The survey was mailed to approximately 7,750 NFIB members and a follow-up survey was mailed two weeks later.[13] A 19 percent response rate was reported (based on usable responses), which was 11 percentage points lower than that of other NFIB surveys. The survey was used extensively in chapters IV through V and formed the basis of the policy simulations conducted in chapter VII.

Sample Characteristics—The NFIB reported that the survey may overrepresent small employers in manufacturing and underrepresent those in services. Firms with one to four employees and businesses in the east may be underrepresented as well. Businesses in rural areas may be overrepresented. NFIB members probably have older and more stable businesses than the universe of small employers, as their firms have been in business on average a total of nine to ten years. While the NFIB report indicates that the sample is generally similar to the universe of small employers, pension coverage rates for full-time employees are higher than those calculated using the nationally representative 1983 CPS pension supplement. Higher benefit sponsorship by more stable employers would be expected (see chapter IV). The higher than anticipated NFIB coverage rates affected the way in which the simulations in chapter VII were conducted (see appendix B).

The Data Used in This Study—In chapter IV, the raw NFIB survey responses on benefit provision (arrayed in categories by percentage of full-time employees) were weighted according to group means to determine the percentage of full-time employees covered by particular employee benefits by

---

[13]If two responses were received (approximately 5 percent of the file), the first was used.

firm size.[14] In chapters IV and V, firms were considered to sponsor a pension plan if they either answered the question on pension provision or indicated the type of plan they provided. Only firms with fewer than 100 full-time employees were included in the analysis presented in chapters V through VII (reported in appendix B). Firms reporting payrolls of $50,000 or more per employee were also omitted to improve the quality of the data. This omission may have biased the analysis against a few firms with fewer than five employees and one highly compensated owner-manager. Several dollar-value variables were recoded by EBRI from the survey documents to remove topcoding; only EBRI's NFIB file contains complete financial data.

Survey of Income and Program Participation

The Census Bureau's SIPP was designed to measure household income and participation in private and public insurance and welfare programs.[15] The sample is approximately the same size as the Census Bureau's CPS pension supplement and is nationally representative. In chapter V, SIPP analysis is compared to similar findings from other data bases.

The Survey of Income and Program Participation—Starting October 1983, the same panel of households was interviewed by the Bureau of the Census for a period of two and one-half years. The panel represented the noninstitutional resident population of the United States. Households were randomly divided into four nationally representative "rotation" groups. One group was interviewed each month. Each year a new panel is added so that two and sometimes three panels are interviewed at one time.

Every four months a Census interviewer collected data from one of the groups for the preceding four-month period. A complete series of interviews for all four groups is called a wave. The survey included all persons 15 years old and over in the noninstitutional civilian population who were present in the sample household at the time of the initial interview. These individuals were called original sample persons.[16] Individuals who moved into the household of an original sample person were only included in

---

[14]The CPS pension supplement could not be used because it does not contain information on the entire spectrum of benefits.

[15]SIPP is currently overseen by a SIPP Advisory Committee chaired by a representative from the Office of Management and Budget and the Social Science Research Council's Committee on SIPP, organized through a grant from the National Science Foundation.

[16]Persons in noninstitutional group quarters, such as college dormitories as well as rooming and boarding houses, convents or monasteries, are eligible for inclusion if the address was selected for the sample and was their usual residence. Thus, college students in dormitories generally would not be interviewed, as their usual residences was at their family home.

the survey during the time that they were residing with the original sample person. For most of the 1984 panel, including the waves used here, original sample persons who left the United States, entered institutions, or entered the armed forces were not followed even if they later reentered the civilian noninstitutional population.

Certain questions were asked in each interview. These are called "core" questions. All eligible persons were asked about their labor-force status during every week of the four-month reference period. If a person was employed, looking for work, or laid off, that person was included in the labor force.[17] The Census Bureau also provided sample weights based on age, race, and sex to produce accurate national population estimates. The Census Bureau imputed responses to missing questions based on responses from individuals with similar characteristics. These imputations can be identified by the user.

Topical Modules—There are some questions in SIPP that were not asked in each interview but only during certain waves. This group of questions is called a topical module. The topical modules provided detailed information on a number of subjects including work history and training, asset ownership and income, and employee benefits.

Data Used in This Study—For the analysis in chapter V, data were merged from interview waves 3 and 4 and their associated topical modules. The wave 3 "core" interview provided data on age, sex, education, industry, and business sector (public, private, or self-employed). Wave 3 and wave 4 interviews were matched for men aged 25 through 64 in the private sector. The wave 3 topical module provided information about job tenure, establishment and firm size,[18] and whether the job was under a union contract. Wave 4 provided information on pension coverage and participation. While some workers may have changed jobs between wave 3 and wave 4,[19] they would have been unlikely to be plan participants in their new jobs since many firms have a one-year waiting period. Thus, some participants in wave 3 may have been counted as nonparticipants in the

---

[17]The two jobs with the most hours worked during the reference period were included. Self-employed persons with up to two businesses were asked for the legal type of business, the value of the business, and the net profits for the year, again depending on those with the most hours worked.

[18]While the wave 4 topical module also had information on firm and establishment size, these data are not considered reliable according to SIPP users groups. In particular, the item nonresponse was high and Census Bureau imputations appeared to weight the data toward large firms.

[19]It was not possible to use SIPP data to verify that these workers had the same job in the next wave. The most likely candidate would have been to control for industry changes. Substantial differences in industry codes between waves suggested that this method was unreliable. Furthermore, nonresponse to the industry question in wave 4 was higher than wave 3 nonresponse.

analysis. Restricting the analysis to prime-age men working for small employers provided information about the factors affecting pension coverage for a relatively homogeneous group of workers that was likely to expect a continuing employment relationship with a firm.[20]

---

[20]This sample was also used in Andrews, 1989c.

Appendix B. Technical Appendix

Introduction

This appendix presents in greater detail the statistical analysis cited in chapters V through VII. The chapters in which the findings are cited are cross-referenced in the text. The first four sections of this appendix review findings from the four data sets discussed in appendix A. These are (1) the 1979 and 1983 Current Population Survey (CPS) pension supplements; (2) the Small Business Administration/Internal Revenue Service (SBA/IRS) corporate tax record match file; (3) the National Federation of Independent Business (NFIB) survey of small employers; and (4) the 1984 Survey of Income and Program Participation (SIPP). The final section of this appendix provides more detailed information on how the simulations presented in chapter VII were conducted.

Analysis Using the CPS Pension Supplements

Table B.1 and table B.2 consist of logit equations[1] that estimate the probability of pension coverage for private-sector workers in firms of all sizes. Table B.1 findings are used in chapter V to demonstrate the joint impact of firm size and establishment size on pension coverage. They indicate the effect of attributes of the work force, such as job tenure, hours worked, and earnings, on the likelihood of pension coverage for employees. The equation also demonstrates that the impact of industry is not straightforward.

Table B.2 uses both the 1979 and 1983 CPS pension supplements to investigate whether the change in the coverage rate between those years can be explained by shifts in other variables such as firm size, establishment size, unionization, and industry. As chapter II indicates, there have been significant shifts in the importance of the last three variables over time for the labor market. Nonetheless, an unexplained decrease in the likelihood of pension coverage is apparent between 1979 and 1983.

---

[1] In cases in which the dependent variable is dichotomous, ordinary least squares (OLS) regressions suffer from a number of inadequacies. Consequently, a maximum likelihood procedure is preferred.

TABLE B.1
Pension Coverage Logit Analysis, May 1983 EBRI/HHS Current Population Survey Pension Supplement
(dependent variable: likelihood of coverage)

Variable	Parameter	t-Statistic
Constant	−0.569	−1.59
Firm Size Variables		
Fewer than 25 workers	−2.093	−29.58
25–99 workers	−1.34	−19.26
100–499 workers	−0.661	−11.70
Establishment Size		
Fewer than 25 workers	−0.434	−6.95
25–99 workers	−0.279	−4.71
Union Variables		
Union	0.793	12.18
Union*F1[a]	1.566	8.86
Union*F2[b]	0.439	2.88
Industry Variables		
Construction	−0.505	−5.08
Durable goods	0.283	4.04
Communications	0.909	6.41
Wholesale trade	0.510	5.55
Retail trade	−0.282	−4.27
Finance, insurance, and real estate	0.813	9.66
Professional services	0.477	7.10
Business and personal services	−0.674	−8.27
Job Tenure		
Less than one year	−0.563	−10.47
Years of tenure	0.054	15.94
Wage Rate	0.0923	18.16
Annual Hours Worked	0.00029	8.18
Over 65 Years of Age	−1.025	−6.74
Likelihood Ratio Index	0.332	
Number of Observations	18,071	

Source: Employee Benefit Research Institute.
[a]Fewer than 25 workers.
[b]25–99 workers.

TABLE B.2
Pension Coverage Logit Analysis, May 1979/1983
Current Population Survey Pension Supplements
(dependent variable: likelihood of coverage)

Variable	Parameter	t-Statistic
Constant	−0.126	−1.90
Firm Size Variables		
Fewer than 25 workers	−2.130	−44.12
25–99 workers	−1.339	−28.02
100–499 workers	−0.605	−15.40
Establishment Size		
Fewer than 25 workers	−0.317	−7.51
25–99 workers	−0.175	−4.32
Union Variables		
Union	0.931	21.29
Union*F1[a]	1.253	10.83
Union*F2[b]	0.487	4.78
Industry Variables		
Construction	−0.546	−8.44
Durable goods	0.0345	7.23
Communications	0.693	6.81
Wholesale trade	0.152	2.33
Retail trade	−0.587	−13.08
Finance, insurance, and real estate	0.477	8.15
Professional services	0.376	8.57
Business and personal services	−1.022	17.58
Job Tenure		
Less than one year	−0.439	−12.56
Years of tenure	0.0553	23.08
Wage Rate	0.0911	23.54
Annual Hours Worked	0.000364	15.10
Over 65 Years of Age	−0.882	−8.97
1983 Survey Only	−0.485	−17.64
Likelihood Ratio Index	0.334	
Number of Observations	39,364	

Source: Employee Benefit Research Institute.
[a]Fewer than 25 workers.
[b]25–99 workers.

Analysis Using the SBA/IRS Corporate Tax Record Match File

Analysis using the SBA/IRS match file of corporate tax returns uses grouped logit[2] to investigate the likelihood that a corporation made a contribution to a pension fund. The grouped logit equation uses combined data for all firms whether or not they sponsor a pension plan. The analysis confirms findings of the other data sets about the factors that influence pension sponsorship. The dependent variable represents the percentage of corporations in particular industry/firm-size groups making a pension contribution. It indicates the likelihood that a firm will contribute to a pension plan. Unlike the analysis using the CPS and the NFIB data sets, the analysis using these data was constrained by the grouping procedures.

Table B.3 indicates that firm size, average payroll, and the capital-labor ratio each influence the likelihood of a plan contribution. These findings are cited in chapter V. Table B.4 adds to that analysis, indicating that the addition of industry variables reflects differences in average pay and the

TABLE B.3
Pension Coverage Grouped Logit Analysis,[a]
SBA/IRS Corporate Match File
(dependent variable: percentage of corporations with pension contributions)

Variable	Parameter	t-Statistic
Constant	− 1.559	− 5.47
Firm Size		
Fewer than 50 Workers	− 1.410	− 5.89
Payroll per Employee	0.114	7.92
Assets per Employee	0.000512	1.57
Adjusted R-square	0.428	
Number of Observations	108	

Source: Employee Benefit Research Institute.
[a]Weighted by number of tax returns in each cell.

---

[2]Because the file consists of group averages arrayed by firm size, industry, and coverage status, the usual logit procedures are not appropriate.

TABLE B.4
Pension Coverage Grouped Logit Analysis,[a]
SBA/IRS Corporate Match File,
Industry Variables Included
(dependent variable: percentage of corporations
with pension contributions)

Variable	Parameter	t-Statistic
Constant	− 0.630	− 2.20
Firm Size		
Fewer than 50 Workers	− 1.422	− 7.07
Payroll per Employee	0.0287	1.43
Assets per Employee	− 0.000552	− 0.79
Industry Variables		
Wholesale trade	0.759	4.22
Finance, insurance, and real estate	2.217	2.10
Professional services	1.461	5.7
Adjusted R-square	0.598	
Number of Observations	108	

Source: Employee Benefit Research Institute.
[a]Weighted by number of tax returns in each cell.

capital-labor ratio. While the opposite hypothesis could be proposed—
that earnings and the degree of capitalization are proxies for industry,
both theory and analysis using the CPS and NFIB data suggest that this
is not the case. The industry variables appear to reduce the significance
of payroll per employee and assets per employee because of the grouping procedures. If individual observations had been available to EBRI to
conduct the analysis, the theoretically appropriate variables should have
reduced or changed the coefficients on each of the industry dummies.
Nonetheless, the variable representing professional services is positive and
significant, suggesting that professional practices are more likely to have
a pension plan. These findings are reviewed in chapter V.

Since individual observations were not available for the SBA/IRS match
file, t-tests were conducted to see whether profit rates and the capital-labor

ratio differed for firms making a pension contribution and those not making a contribution to a pension fund (table B.5). T-tests indicate that pretax profits and assets per employee were higher in firms making pension contributions. These findings, indicated in chapter V, support the theory that the economic circumstances of the firm determine plan provision. An analysis of the impact of profits on plan sponsorship based on data containing observations of individual corporations would strengthen this finding. Many observers of the small-business sector indicate that the profit rate in small firms is of paramount importance to plan provision. Unfortunately, better data were not available to test this hypothesis more carefully.

Analysis Using the NFIB Survey of Small Employers

Table B.6 through table B.11 are based on the NFIB small-employer survey. The first four tables model pension provision. Administrative expenses are estimated for all firms using the first three equations. These estimates reflect the administrative costs that each employer who decided to sponsor a pension plan would face. Naturally, actual data on administrative costs are provided only for firms that sponsor pension plans.

TABLE B.5
Tests of Equality of Means,
Pretax Profits and Capital-Labor Ratios,
Corporations Reporting Pension Contribution and Others,[a]
SBA/IRS Corporate Match File

Means Being Tested	Means	t-Statistic
Pretax Profits		
Those with contribution	10.91%	2.653
		(214 d.f.)
Those without contribution	3.38%	
Capital-Labor Ratio[b]		
Those with contribution	$330	2.577
		(214 d.f.)
Those without contribution	$127	

Source: Employee Benefit Research Institute.
[a]Data grouped by firm size, industry, and pension contribution status.
[b]Capital-labor ratios equal reported corporate assets per employee in thousands of dollars.

TABLE B.6

Administrative Cost Equation in Log Form, NFIB Survey of Small Employers
(dependent variable: administrative costs)

Variable[a]	Parameter	t-Statistic
Constant	2.342	3.58
Participants	0.4062	4.69
Fund Contribution	0.347	4.52
Adjusted R-square	0.415	
Number of Observations	148	

Source: Employee Benefit Research Institute.
[a]All continuous variables in log form.

TABLE B.7

Participant Equation in Log Form, NFIB Survey of Small Employers
(dependent variable: plan participants)

Variable[a]	Parameter	t-Statistic
Constant	− 2.558	− 4.21
Total Employment	0.961	26.67
Payroll per Employee[b]	0.247	3.99
Adjusted R-square	0.758	
Number of Observations	236	

Source: Employee Benefit Research Institute.
[a]All continuous variables in log form.
[b]Payroll in thousands of dollars.

179

Fund Contribution Equation in Log Form, NFIB Survey of Small Employers
(dependent variable: annual fund contribution)

Variable[a]	Parameter	t-Statistic
Constant	−0.178	−0.14
Total Employment	0.619	10.16
Payroll per Employee[b]	0.847	6.71
Nonprofessional Services and Retail Sales	−0.360	−2.48
Adjusted R-square	0.452	
Number of Observations	201	

Source: Employee Benefit Research Institute.
[a]All continuous variables in log form.
[b]Payroll in thousands of dollars.

Nevertheless, nonsponsors would also pay administrative costs if they started a plan, and these costs generally depend upon the size of the plan. The estimated value of administrative costs for each firm (on a per employee basis) are entered into the equation in table B.9 to predict the likelihood that a small employer will sponsor a pension plan.[3]

Findings based on the equation presented in table B.9 are found in chapter V where the effects of each of the variables included in the analysis on the likelihood of plan sponsorship are discussed. By changing the values of some of the variables included in the equation, different economic and public policy scenarios are simulated for chapter VII, including the effect of a 14 percent tax credit on plan formation. The simulation methodology is discussed in greater detail below.

The equation presented in table B.10 is identical to that of table B.9, but assets per employee are substituted for sales and industry dummies. Assets per employee are taken from the SBA/IRS match file and are matched to the firm-level observations in the NFIB survey by firm size and industry. The SBA/IRS observations attached to the NFIB file are averages for all tax returns combined—that is, the figures are the same for

---

[3]More information on the use of these equations is provided in Andrews, 1989a.

TABLE B.9
Pension Coverage Logit Analysis,
NFIB Survey of Small Employers
(dependent variable: likelihood firm sponsors pension plan)

Variable	Parameter	t-Statistic
Constant	− 3.154	− 7.23
Employment	0.015	2.12
Payroll per Employee[a]	0.077	5.64
Sales		
Under $100,000	0.352	0.87
$100,000–199,999	− 0.857	− 2.37
$200,000–499,999	− 0.555	− 2.22
$1.5–2.9 million	0.555	2.13
$3.0–10 million and over	0.911	3.04
Industry		
Finance, insurance, and		
real estate	0.846	2.98
Nonprofessional services	− 0.606	− 1.81
Administrative Cost		
per Employee[b]	− 0.00615	− 1.29
Has Health Insurance	1.064	3.74
Advisor[c]		
Trade association	0.739	2.57
Financial planner	1.080	4.65
Other source	1.098	4.17
Likelihood Ratio Index	0.266	
Number of Observations	939	

Source: Employee Benefit Research Institute.
[a]Payroll in thousands of dollars.
[b]Predicted costs for sponsors and nonsponsors. See table B.6 for forecasting equation.
[c]Excluded group consists of accountants and attorneys.

TABLE B.10
Pension Coverage Logit Analysis,
NFIB Survey of Small Employers
Matched with SBA/IRS Data
(dependent variable: likelihood firm sponsors pension plan)

Variable	Parameter	t-Statistic
Constant	− 3.388	− 8.30
Employment	0.0277	4.30
Payroll per Employee[a]	0.0836	7.14
Assets per Employee[b]	0.000549	3.28
Administrative Costs per Employee[c]	− 0.00902	− 1.99
Has Health Insurance	1.173	4.38
Advisor[d]		
Trade association	0.732	2.73
Financial planner	0.960	4.33
Other source	1.204	4.05
Likelihood Ratio Index	0.227	
Number of Observations	958	

Source: Employee Benefit Research Institute.
[a]Payroll in thousands of dollars.
[b]Average assets per employee in industry/firm-size group in thousands of dollars.
[c]Predicted costs for sponsors and nonsponsors. See table B.6 for forecasting equation.
[d]Excluded group consists of accountants and attorneys.

providers and nonproviders. While these findings are not conclusive, they provide further evidence that (1) capitalization affects plan provisions and that (2) industrial classifications may proxy other employer attributes that are primary influences on plan sponsorship. These findings are noted in a footnote to chapter V.

Table B.11 examines the relationship between the percentage of employees participating in a small-employer plan and other variables to provide confirming evidence to the CPS findings that employees working for

Pension Participation Regression Analysis,[a]
NFIB Survey of Small Employers
(dependent variable: percentage of
participants in pension plan)

Variable	Parameter	t-Statistic
Constant	0.797	17.13
Sales over $500,999	0.152	3.23
Industry Variables		
Construction	− 0.0875	− 2.69
Retail trade	− 0.207	− 6.08
Business and personal services	− 0.292	4.29
Adjusted R-square	0.167	
Number of Observations	323	

Source: Employee Benefit Research Institute.
[a]Observations weighted by employment.

professional offices and practices are more likely to have a pension plan on the job than other employees in small firms but are less likely to participate in that plan. This hypothesis was not confirmed for small employers. These findings are incorporated in a footnote to chapter V.

Analysis Using the 1984 Survey of Income and Program Participation

Table B.12 through table B.13 model pension coverage and participation for men aged 25 to 64 working for small employers to determine whether the findings from the data bases just discussed can be supported by a wide range of data. The effect of firm size, unionization, wage rates, and job tenure is similar to those found earlier. Pension coverage rates are affected by some of the same industries in the SIPP analysis as in the CPS analysis presented in table B.1. Nonetheless, the participant equation does not confirm that workers in professional services are less likely than others to be covered by an employer-sponsored pension plan, suggesting that professional offices do not discriminate in pension coverage against prime-age men. These findings are reported in a footnote to chapter V.

Pension Coverage Logit Analysis,
Men Aged 25–64 Working for Small Employers,[a]
1984 Survey of Income and Program Participation
(dependent variable: likelihood of coverage)

Variable	Parameter	t-Statistic
Constant	−0.738	−5.40
Firm Size		
Fewer than 25 Workers	−0.723	−6.95
Union Contract	1.444	9.29
Industry Variables		
Construction	−0.728	−4.43
Retail trade	0.517	−3.49
Professional services	0.310	1.83
Other services	−0.453	−2.38
Wage Rate	0.0425	4.77
Job Tenure	0.0187	0.91
Likelihood Ratio Index	0.114	
Number of Observations	1,914	

Source: Employee Benefit Research Institute.
[a]Restricted to those with one year or more of tenure.

Economic and Public Policy Simulations

Table B.14 through table B.16 provide the basic input to the eight simulations of changes that would affect the probability of pension coverage among small employers. The effect of a tax credit equal to 14 percent of plan contributions on plan provision is the first simulation. (The proposal is explained in greater detail in chapter VII.) In this simulation, administrative costs per employee were recalculated for each small business in the sample, assuming that a 14 percent tax credit against plan contributions was granted to small employers. In effect, the tax credit would reduce administrative costs. The new administrative cost forecasts were substituted in the logit coverage equation reported in table B.9. The

TABLE B.13

Pension Participation Logit Analysis, Men Aged 25–64 Working for Small Employers,[a] Covered by a Pension Plan, 1984 Survey of Income and Program Participation (dependent variable: likelihood of participation)

Variable	Parameter	t-Statistic
Constant	0.197	0.53
Firm Size		
Fewer than 25 Workers	0.0867	0.36
Union Contract	0.938	2.48
Industry Variables		
Construction	0.260	0.51
Retail trade	0.159	0.40
Wholesale trade	−0.305	−0.84
Professional services	0.375	0.88
Other services	−0.606	−1.41
Communications and utilities	−0.973	−1.66
Other nonmanufacturing	−0.109	−0.26
Wage Rate	0.042	1.75
Job Tenure	0.157	5.47
Likelihood Ratio Index	0.160	
Number of Observations	708	

Source: Employee Benefit Research Institute.
[a]Restricted to those with one year or more of tenure.

percentage of employees in the small-firm sample with pension coverage was calculated by weighting the predicted firm-specific coverage rates by the number of employees in each firm. Coverage rates before and after the tax credit were calculated for two firm-size categories—fewer than 5 employees and 5 to 24 employees. These rates for the 14 percent tax credit (and the other seven simulations) are presented in table B.14.

Changes in coverage based on these firm-size categories were applied to coverage rates for workers in firms with fewer than 25 employees and

Simulated NFIB Coverage Rates[a]
Used to Adjust Nationwide Data
under Different Scenarios,
Firms with Fewer than 100 Employees

Firm Size[b]	1-4 Workers	5-24 Workers
Base Case	.1666	.3456
14 Percent Tax Subsidy	.3659	.5125
Real Wage Growth		
$5,000	.2128	.4135
$8,500	.2499	.5204
$12,500	.2969	.5204
Better Advice	.2447	.4608
Real Wage Gains and Better Advice	.3049	.5354
Real Wage Gains and Tax Subsidy	.4243	.5779
Real Wage Gains, Better Advice, and Tax Subsidy	.5322	.6885

Source: Employee Benefit Research Institute.
[a]Based on simulations using logit coverage equation reported in table B.9.
[b]Rates are simulated for firms with 1-4 employees and 5-24 employees, respectively. Changes in coverage based on these rates were applied to coverage rates for workers in firms with fewer than 25 employees and firms with 25-100 workers, using the May 1983 EBRI/HHS Current Population Survey pension supplement (based on table B.15) to account for the higher coverage rates reported by NFIB employers.

firms with 25 to 100 employees, using the May 1983 CPS pension supplement. The base employment and coverage figures used to calculate these rates are presented in table B.15. Using coverage-rate forecasts that do not apply directly to the employment-size categories in question makes the behavioral responses less accurate than they would be if the NFIB sample were representative of all small employers. Directly using the rates for most employers and Form 943 for agricultural employers). The match was undertaken to provide accurate economic information on assets, receipts, and other financial variables for large and small employers. (Employment and payroll data found on the business tax forms were known to be flawed.) The IRS conducted the match under contract to the SBA and the two files were linked using the employer identification number (EIN) common to both files.[4] Tabulations from the SBA/IRS match file are used in chapters II, IV, and V.

Employment Tax Forms—Most employers must file employment tax Form 941 or Form 943 (for nonagricultural and agricultural employers, respectively).[5] These forms may be filed by subsidiaries or by the parent company. Form 941 is filed quarterly by nonagricultural employers who withhold income taxes, Social Security taxes, or both.[6] Form 943 is similar to Form 941 but is filed annually by agricultural employers.[7]

Employment is reported for the pay period including March 12. If the business is sold or transferred (including changing the legal form of the business) during the quarter, both businesses file a form.[8] If the firm merges or is consolidated with another, the original firm must file for that quarter and show all wages paid for that quarter. The Census Bureau receives a tape of 941/943 forms from the IRS, validates the information, and imputes employment and payroll when necessary.

Business Tax Forms—Business tax Form 1120 is filed by all domestic corporations, real estate, investment trusts, regulated investment companies, insurance companies, and foreign corporations doing business in the United States. This form reports income, gains, losses, deductions, and credits of U.S. corporations. For the 1979 sample, returns with accounting periods that ended from July 1979 through June 1980 were included.[9]

The Sample—A stratified probability sample of 80,000 firms was selected by the IRS out of a total of 2.6 million firms. The sample included all firms

---

[4] Three files were actually assembled—one for sole proprietorship, one for partnerships, and one for corporations.

[5] Those employing only household employees file Form 942 and are not included in the match file.

[6] "Wages" are defined as the total of all wages paid, tips reported, taxable fringe benefits provided, and other compensation paid to employees, even if income or Social Security taxes are not withheld. This does not include pension distributions, annuities, third-party sick pay, supplemental unemployment compensation benefits, or gambling winnings, even if income taxes were withheld on them.

[7] In this case, "wages" are taxable cash wages paid.

[8] The change and the date of the change must be noted on the form as well as the name of the new owner or new business name.

[9] The IRS has recently completed a 1982 match that was not available for this study. In that match file, returns with accounting periods ending January 1981 to December 1983 are included.

TABLE B.16
Simulated Nationwide Coverage Rates[a]
under Different Scenarios,
Firms with Fewer than 100 Employees

Firm Size	1–24 Workers	25–99 Workers	Total
Base Case	.1560	.3603	.2196
14 Percent Tax Subsidy	.3427	.5342	.4023
Real Wage Growth			
$5,000	.1996	.4310	.2715
$8,500	.2341	.4826	.3115
$12,500	.2781	.5425	.3604
Better Advice	.2292	.4803	.3074
Real Wage Gains and Better Advice	.2856	.5581	.3704
Real Wage Gains and Tax Subsidy	.3974	.6024	.4612
Real Wage Gains, Better Advice, and Tax Subsidy	.4984	.7177	.5667

Source: Employee Benefit Research Institute.

[a]Based on simulated changes in coverage rates by firm size under different scenarios reported in table B.14 applied to nationwide coverage rates and employment totals from the May 1983 EBRI/HHS Current Population Survey pension supplement.

Bibliography

Aaron, Henry J., Barry P. Bosworth, and Gary Burtless. *Can America Afford to Grow Old?* Washington, DC: The Brookings Institution, 1989.

Allen, Steven G., and Robert L. Clark. "Pensions and Firm Performance." In Morris Kleiner, Richard Block, Myron Roomkin, and Sidney Salsburg, eds., *Human Resources and the Performance of the Firm*. Madison, WI: Industrial Relations Research Association, 1987.

Alvey, Wendy, and Beth Kilss, eds. *Statistics of Income and Related Administrative Record Research: 1982*. Selected papers presented at the 1982 annual meetings of the American Statistical Association in Cincinnati, Ohio, August 16–19, 1982. Washington, DC: U.S. Department of the Treasury, Internal Revenue Service, 1982.

Andrews, Emily S. "Changing Pension Policy and the Aging of America." *Contemporary Policy Issues* (September 1987): 84–97.

_____. *The Changing Profile of Pensions in America*. Washington, DC: Employee Benefit Research Institute, 1985.

_____. "Pension Policy and Small Employers." In *Industrial Relations Research Association Series: Proceedings of the Forty-First Annual Meeting*. Madison, WI: Industrial Relations Research Association, Summer 1989a.

_____. "Pension Provision by Small Employers: Coverage, Administrative Costs, and the Pension Share of Compensation." Unpublished manuscript, January 1989b.

_____. "Wage-Pension Tradeoffs for Workers in Small Firms." Paper presented at Eastern Economic Association meetings, March 6, 1987, revised April 1989c.

Andrews, Emily S., and Deborah J. Chollet. "Future Sources of Retirement Income: Whither the Baby Boom?" In Susan M. Wachter, ed., *Social Security and Private Pensions: Providing for Retirement in the Twenty-First Century*. Lexington, MA: Lexington Books, 1988.

Andrews, Emily S., and Olivia S. Mitchell. "The Current and Future Role of Pensions in Old Age Economic Security." *Benefits Quarterly* (1986, second quarter): 26–35.

Annual Report of the Board of Trustees of the Federal Old-Age and Survivors Insurance and Disability Insurance (OASDI) Trust Funds. Baltimore, MD: Social Security Administration, 1988 and 1989.

Arthur Andersen & Co. "Special Report: The 1986 White House Conference on Small Business." *Small Business Forum*. Washington, DC: Arthur Andersen & Co, 1986.

Armington, Catherine. "Further Examination of Sources of Recent Employment Growth Analysis of USEEM Data for 1976 to 1980." The Brookings Institution. Unpublished manuscript, March 1983.

Armington, Catherine, and Marjorie Odle. "Small Business—How Many Jobs?" *The Brookings Review* (Winter 1982): 14–16.

Atkins, G. Lawrence. *Spend It or Save It? Pension Lump-Sum Distributions and Tax Reform*. Washington, DC: Employee Benefit Research Institute, 1986.

Barron, John M., Dan A. Black, and Mark A. Loewenstein. "Employer Size: The Implications for Search, Training, Capital Investment, Starting Wages, and Wage Growth. *Journal of Labor Economics* (January 1987): 76–89.

Barth, James R., Joseph J. Cordes, and Robert B. Friedland. "Some New Evidence on How Taxes Affect the Wage-Fringe Benefit Tradeoff." Discussion paper of the Department of Economics, George Washington University (D–8416), 1984.

Birch, David, and Susan MacCracken. "Assumptions vs. Reality in the Brookings Analysis of Small Business Job Creation." Submitted to a hearing before the Subcommittee on Employment and Productivity of the Committee on Labor and Human Resources, U.S. Senate, 12 January 1983.

Bluestone, Barry, and Bennett Harrison. "The Great American Job Machine: The Proliferation of Low Wage Employment in the U.S. Economy." Paper prepared for the Joint Economic Committee of Congress, December 1986.

Boskin, Michael J. *Too Many Promises: The Uncertain Future of Social Security*. Homewood, IL: Dow Jones-Irwin, 1986.

Bradford, David F., and the U.S. Treasury Tax Policy Staff. *Blueprints for Basic Tax Reform*. Arlington, VA: Tax Analysts, 1984.

Brock, William A., and David S. Evans. *The Economics of Small Business*. New York: Holmes and Meier Publishers, Inc., 1986.

Brown, Charles, and James L. Medoff. "The Employer Size Wage Effect." Discussion paper no. 1202. Harvard Institute of Economic Research, Harvard University, January 1986.

Brown, Paul B. "*Inc.*'s Guide to Writing Your Own Ticket." *Inc.* (September 1988): 80–86.

Bulow, Jeremy I., and Lawrence H. Summers. "A Theory of Dual Labor Markets with Application to Industrial Policy, Discrimination, and Keynesian Unemployment." *Journal of Labor Economics* (July 1986, part 1): 376–414.

Burkhauser, Richard V. "The Pension Acceptance Decision of Older Workers." *Journal of Human Resources* (Winter 1979): 63–75.

Burtless, Gary, and Robert A. Moffitt. "The Joint Choice of Retirement Age and Post Retirement Hours of Work." *Journal of Labor Economics* (April 1985): 209–236.

Calimafde, Paula. "The Impact of the Top-Heavy Rules on Small Business Retirement Plans: Do the Costs Outweigh the Benefits Following the Tax Reform Act of 1986?" Report submitted to the Office of Advocacy, U.S. Small Business Administration, 1987.

Clark, Robert L. "Defined Contribution Plans: Are They the Pension of the Future?" In *What Is the Future for Defined Benefit Pension Plans?* Washington, DC: Employee Benefit Research Institute, 1989.

Clark, Robert L., Stephen F. Gohmann, and Ann A. McDermed. "Declining Use of Defined Benefit Pension Plans: Is Federal Regulation the Reason?" Unpublished manuscript, April 1988.

Clark, Robert L., and Ann A. McDermed. "Labor Contracts, Pension Plans and Lifetime Earnings." Unpublished manuscript, September 1986.

Cooley, Phillip L., and Charles E. Edwards. "Age Effects on Managerial Compensation in Small Firms." *American Journal of Small Business* (Spring 1985): 41–48.

Cooper, Robert D. *Pension Fund Operating Expenses, The Summary Report and Fact Book*. Brookfield, WI: International Foundation of Employee Benefit Plans, 1984.

Cooper, Robert D., and Melody A. Carlsen. *Pension Fund Operations and Expenses, The Technical Report*. Brookfield, WI: International Foundation of Employee Benefit Plans, 1980.

Day, C.D. "1979 Corporation, Partnership, and Sole Proprietorship Employment and Payroll Studies: An Initial Look at the Relative Efficiency of Small and Large Business." Internal Revenue Service, Statistics of Income Division. Unpublished manuscript, October 1985.

Denison, Edward F. "The Shift to Services and the Rate of Productivity Change." *Survey of Current Business* (October 1973): 20–35.

Dennis, William J., Jr. *Small Business Employee Benefits, December 1985*. Washington, DC: National Federation of Independent Business Research and Education Foundation, 1985.

Dorsey, Stuart. "A Model and Empirical Estimates of Worker Pension Coverage in the U.S." *Southern Economic Journal* (October 1982): 506–520.

Dunn, Lucia F. "The Effects of Firm Size on Wages, Fringe Benefits, and Work Disutility." In Betty Bock, Harvey J. Goldschmid, Ira M. Millstein, and F.M. Scherer, eds., *The Impact of the Modern Corporation*. New York: Columbia University Press, 1984.

Dye, Richard F. "Evidence on the Effects of Payroll Tax Changes on Wage Growth and Price Inflation: A Review and Reconciliation." ORS Working Papers 34. Washington, DC: Social Security Administration, April 1984.

191

Ehrenberg, Ronald J. "Retirement System Characteristics and Compensating Differentials in the Pubic Sector." *Industrial and Labor Relations Review* (July 1980): 470–483.

Employee Benefit Research Institute. "After Tax Reform: Revisiting 401(k)s." *EBRI Issue Brief* no. 72 (November 1987).

_____. "Number of Pension Plans Rises in 1987." *Employee Benefit Notes* (January 1989): 4.

_____. "Pension Portability and Benefit Adequacy." *EBRI Issue Brief* no. 56 (July 1986).

_____. "Pension Portability and What It Can Do for Retirement Income: A Simulation Approach." *EBRI Issue Brief* no. 65 (April 1987).

_____. "Small Employers and Pension Plans." *Employee Benefit Notes* (May 1986): 2–4.

"Federal Aid for Destitute Reaching Just Half of Those Eligible." *The New York Times*, 10 May 1988, p. A21.

Fields, Gary, and Olivia S. Mitchell. *Retirement, Pensions and Social Security.* Cambridge, MA: MIT Press, 1984.

Fini, Christine. "The Retirement Equity Act of 1984 and the Earnings Sharing Proposal: An Analysis." Unpublished manuscript, 1988.

Fox, Alan, "Earnings Replacement Rates and Total Income: Findings from the Retirement History Study." *Social Security Bulletin* (October 1982): 3–23, 53.

Freeman, Richard B. "Unions, Pensions and Union Pension Funds." In David A. Wise, ed., *Pensions, Labor, and Individual Choice.* Chicago: University of Chicago Press, 1985.

Goldstein, G.S., and M.V. Pauly. "Group Health Insurance as a Local Public Good." In Richard N. Rossett, ed., *The Role of Health Insurance in the Health Service Sector.* New York: Columbia University Press, 1976.

Grad, Susan. *Income of the Population Age 55 and Over, 1986.* U.S. Department of Health and Human Services, Social Security Administration, Office of Policy. Washington, DC: U.S. Government Printing Office, 1977–1988.

Greenia, Nicholas. "Processing and Imputation Methodology, Forms 1065/941/943 Link Study." Internal Revenue Service, Statistics of Income Division, Corporation Statistics Branch. Unpublished manuscript, November 1983.

Gustman, Alan L., and Thomas L. Steinmeier. "A Structural Retirement Model." *Econometrica* (May 1986): 555–584.

_____. "Partial Retirement and the Analysis of Retirement Behavior." *Industrial and Labor Relations Review* (April 1984): 403–415.

_____. "Pensions and Unions." Report submitted to the Department of Labor, Office of the Assistant Secretary for Policy, May 1986.

_____. "The Pension Innovation, the Evolution of Accounting Standards and Pension Regulation, and Trends Toward Defined Contribution Pension Plans." Unpublished manuscript, November 1980.

Haber, Sheldon D., Enrique J. Lamas, and Jules H. Lichtenstein. "On Their Own: The Self-Employed and Others in Private Business." *Monthly Labor Review* (May 1987): 17–23.

Hagens, John B., and John C. Hambor. "The Macroeconomic Effects of a Payroll Tax Rollback." *Eastern Economic Journal* (January 1980): 21–32.

Hall, Robert E. "The Importance of Lifetime Jobs in the U.S. Economy." *American Economic Review* (September 1982): 716–724.

Hallenbeck, Gary T., and Russell E. Hall. "When May Plan Assets Be Used to Pay Administrative Expenses." *Pension World* (January 1988): 46–48.

Halpern, J.H., and Alicia H. Munnell. "The Inflationary Impact of Increases in the Social Security Payroll Tax." *New England Economic Review* (March/April 1980): 23–34.

Hamilton, James, and James Medoff. "Small Business Monkey Business." *The Washington Post*, 24 April 1988, p. D2.

Hammermesh, Daniel S. "Commentary." In John J. Siegfried, ed., *The Economics of Firm Size, Market Structure, and Social Performance.* Washington, DC: U.S. Government Printing Office, 1980.

_____. "New Estimates of the Incidence of the Payroll Tax." *Southern Economic Journal* (April 1979): 1208–1219.

Harris, Candee. "The Role of Small Business in a Changing Economy, 1976–1982." Unpublished manuscript, 1985.

Haworth, Charles T., and Carol Jean Reuther. "Industrial Concentration and Inter-Industry Wage Determination." *Review of Economics and Statistics* (February 1978): 85–95.

Hewitt Associates and the Profit Sharing Council of America. *1988 Profit Sharing Survey.* Chicago: The Profit Sharing Council of America, 1988.

Ippolito, Richard A. "A Study of the Regulatory Effect of the Employee Retirement Income Security Act." *Journal of Law & Economics* (April 1988): 85–125.

_____. *Pensions, Economics and Public Policy.* Homewood, IL: Dow Jones-Irwin, 1986.

_____. "The Implicit Pension Contract: Developments and New Directions." *Journal of Human Resources* (Summer 1987): 441–467.

James Bell and Associates, Inc., and ICF Incorporated. "Coverage, Characteristics, Administration, and Costs of Pension and Health Care Benefits in Small Businesses." Report submitted to the U.S. Small Business Administration, Office of Advocacy, March 1984.

Justin Research Associates. "Issues Relating to Small Business Pension Plans." Report submitted to the U.S. Small Business Administration, Office of Advocacy, May 1985.

Kasprzyk, Daniel, and Roger A. Herriot. "Some Aspects of the Survey of Income and Program Participation." Survey of Income and Program Participation Working Paper no. 8601. Prepared for the U.S. Department of Commerce, Bureau of the Census, April 1986.

Kendrick, John W. "Measurement of Output and Productivity in the Service Sector." In Robert P. Inman, ed., *Managing the Service Economy: Prospects and Problems.* New York: Cambridge University Press, 1985.

Kennell, David I., and John F. Shiels. "Summary of Assumptions for PRISM Simulations." Paper submitted to the American Association of Retired Persons, 1986.

Kirchoff, Bruce, and Bruce Phillips. "Examining Entrepreneurship's Role in Economic Growth." Paper presented at the Seventh Annual Babson Entrepreneurship Research Conference in Malibu, California, April 30, 1987.

Korczyk, Sophie M. "The NRECA Survey of Retirement Coverage in Smaller Firms: Evidence and Policy Implications." Report to the National Rural Electric Cooperative Association, October 1988.

Kosters, Marvin H., and Murray N. Ross. "The Influence of Employment Shifts and New Job Opportunities on the Growth and Distribution of Real Wages." In Phillip Cagan, ed., *Deficits, Taxes, and Economic Adjustments.* Washington, DC: American Enterprise Institute, 1987.

Kotlikoff, Laurence J., and Daniel E. Smith. *Pensions in the American Economy.* Chicago: University of Chicago Press, 1983.

Kotlikoff, Laurence J., and David Wise. "Labor Compensation and the Structure of Private Pension Plans: Evidence for Contractual Versus Spot Labor Market." In David Wise, ed., *Pensions, Labor, and Individual Choice.* Chicago: University of Chicago Press, 1985.

Kutscher, R.E, J.A. Mark, and J.R. Norsworthy. "The Productivity Slowdown and Outlook to 1985." *Monthly Labor Review* (May 1977): 3–8.

Kwoka, John E., Jr. "Establishment Size, Wages and Job Satisfaction: The Trade-Offs." In John J. Siegfried, ed., *The Economics of Firm Size, Market Structure, and Social Performance.* Washington, DC: U.S. Government Printing Office, 1980.

Lazear, Edward. "Agency, Earnings Profiles, Productivity and Hours Restrictions. " *American Economic Review* (September 1981): 606–620.

———. "Pensions as Severance Pay." In Zvi Bodie and John B. Shoven, eds., *Financial Aspects of the United States Pension System.* Chicago: University of Chicago Press, 1983.

———. "Why Is There Mandatory Retirement?" *Journal of Political Economy* (December 1979): 1261–1284.

Leonard, Jonathan S. "Carrots and Sticks: Pay, Supervision, and Turnover." *Journal of Labor Economics* (October 1987, part 2): S136–S152.

————. "On the Size Distribution of Employment and Establishments." Working Paper no. 1951. Washington, DC: National Bureau of Economic Research, June 1986.

Long, James E., and Frank A. Scott. "The Income Tax and Nonwage Compensation." *Review of Economics and Statistics* (May 1982): 211–219.

Louis Harris and Associates. "Strategies to Increase Participation in the Supplemental Security Income Program: Follow-Up Study of Poor Elderly People." Report submitted to the American Association of Retired Persons under a grant from the Commonwealth Fund Commission on Elderly People Living Alone, February 1988.

Masters, Stanley H. "Wages and Plant Size: An Interindustry Analysis." *Review of Economics and Statistics* (August 1969): 341–345.

Mellow, Wesley. "Employer Size and Wages." *Review of Economics and Statistics* (August 1982): 495–501.

Mincer, Jacob. *Schooling, Experience, and Earnings.* New York: Columbia University Press, 1974.

Mitchell, Olivia S. "Fringe Benefits and Labor Mobility." *Journal of Human Resources* (Spring 1982): 286–298.

————. "Fringe Benefits and the Cost of Changing Jobs." *Industrial and Labor Relations Review* (October 1983): 70–78.

————. "Worker Knowledge of Pension Provisions." *Journal of Labor Economics* (January 1988): 21–39.

Mitchell, Olivia S., and Emily S. Andrews. "Scale Economies in Private Multiemployer Pension Systems." *Industrial and Labor Relations Review* (July 1981): 522–530.

Mitchell, Olivia S., and Rebecca A. Luzadis. "A Multinominal Logit Model of Pension Outcomes." Unpublished manuscript, October 1987, revised.

Mitchell, Olivia S., and Silvana Pozzebon. "Wages, Pensions and the Wage-Pension Tradeoff." Unpublished manuscript, July 1987, revised.

Moglen, Gain, Charles Day, and Thomas Petska. "Record Linkage and Imputation Strategies in the 1982 Business Employment and Payroll Studies." In *Statistics of Income and Related Administrative Record Research.* Washington, DC: U.S. Department of the Treasury, Internal Revenue Service, 1987.

Munnell, Alicia H. *The Economics of Private Pensions.* Washington, DC: The Brookings Institution, 1982.

Nalebuff, Barry, and Richard J. Zeckhauser. "Pensions and the Retirement Decision." In David Wise, ed., *Pensions, Labor, and Individual Choice.* Chicago: University of Chicago Press, 1985.

Nordhaus, W.D. "The Recent Productivity Slowdown." *Brookings Papers on Economic Activity* no. 3 (1972): 493–536.

Oi, Walter Y. "Heterogeneous Firms and the Organization of Production." *Economic Inquiry* (April 1983): 147–171.

_____. "Low Wages and Small Firms." Report submitted to the U.S. Department of Labor, Contract no. B9-M4-2651, 13 November 1985.

Oi, Walter Y., and John Rasian. "Impact of Firm Size on Wages and Work." Unpublished manuscript, preliminary draft, 13 August 1985.

Opinion Research Corporation. "Report on a Focus Group Study of Retirement Benefits in Small U.S. Business." Report prepared for the Employee Benefit Research Institute and the American Association of Retired Persons, February 1986.

Personick, Valerie A. "Industry Output and Employment through the End of the Century." *Monthly Labor Review* (September 1987): 30–45.

Pope, Ralph A. "Economies of Scale in Large State and Municipal Retirement Systems." *Public Budgeting and Finance* (Autumn 1986): 70–80.

President's Commission on Pension Policy. *Coming of Age: Toward a National Retirement Income Policy*. Washington, DC: U.S. Government Printing Office, 1981.

Pugel, Thomas A. "Profitability, Concentration and the Interindustry Variation in Wages." *Review of Economics and Statistics* (May 1980): 248–253.

Quinn, Joseph F. "Microeconomic Determinants of Early Retirement: A Cross-Sectional View of White Married Men." *Journal of Human Resources* (Summer 1977): 329–346.

Radner, Daniel B. "Money Incomes of Aged and Nonaged Family Units, 1967–1984." *Social Security Bulletin* (August 1987): 9–28.

Rogers, Gayle T. "Vesting of Private Pension Benefits in 1979 and Changes from 1972." *Social Security Bulletin* (July 1981): 12–29.

Rosen, Sherwin. "Unionism and the Occupational Wage Structure in the United States." *International Economic Review* (June 1979): 269–286.

Schiller, Bradley R., and Randall D. Weiss. "The Impact of Private Pensions on Firm Attachments." *Review of Economics and Statistics* (August 1979): 369–380.

_____. "Pensions and Wages: A Test for Equalizing Differences." *Review of Economics and Statistics* (November 1980): 463–468.

Skolnick, Alfred M. "Private Pension Plans, 1950–1974." *Social Security Bulletin* (June 1976): 3–17.

Smith, Robert S. "Compensating Differentials for Pensions and Underfunding in the Public Sector." *Review of Economics and Statistics* (August 1981): 463–468.

Smith, Robert S., and Ronald G. Ehrenberg. "Estimating Wage-Fringe Trade-Offs: Some Data Problems." In Jack E. Triplett, ed., *The Measurement of Labor Cost.* Chicago: University of Chicago Press, 1983.

Stafford, Frank P. "Firm Size, Work Place Public Goods, and Worker Welfare." In John J. Siegfried, ed., *The Economics of Firm Size, Market Structure, and Social Performance.* Washington, DC: U.S. Government Printing Office, 1980.

Teachers Insurance and Annuity Association and College Retirement Equities Fund and Education Research Unit. *Research Dialogues* (January 1987).

Thompson, Lawrence H. "Altering the Public/Private Mix of Retirement Income. In Susan M. Wachter, ed. *Social Security and Private Pensions.* Lexington, MA: D.C. Heath and Company, 1988.

Thurow, Lester. "The U.S. Productivity Problem." *Data Resource Review* (August 1979).

U.S. Congress. Congressional Budget Office. *Tax Policy for Pensions and Other Retirement Saving.* Washington, DC: Congressional Budget Office, 1987.

_____. *The Changing Distribution of Federal Taxes: 1975–1990.* Washington, DC: Congressional Budget Office, 1987.

U.S. Department of Commerce. Bureau of the Census. "Pensions: Worker Coverage and Retirement Income, 1984." *Current Population Reports.* Household Economic Studies, Series P–70, no. 12. Washington, DC: U.S. Government Printing Office, 1987.

_____. *Survey of Income and Program Participation Users' Guide.* Washington, DC: U.S. Department of Commerce, Bureau of the Census, 1987.

U.S. Department of Commerce. Bureau of Economic Analysis. *The National Income and Product Accounts of the United States, 1929–1982.* Washington, DC: Government Printing Office, 1988.

_____. *The Survey of Current Business.* Washington, DC: U.S. Government Printing Office, 1988.

U.S. Department of Labor. Bureau of Labor Statistics. *Employee Benefits in Medium and Large Firms, 1985.* Washington, DC: U.S. Government Printing Office, 1986.

U.S. Department of the Treasury. Internal Revenue Service. News release IR-88-7, 14 January 1988.

U.S. Small Business Administration. *The State of Small Business: A Report of the President.* Washington, DC: U.S. Government Printing Office, 1986.

U.S. Small Business Administration. Office of Advocacy. "A Guide to Understanding U.S. and State Small Business Job Generation Data." Unpublished manuscript, revised June 1987.

_____. *Linked 1976–1984 USEEM User's Guide.* Washington, DC: U.S. Government Printing Office, 1987.

Van de Water, Paul N., and Paul R. Cullinan. "Government Budget Trends." In *Business, Work, and Benefits: Adjusting to Change.* Washington, DC: Employee Benefit Research Institute, 1988.

Viscusi, W. Kip. "The Structure of Uncertainty and the Use of Nontransferable Pensions as a Mobility-Reduction Device." In David Wise, ed., *Pensions, Labor, and Individual Choice.* Chicago: University of Chicago Press, 1985.

Wessell, David, and Buck Brown, "The Hyping of Small-Firm Job Growth." *The Wall Street Journal,* 8 November 1988.

Wolfe, Edward N. "The Magnitude and Causes of the Recent Productivity Slowdown in the United States: A Survey of Recent Studies." In William J. Baumol and Kenneth McLennan, eds., *Productivity Growth and U.S. Competitiveness.* New York: Oxford University Press, 1985.

Woodbury, Stephen A. "Substitution between Wage and Nonwage Benefits." *American Economic Review* (March 1983): 166–182.

Index

199

Information sources
plan formation and, 85–86,
98, 100, 140–141, 146
proposed DOL outreach legislation, 137, 140
Integration, 18, 107, 120
Internal Revenue Service (IRS)
user fees, 131
IRAs *see* Individual retirement
accounts

J

Job creation, 27–30
Job tenure
compensation structure and,
58–62, 82
coverage rates and, 71, 92
firm size and, 40–41
Joint-and-survivor benefits, 118,
126

K

Keogh plans, 108, 125
contributions under ERTA, 115
Key employees, 116
taxation of distributions, 119

L

Labor force composition
compensation and, 46–47
plan type and, 85
Lawyers *see* Professionals
Legislation
pension plans and, 105–122
portability and preservation
proposals, 135–138
Lump-sum distributions, 132,
144 *see also* Distributions
taxation of, 119, 120

M

Management ratio
coverage rates and, 68
firm size and, 41–42, 54
Manufacturing industries
capital intensity and, 37,
67–68
coverage rates and, 67, 96
employment and establish-
ment size, 26
employment and firm size, 24,
36
job tenure and, 40–41
productivity, 32
small employers and, 36
unionization and firm size, 38
wages and firm size, 48–49
Marginal tax rates, 93n
Medicaid, 3–4
Medicare, 3
MEPPAA *see* Multiemployer
Pension Plan Amendments
Act of 1980
Minimum universal pension
system (MUPS), 156–158
Model SEPs, 113
Multiemployer Pension Plan
Amendments Act of 1980
(MEPPAA)
provisions of, 115
Multiemployer plans, 58, 115
MUPS *see* Minimum universal
pension system

N

National Federation of Independent Business (NFIB)
survey, 94n, 102n
small-employer plan sponsorship decisions, 75–77